Black America Series

Tallahassee
Florida

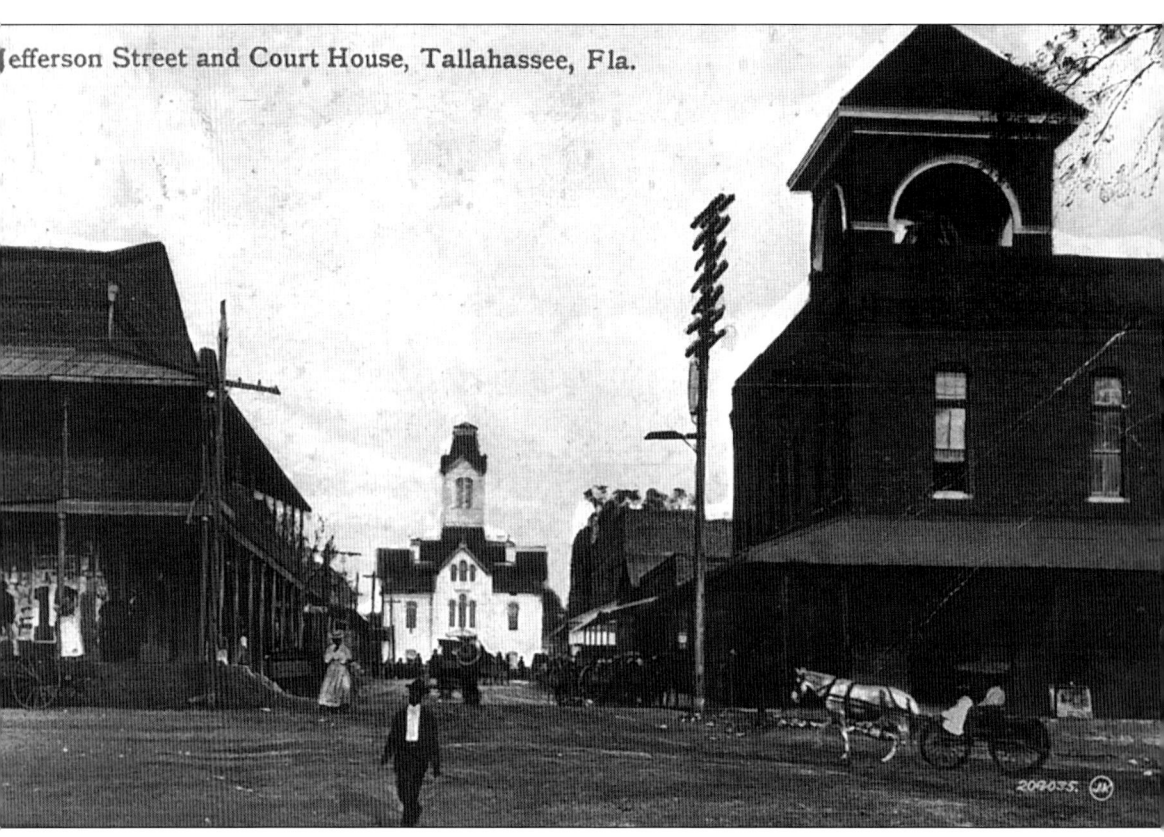

This is Jefferson Street and the courthouse in Tallahassee, Florida, during the early 20th century. (Courtesy of the Florida State Archives.)

BLACK AMERICA SERIES

TALLAHASSEE
FLORIDA

Althemese Barnes and Ann Roberts

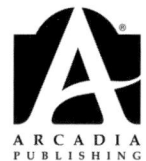

ARCADIA
PUBLISHING

Copyright © 2000 by Althemese Barnes and Ann Roberts
ISBN 978-0-7385-0551-0

Published by Arcadia Publishing
Charleston SC, Chicago IL, Portsmouth NH, San Francisco CA

Printed in the United States of America

Library of Congress Catalog Card Number: 99-068582

For all general information contact Arcadia Publishing at:
Telephone 843-853-2070
Fax 843-853-0044
E-Mail sales@arcadiapublishing.com
For customer service and orders:
Toll-Free 1-888-313-2665

Visit us on the Internet at www.arcadiapublishing.com

We dedicate this book to our parents—Pete Birdie Grant Roberts, Simon Peter Roberts, Mary Pemberton, and Moses Pemberton—our grandparents, and other ancestors who were our inspiration and aspiration. We pay tribute to the teachers, principals, matriarchs, and patriarchs of African-American communities, all of whom helped to shape and mold our lives. And finally, to family members and friends who shared the vision and gave continued support and encouragement, thank you.

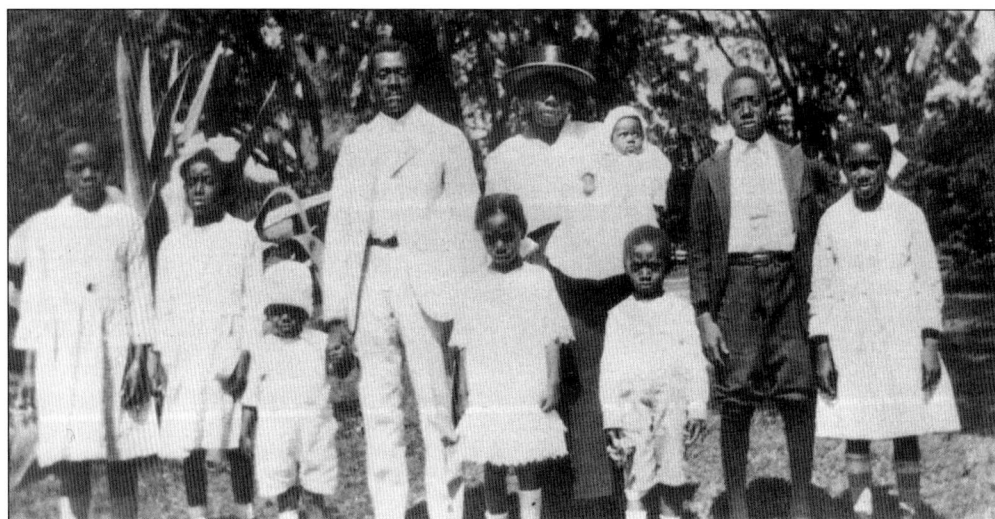

Austin Porter II, the overseer at Waverly Plantation, was photographed during the 1920s with his wife, Rebecca Edwards, and eight of their twelve children. The Porters maintained and farmed the property of the Hoffmans, who were its wealthy Northern owners. The children are, from left to right, Mary, Ida, Austin, Lula, Martha (in her mother's arms), Buddy, Willie, and Patsy.

Contents

Acknowledgments		6
Introduction		7
1.	Pioneers	9
2.	Businesses	19
3.	Caregivers	27
4.	The Civil Rights Movement	35
5.	Faces and Places	43
6.	Matriarchs and Patriarchs	61
7.	Events and Celebrations	75
8.	Education	93
9.	Worship	109
10.	Legacy of Avery	121

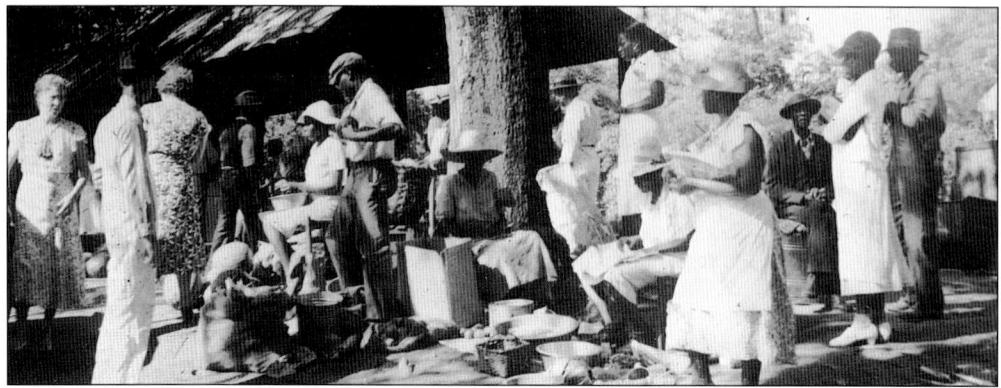
Black farmers are at the Curb Market on Boulevard Street in 1938. This location is now the site of the Tallahassee Leon County Civic Center.

ACKNOWLEDGMENTS

A debt of gratitude is owed to the many who opened their doors, with and without invitation, to Ann Roberts and Althemese Barnes, former classmates of the original Lincoln High School and of Florida A&M University, who decided to devote their time to researching and documenting the past. Driven by the desire to help individuals build awareness of, develop an appreciation for, and place in context the valuable contributions that African Americans have made in shaping the overall fabric of America, we have created this publication as a labor of love. We acknowledge the board of directors, members, and volunteers of the John G. Riley House Museum who, since the establishment of the museum in January 1996, have helped to preserve the Riley House, one of Tallahassee's significant African-American landmarks.

There are many that deserve credit for the success of this publication. Most notable are the contributing families: Wilhemina and Leroy Wester; Orynthia Ellis; Carl and Pearl Crawford; Leroy Burgess; Freeman and Thelma Lawrence; Philip and Annie Bell Nelson; Devurn and Allie Mae Glen; Paul and Betty Roberts; Anita McGhee Davis; Bennie Moseley; James McCloud Bryant; Mary Abner Williams; Bettye Stevens; Annie Ruth Mann; Sam and Elaine Sims; Carrie Ross; Myrtle Edwards Williams; Aquilina Howell; Inez Gardner Robinson; Eve Mannings; Tom and Barbara Rollins; Willie Mae Carter; George Russ; Lloyd and Mary Hadley; Betty and Thomas Hadley; Aldonia Flowers; Jeanette Gaines; Tawana Martin; Mary Caldwell; James and Buelah Smith; Mary King; Ike Gilliam; Edwina Martin; Irene Perry; Mary Porter Pemberton; Lillie Franklin Davis; Jacquelyn West Daniels; James and Annie Mae Oliver; Gwendolyn Oliver Parker; Flora Hall; Charlotte Griffin; Mary Martin; Irvin Holiday; Edwina Stephens; Beatrice Clarke; Rosa Brown; Ruth Orr; Gladys Anderson; Aurestine Huette Dupont Higgs; Linda Swilley-Meeks; Barrie Ashcroft; Vivian Williams; Na'im Akbar; Laura Dixie; Annie McKinney; Bernice Simmons; Lessie Sanford; Marie Spencer; Jerome Colson; Emily James; Dorothy W. Henry; Lucille Brown; Barbara Black; and Flora Hunter.

The Florida State Archives and the Riley House Museum were valuable sources of information. Historians Sharyn Thompson and Vivian Young were a constant source of inspiration. They, along with Byron Spice, a dedicated friend and supporter of the Riley House Museum, frequently cheered the project on and dropped off significant information and documentation to support the research. These contributors shall, like their predecessors, be forever etched on the pages of Tallahassee's African-American history.

Pete Birdie Grant Roberts, the daughter of African Methodist Episcopal (AME) Bishop R.A. Grant, was photographed in the early 1900s. She was the niece of Margaret Yellowhair, a devoted stewardess and a pastry maker at Dutch Kitchen Restaurant, which was located in the current Chamber of Commerce building. The Roberts home at 512 West Carolina Street is one of the few historic architectural styles (frame vernacular saddlebag) remaining in the historic African-American community of Frenchtown.

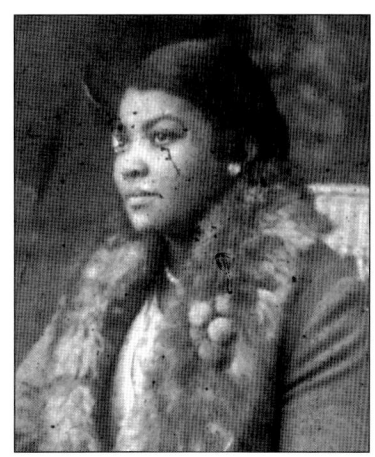

INTRODUCTION

Here are treasured legacies, no longer forgotten in time. Photos and other mementos of African-American history that were once curled up in cigar boxes, piled atop each other in shoe boxes, clinging to the crumbling pages of photo albums, languishing in long-closed drawers and cedar chests, and destined to become faded memories have now come to light. Because many families responded to the diligent search of the authors, significant aspects of history have been retrieved for the benefit of present and future generations. This is just the beginning, a microcosm, of the vast amount of history yet to be unveiled. Hopefully, this publication will serve as a catalyst for families, inspiring them to share their histories and mementos.

A review of the history of African Americans in the capital city of Florida, Tallahassee, and Leon County can be both tantalizing and inspiring. From the early to the mid-1800s, when Leon County's economy was largely dependent on slave labor, to and throughout the period of the Civil Rights Movement, African Americans have played a critical role. From their struggle under the oppressive conditions that prevailed in the slave-based economy that existed until Emancipation in 1865 to their occupation as either tenant farmers or sharecroppers, African Americans have consistently demonstrated perseverance, natural aptitude, and skill. Once denied, by law, the right to read, write, and figure, African Americans emerged as land owners, entrepreneurs, lawyers, doctors, and men and women who distinguished themselves as exemplary matriarchs and patriarchs. Research, including oral histories, shared photographs, and collective memories, document numerous triumphs in spite of the odds.

Including images of the quietude of slave and plantation cemeteries, photographic reminders of those who have gone before, and pictures of the architectural vernacular structures that dotted the landscape of rural Leon County and Tallahassee, this publication helps to write what were once missing pages of the past. Its revelations document the unyielding resolve of a people for independence, as well as pay tribute to their achievements. It is our legacy, as well as our challenge, to continue preserving the ancestral shrines.

Much of Tallahassee's African-American history lies in forgotten, abandoned cemeteries, located on former plantation land. Many contributing ancestors rest in a segregated section of Old City Cemetery and at the predominantly African-American Greenwood and Southside Cemeteries. In many instances, unmarked graves are all that remain of the dedicated lives that were spent making significant contributions to the development of Tallahassee. This publication recognizes and honors the labor, compassion, perseverance, and tenacity of these persons who shall not be forgotten.

This publication is in remembrance of these persons who showed courage and endured pain and suffering to provide inspiration for future generations. As an expression of love, divine inner spirit, and self-awareness, it is a symbol of the legacy that is still present in the Tallahassee community as evidenced by the many college graduates, elected public officials, authors, artists, elegant homes, progressive churches, and beautiful lives that were touched, nourished, and molded by African Americans.

As a result of this publication, a void has been filled, valuable pieces of history documented, and a legacy preserved.

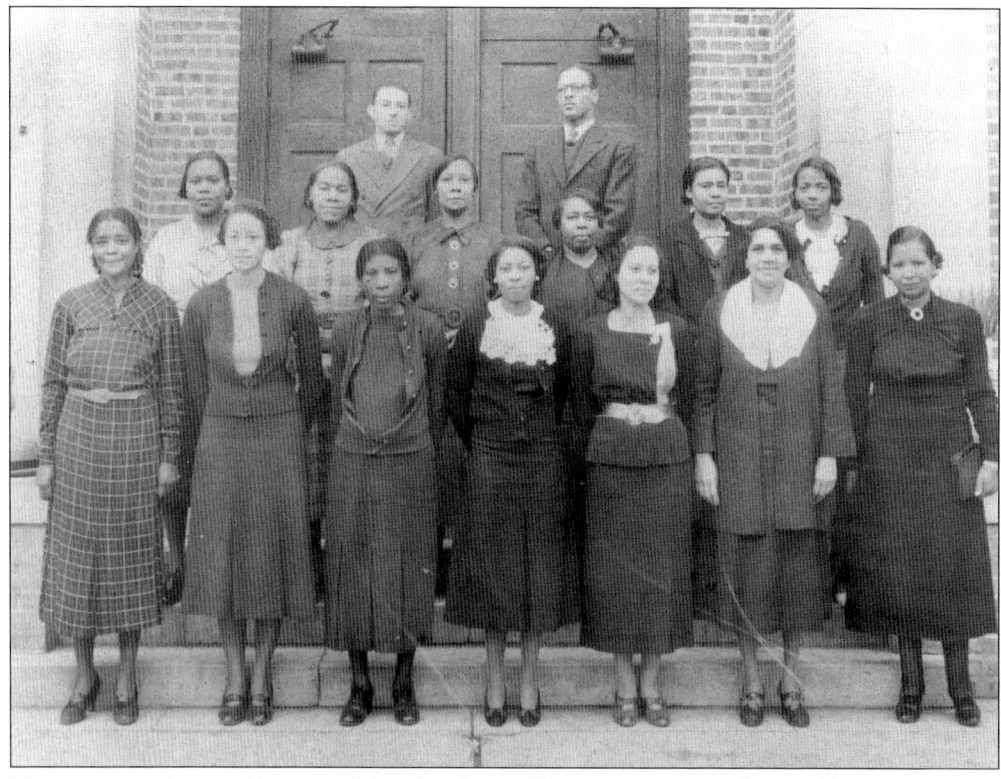

These are teachers at Lincoln High School, c. 1930. From left to right are (front row) Viola Hunter, Ruth Matthews, Jeanette Reid, Alma Myrick, Wilma Cross, Willie K. Perkins, and Alease Twine; (middle row) Daisy Hall, Letitia Taylor Byrd, Henrietta Williams, Alzinia McPherson, Marie Hicks, and Paralee Webb; (back row) R. Frank Nims and Cecil Walker, principal and assistant principal, respectively.

One

PIONEERS

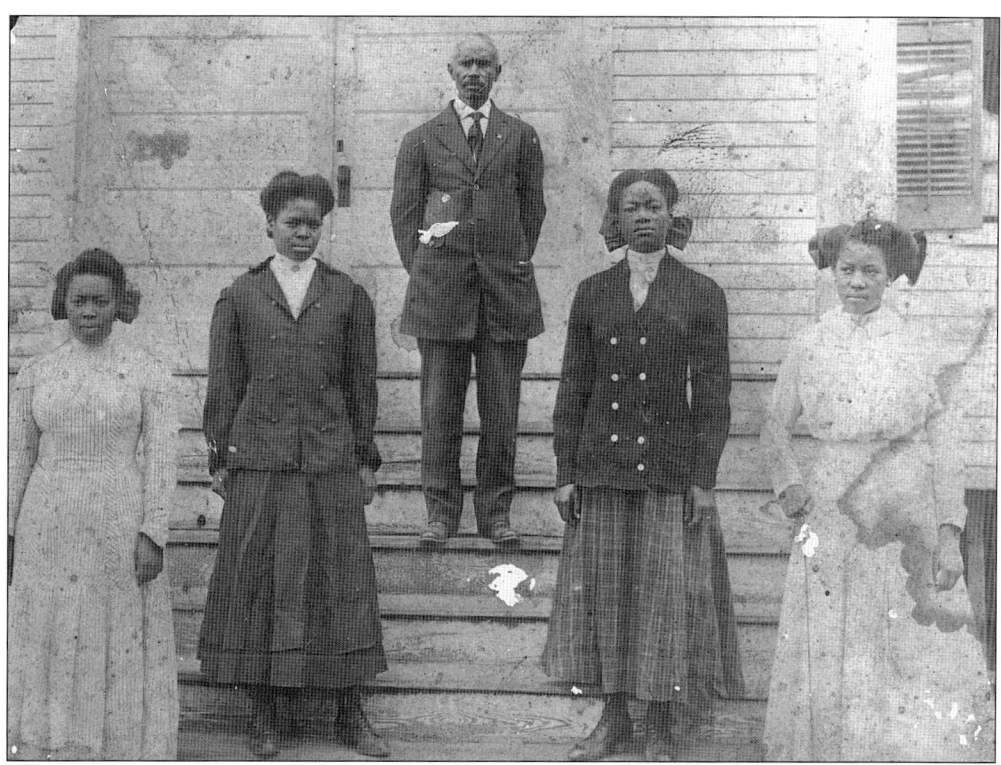

John Gilmore Riley Sr. was photographed in 1898 with teachers on the steps of the Lincoln Normal Institute, later named Lincoln High School. Riley served as a teacher and, later, as principal of Lincoln from 1893 until retiring in 1926. At the time of his death in 1954 at age 97, Riley owned over 150 pieces of real estate, much of it in what is now downtown Tallahassee.

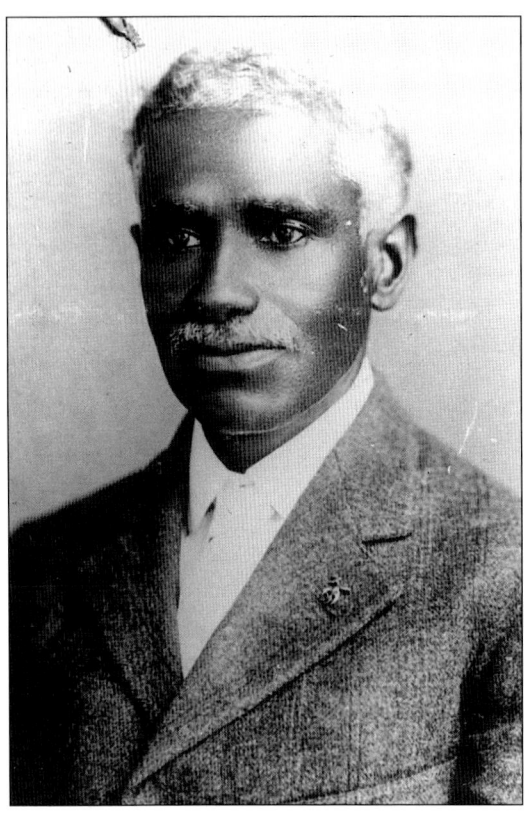

John Gilmore Riley Sr. (1857–1954), who was born into slavery, was a self-taught educator, civic leader, civil rights activist, businessman, and the Grand High Priest of the Royal Arch Masons of Florida. He was the first Tallahassee Mason to achieve the rank of Grand Senior Warden representing the Grand Union Lodge of Florida F&AM, PHA (Free and Accepted Masons, Prince Hall Affiliate). Riley was the first black principal of the original Lincoln High School, one of three freedmen schools built for blacks during Reconstruction. His was a phenomenal rise that defied all odds.

The following letter, dated April 24, 1939, was sent from John G. Riley to Walter White, the president of the National Association for the Advancement of Colored People (NAACP).

Mr. Dear Mr. White,

Here is the second and, perhaps, final report on the Panama City lynching. Clipping from the Jacksonville Journal. I think Florida has a very conscientious prosecuting officer in the person of Attorney General George Cooper Gibbs who will give Florida lynchers some trouble.

The fight is on to the finish between Democracy and mobocracy and one or the other or both must go for a more dynamic government that will protect the life, liberty and property of the people. The filibustering of mobrocracy in the Senate over the Anti-lynching bill was a stunning blow to Democracy which will cost the tax payers $560,000.00.

The layman doubts the survival of Democracy should mobocracy succeed again with a similar attack. Do every thing possible to avert the repetition of success. We have written Senator Andrews to help you. Our other Senator is in sympathy with mobocracy.

We appreciate very much your brainy and diplomatic way of handling the lynching problem and feel grateful to other Congressmen who have the moral courage to cooperate with you.

Remember the widow whose constant persistency with the unjust judge avenged her of her adversary. You and all forces will win by keeping everlastingly at it on the battle front. With best wishes for your every success, I am yours most truly,
J.G. Riley (Source: Florida State University, Strozier Library).

Emlin Riley, photographed in the 1960s, was the youngest son of John Gilmore Riley. Emlin was an insurance agent for the Afro American Life Insurance Company.

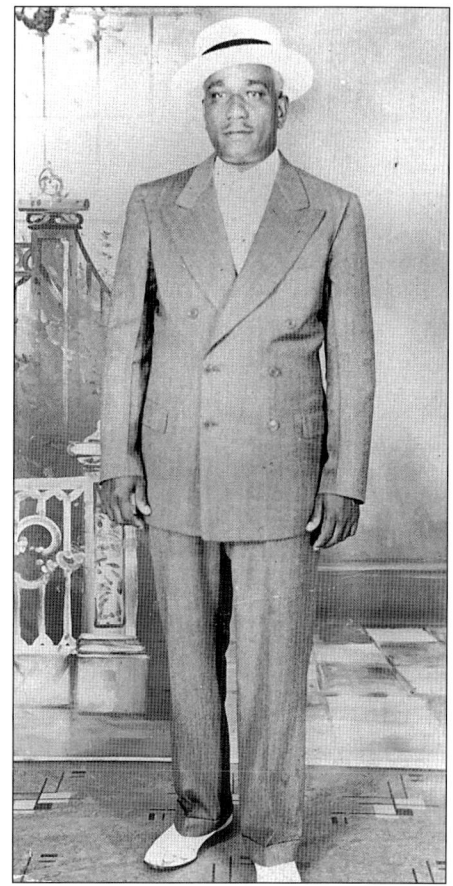

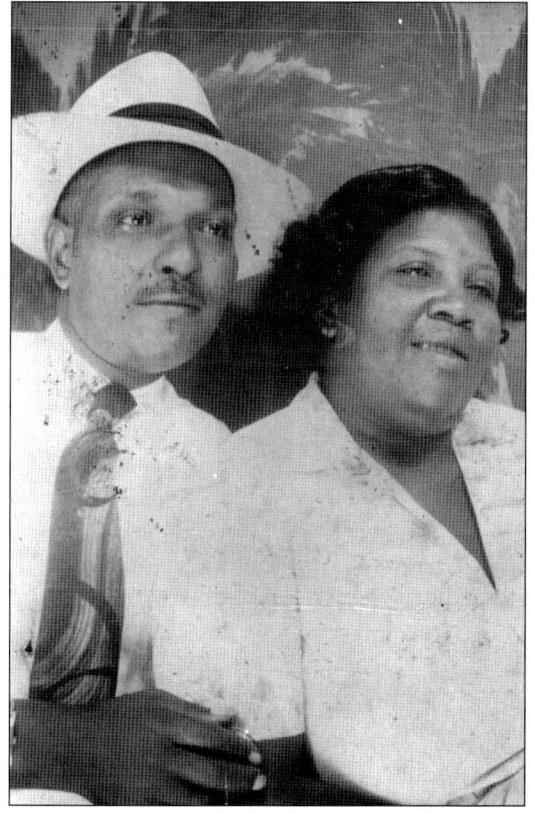

John Riley Jr., son of John Gilmore Riley, is seen here with his wife, Ellen Donaldson Riley, in the 1950s. Ellen Riley had two sisters, Clara Donaldson Givens and Hosea Mills, and a brother who lived in St. Marks, Florida. John Jr. worked at Twine Cleaners on West Brevard Street for many years. In addition to Emlin and John Jr., there were two other siblings: Sarah and Marian, as well as an adopted daughter, Patricia.

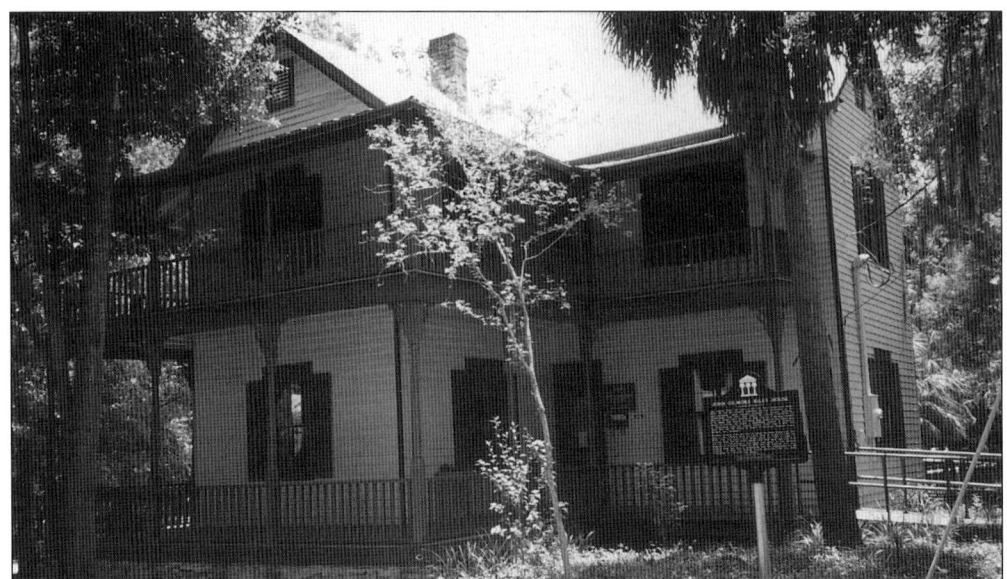

The John Gilmore Riley House, built in 1890 at 419 East Jefferson Street, is the only African-American home in Northwest Florida that is listed in the National Register of Historic Places and was only the second in Florida to receive this designation, which occurred in 1978. The house is located two blocks east of the Leon County Courthouse and four blocks from Florida's Capitol. It is now the Riley House Museum.

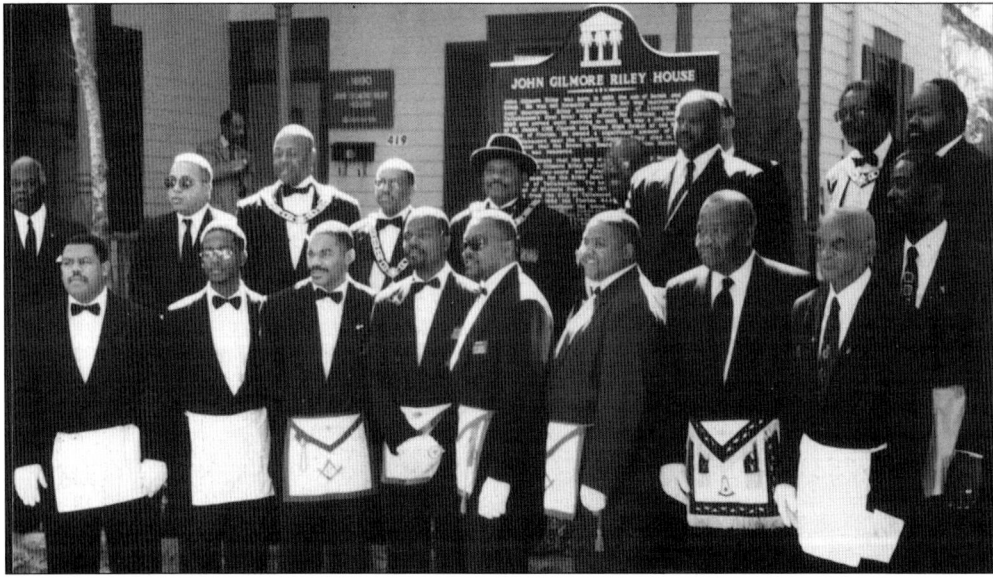

Masons joined government officials in February 1998 to unveil a historic marker at the Riley House. Seen here are, from left to right, (front row) James McElroy, Michael Morgan, Sam Shingles, Arthur Gaines II, Jerome Harris, Drexall Hall, Junious Robinson, Eugene Bailey, and Albert Bush (to the rear of Bailey); (second row) Wilson James, Stanley Youman, Javis Rosier, Charles Jefferson, Michael Moore (Grand Senior Warden representing the Most Worshipful Union Grand Lodge of Florida F&AM, PHA), Osiefield Anderson, Leroy Beverly, Arthur Thompson, and Ben Gaihous. On the porch in the background is attorney Robert Travis, chairman of the Riley House Museum Board.

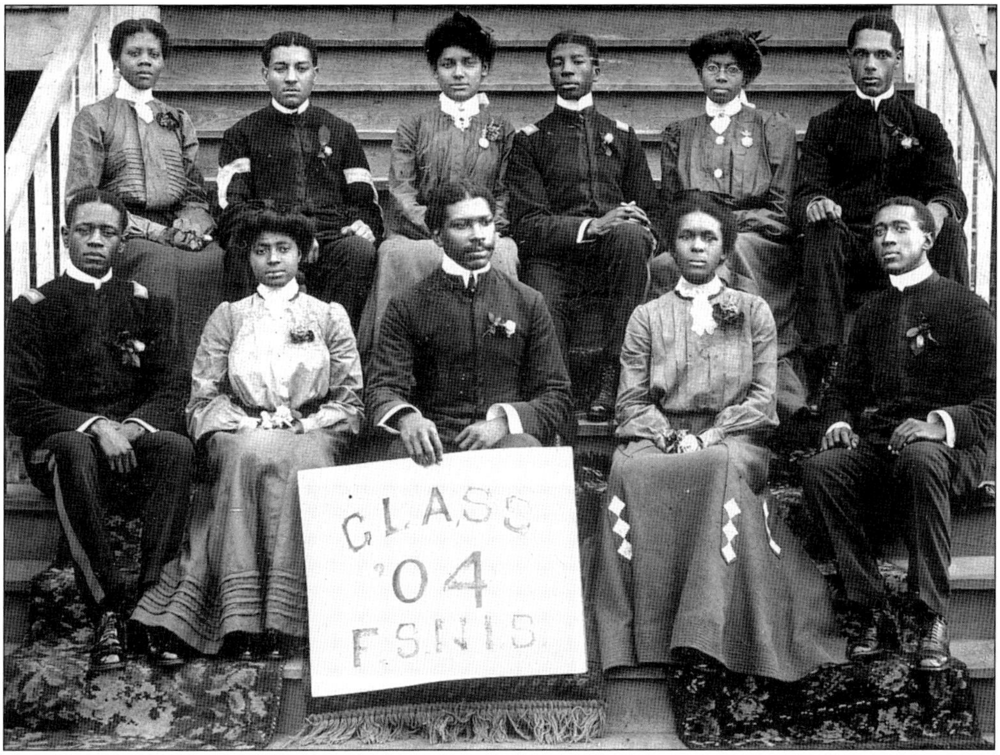

Margaret Yellowhair (first row, second from the right), a 1904 graduate of Florida Normal Institute, now Florida A&M University, taught at Bellaire School and built Capital Theater for blacks during segregation. Her home on what is now Martin Luther King Boulevard still stands and is lived in by her family. She was a member of Bethel AME Church, the president of the A.C.E. (Allen Christian Endeavor) League, a Sunday school teacher, and the grand secretary of the Order of Eastern Star. She is interred in Greenwood Cemetery.

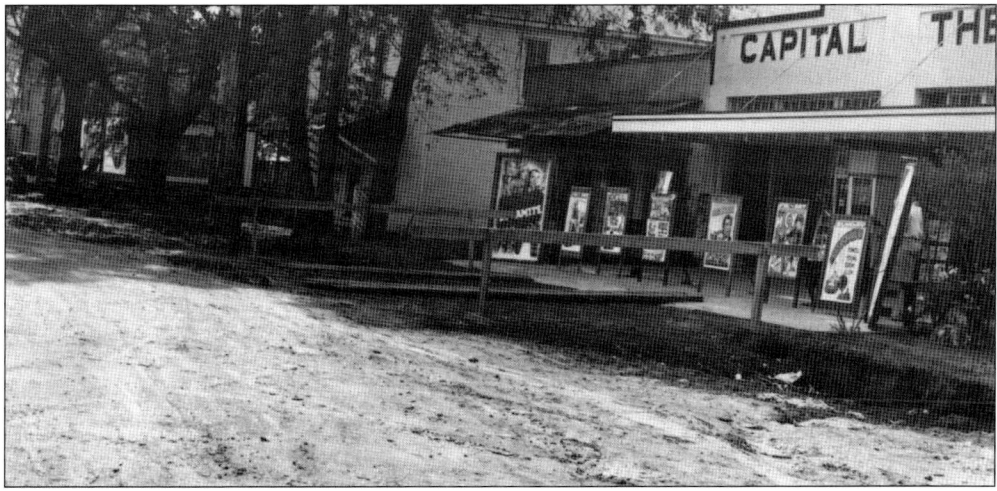

Capital Theater was established by Margaret Yellowhair on Macomb Street in the historic Frenchtown community during the 1930s. Margaret's father, E.H. Yellowhair, was a Tallahassee councilman in 1883–1884 and a tax assessor in 1885. He was born in March 1852 and died in 1926. (Courtesy of the Florida State Archives.)

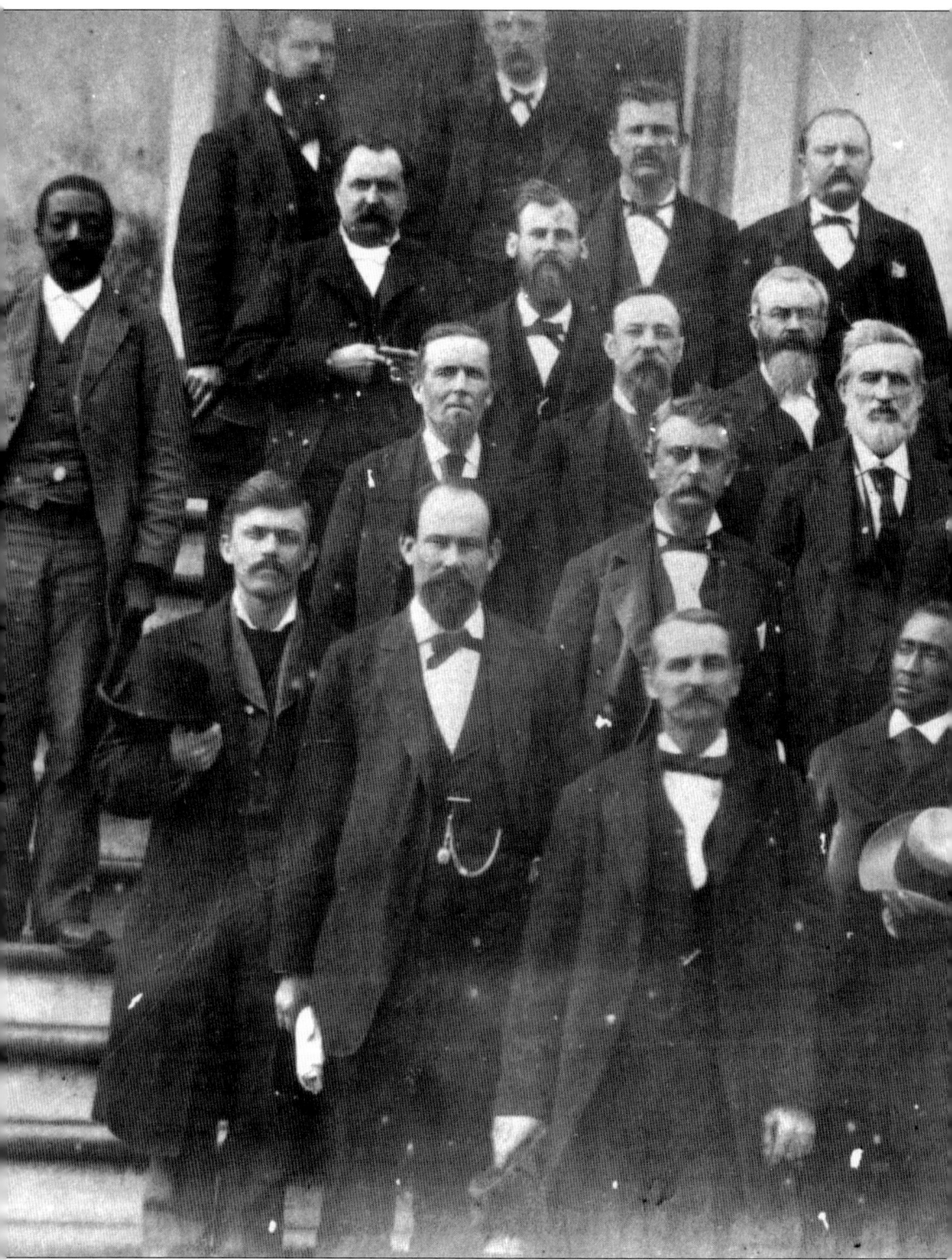

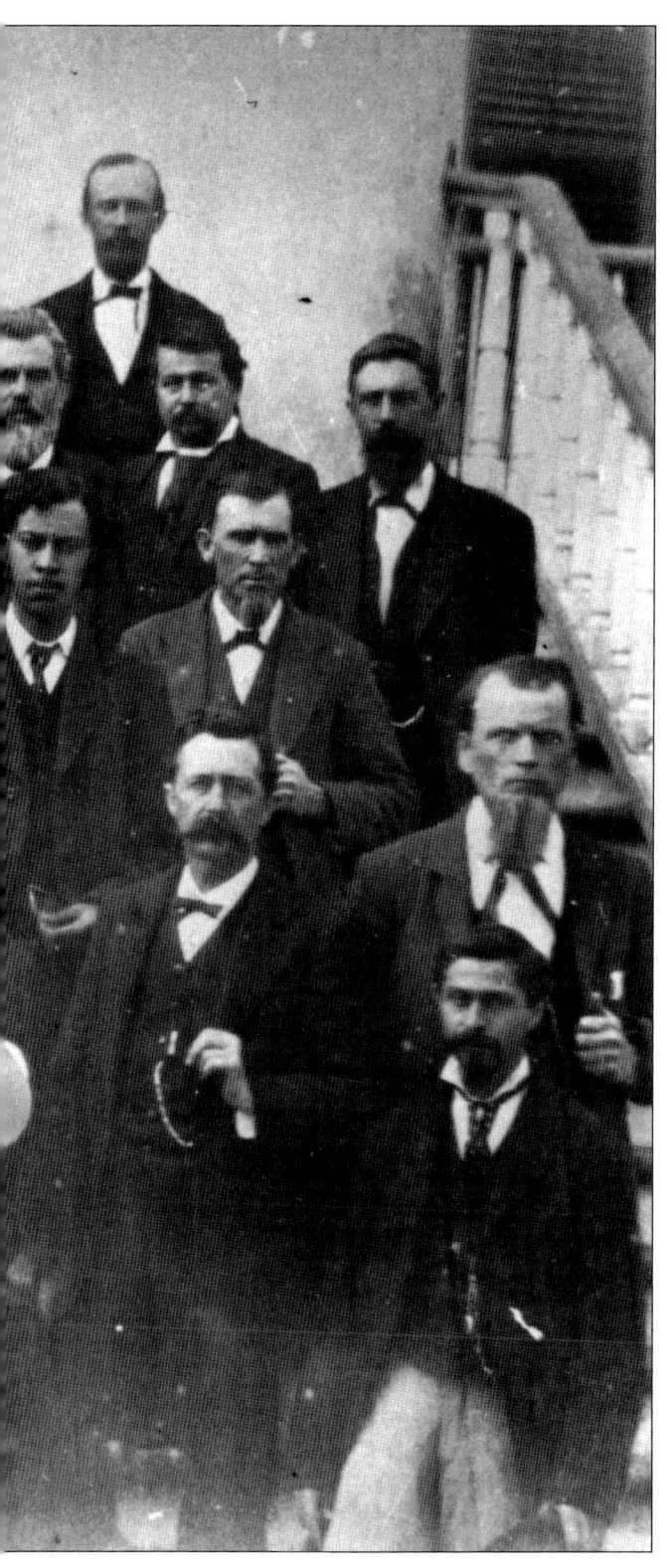

John Wallace (far left), photographed with the Florida senate in 1875, was born into slavery in Gates County, North Carolina, in 1842 and migrated to Leon County at the end of the Civil War. A teacher and a lawyer, he was constable for Leon County for two years, served in the legislature as a representative and senator from 1871 to 1881, and was a justice of the peace in Leon County. Wallace drafted the Carpetbag Rule in Florida. He died on November 25, 1908. Other black legislators shown here are Thomas W. Long (standing in the front row, holding his hat), while directly above and to the right is likely Frederick Hill. Robert Meacham gazes from the second row from the top, third from the right. Standing immediately to the right of Meacham is probably Washington Pope. (Courtesy of the Florida State Archives.)

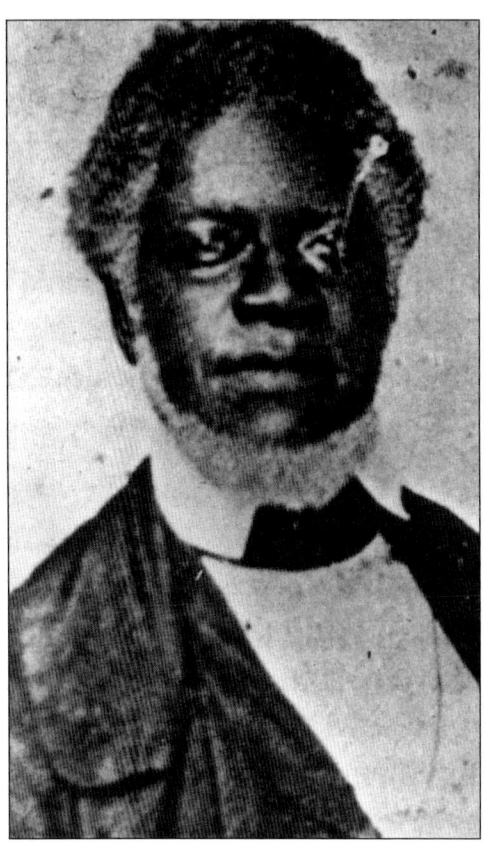

"Father" James Page (1808–1883) taught at Bellaire School on South Adams Street in Tallahassee and founded Bethel Missionary Baptist Church on Martin Luther King Boulevard. Probate case #879 shows him renting a house from Maggie H. Decoursey for $5.50 per month. After his estate claims were settled, $35 was left for his wife, Elizabeth. A former slave, Page was Leon County voter registrar in 1867–1868 and a justice of the peace from 1872 to 1877.

John Elias Proctor, a former slave, is seated on the porch of his Bainbridge Road home in the early 1940s. Proctor served in the House of Representatives from 1873 to 1875 and in 1879, and he served in the Senate in 1883 and 1885. He is listed in a 1977 history of St. Michaels and All Angels Episcopal as a senior warden. Proctor died in 1944 at the age of 100.

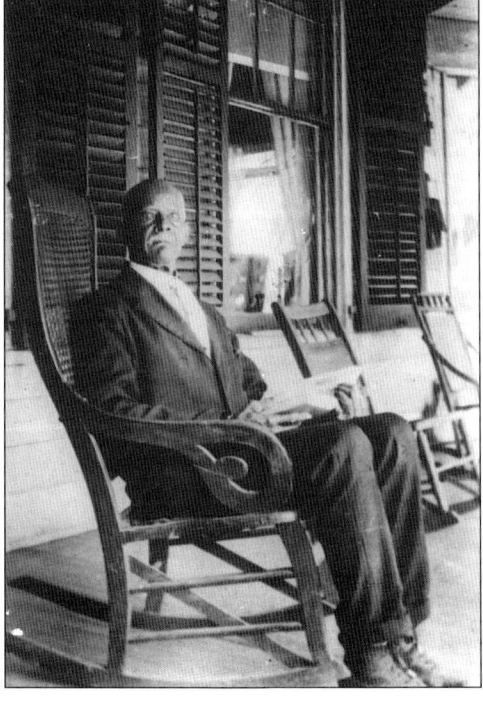

Right: Fred Douglas Lee was the first black policemen in Tallahassee assigned to a regular beat. He was recruited by civil rights activists, including Rev. Charles Kenzie Steele Sr., Fr. David Brooks, Rev. Dan Speed, Rev. K.S. Dupont, Dr. Gilbert Porter, and others to break the color barrier that existed in law enforcement prior to Lee's appointment in the late 1950s.
Lower Left: Maxwell Courtney, a 1962 graduate of the original Lincoln High School, was the first black to attend and graduate from what was then the all-white Florida State University in Tallahassee. His career carried him to Washington, D.C. to work for the federal government. Maxwell met with an untimely death in a drowning accident in the 1970s.
Lower Right: James R. Ford became Tallahassee's first black mayor and, thus, the first black mayor of a capital city in the United States. A native Tallahassean and former educator, Ford ran for commissioner while serving as assistant principal at Leon High School. Prior to public office, he served in the Navy during World War II. A community center, Walker-Ford, is named in his honor.

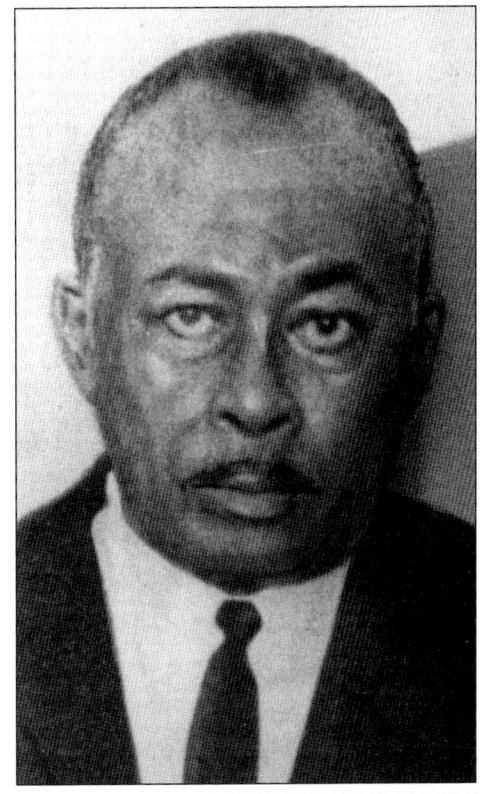

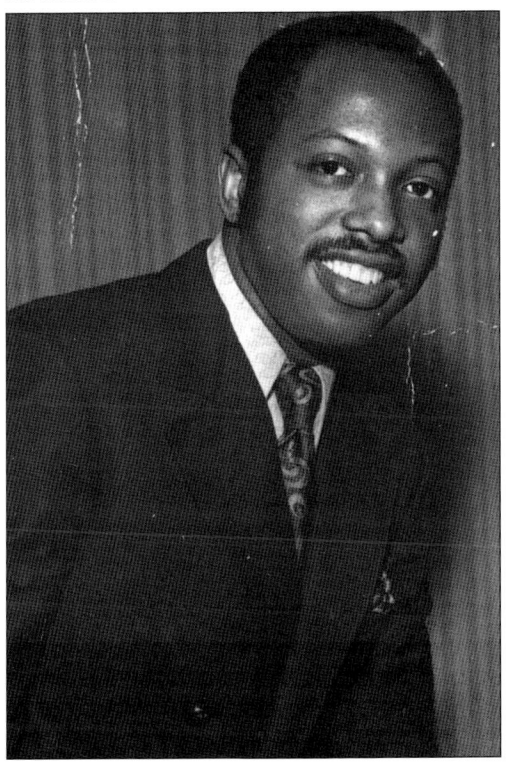

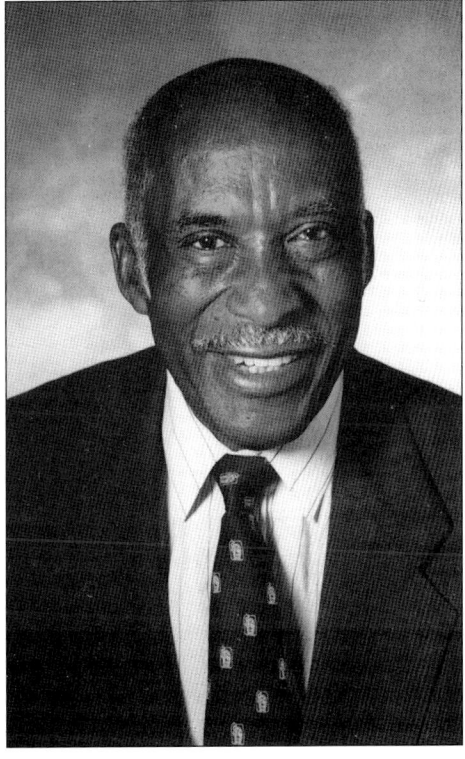

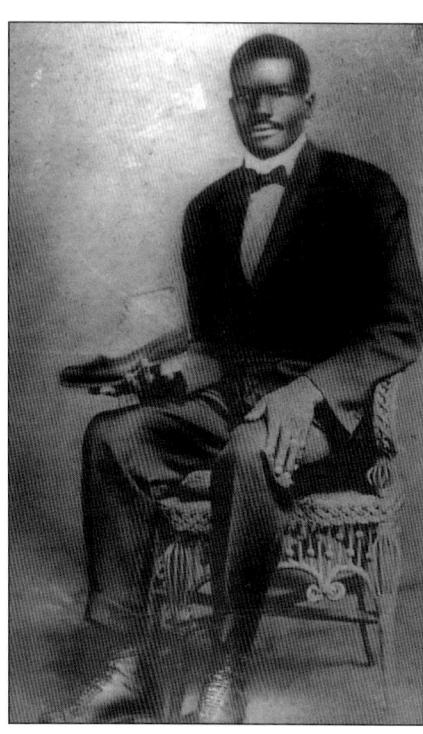

Willis Jiles and his wife, Susie, operated a cobbler business in the Union (Freedmen's) Bank Building. Their children—Willis Jr., James, Sadie, Thelma Jiles Speed, Wilburt, Eleanor Jiles Dupont, Dr. Zola Jiles Sullivan, Samuel, Susie, and Marie Jiles Williams—received college degrees from Florida A&M and Xavier Universities.

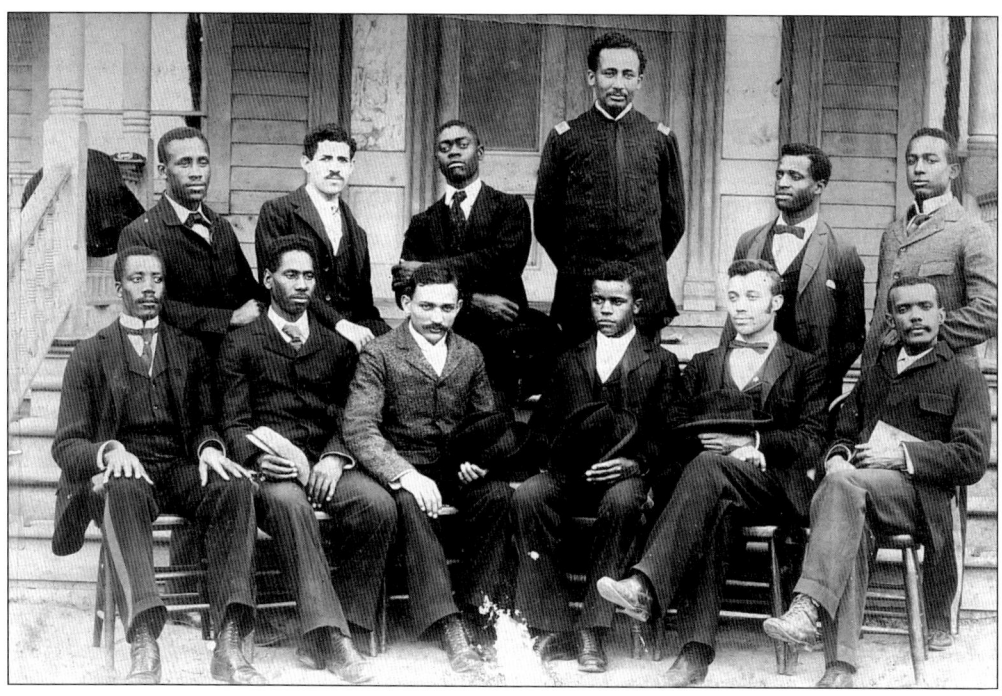

Anatole Emile Martin Sr. (front row, far right), seen here *c.* 1897, plied his trade as a tailor with the armed forces during the Spanish-American War. He later taught tailoring at the State Normal Industrial College, which later became Florida A&M University (FAMU). In 1918, Martin purchased the tailoring business of Perry Hicks at 359 East Jefferson Street. For over 30 years, he served a select clientele with male fashions and alterations.

Two

BUSINESSES

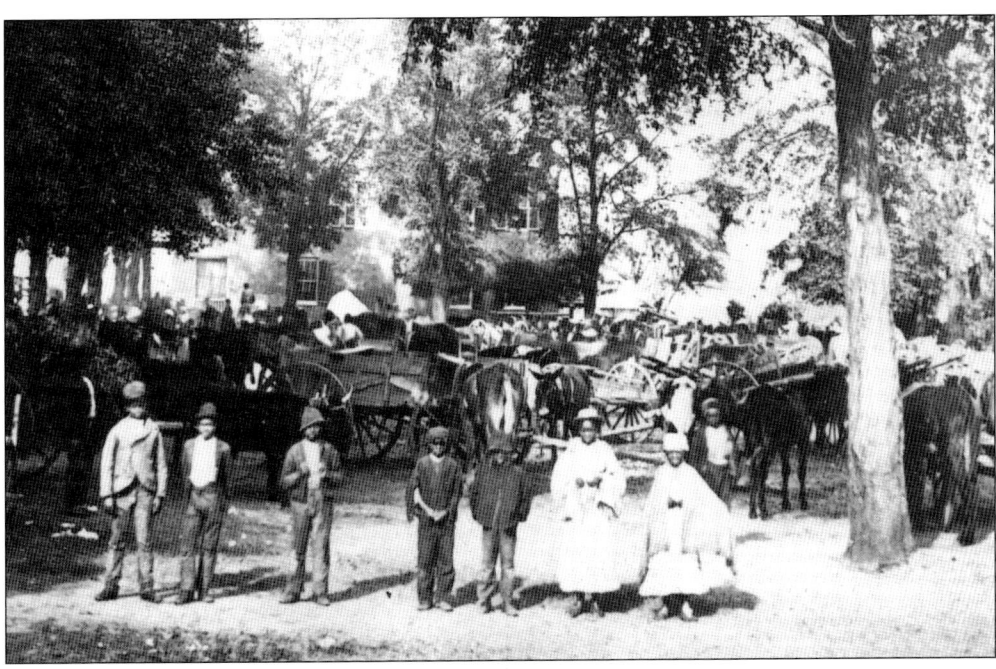

Blacks owned many businesses in Tallahassee after Emancipation; they were farm owners, medical doctors, and ran private businesses. The Market on Washington Square, photographed here in the 1870s, was a venue for many black farmers who brought their produce for sale. It was also a site where families, most of whom lived far apart from each other on farms and plantations, could meet to visit and socialize. (Courtesy of the Florida State Archives.)

William Cats, Pool Hall
William Gunn, physician
Robert Hall, fish market
Emma Hawkins, fish market
George Hicks, grocer
Amos S. Jerry, druggist
Willis Jiles, shoemaker
Henry Magbe, grocer
Oliver Mills, barber
John J. Nims, grocer
Ernest C.A. Norwood, tailor
William Ponder, fruit stand
Edward A. Pottsdamer, cigar maker
Piet Ringling, dentist
George Rollins, meat market
Washington Singleton, pool hall
William G. Stewart, barber
James W. Twine, shoemaker
William Washington, grocer
Lonnie H. Whaley, barber
Tony Williams, blacksmith
Godfrey Wilson, restaurant/grocer
Robert Wilson, tailor
Lizzie Douglas, cafeteria
"Buster" Edwards, Blacksmith
Afro American Insurance
T. McKinnis, restaurant
T. Hadley, grocer
A. Wright, bakery
Artistic Barber Shop
Streamline Cleaners
J. Tookes Villa, hotel
Red Bird
Piet Ringeling, dentist

Benjamin Bryan, butcher
Thomas Chester, huckster
Virgil Croom, barber
Henry Asbury, butcher
Stephen Manor, restaurant
H. Scott, shoemaker
Granville Sheppard, blacksmith
John Sneed, saloon
John Williams, butcher
Alpha O. Campbell, physician
P. G. Hicks, tailor
William Houston, barber
T.P. Pope, fish market
John Nelson, fish market
W.G. Stewart, barber
Thomas Confectionary Co.
L.H. Whaley, barber
J.R.D. Laster, mortician
W. Norris, barber
L. Sims, barber
R. Richardson, dry cleaners
C. Robinson, cleaners
W. Jenkins, dentist
Thomas Strong, mortician
E. Gay, furniture
J. Lincoln, Jewelry
R. Richardson, restaurant
A. Alexander, service station
B. Davis, dry cleaners
Modern Cleaners
Paradise Grill
Chicken Shack
W.H. Hill, Green Lantern Restaurant
A.S. Jerry, MD

The above is a listing of black-owned businesses during the early part of the 20th century. It was compiled from information contained in *Polk's Tallahassee Directories of Householders, Occupants of Office Buildings and other Business Places 1904–1946*, and from oral history interviews.

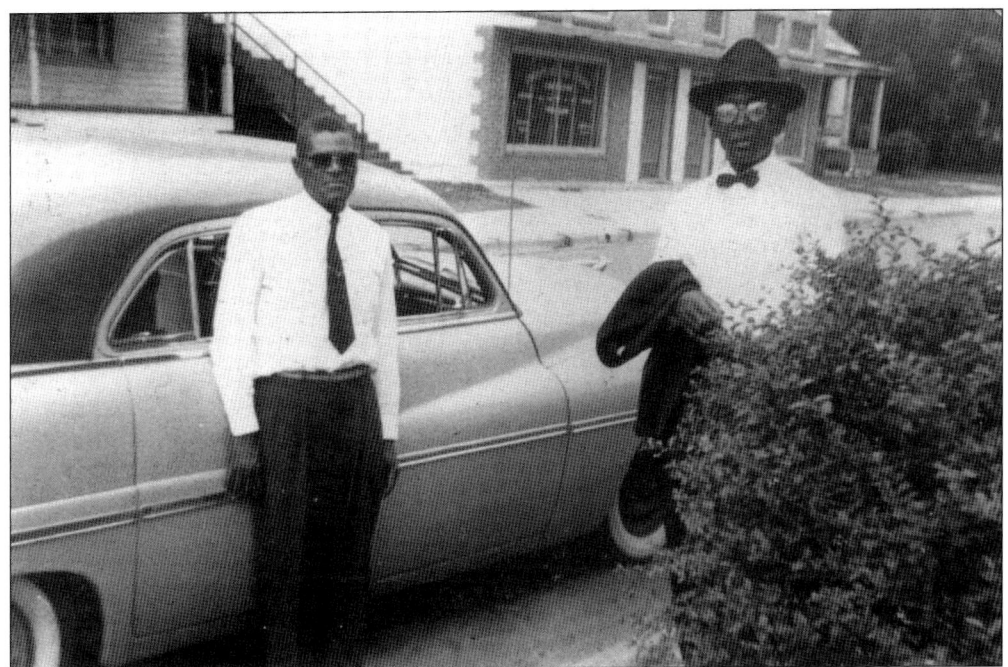

James "Key" Oliver and Arthur "Bim" Johnson stand in front of Twine's Cleaners. Oliver owned extensive property and a store in the historic black community of "Carroll Quarters," located behind the present Miracle Theater Mall on Thomasville Road. Johnson owned and operated a wood yard at the corner of Dunn and Dewey Streets; he delivered wood to numerous citizens, including governors.

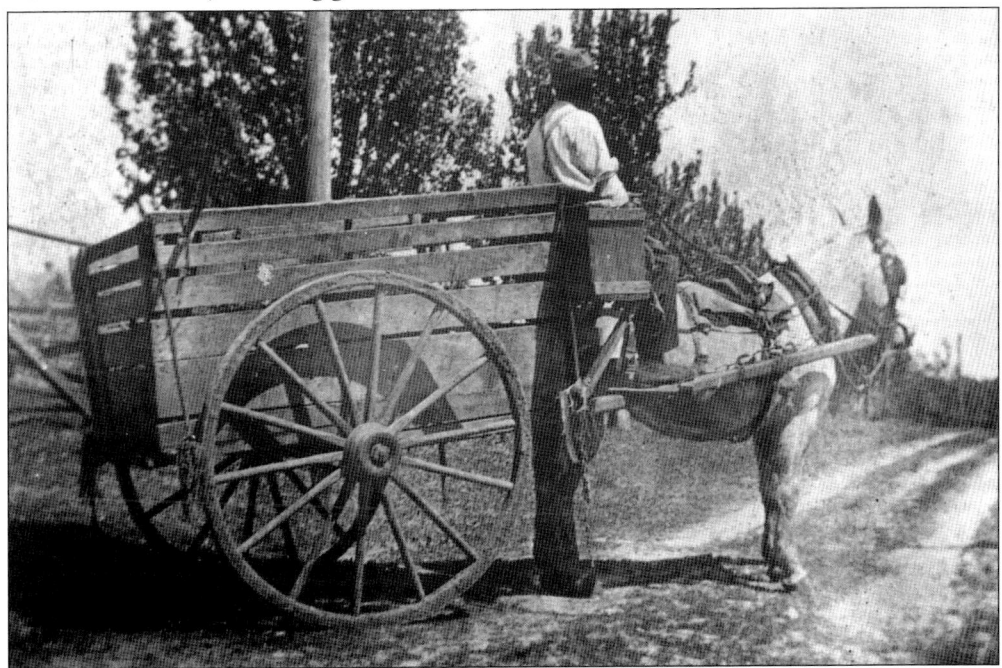

A trash collector was photographed on Tallahassee Street in 1916. At that time, this was a business usually owned and operated by private black citizens.

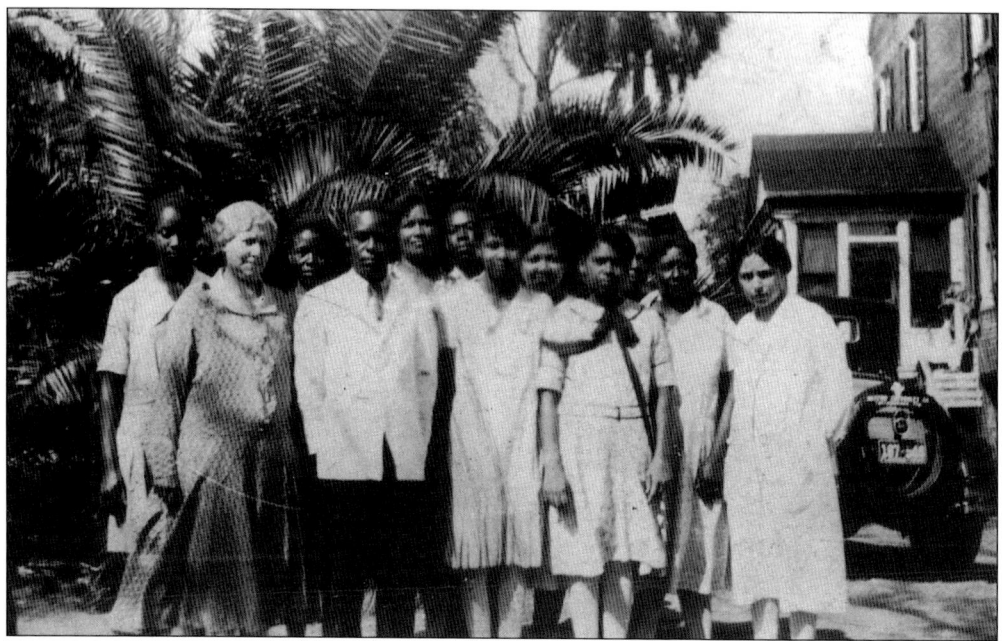

The current Chamber of Commerce building, formerly located at the corner of Park Avenue and Adams Street, housed the Dutch Kitchen. Photographed at the rear of the business is the restaurant staff.

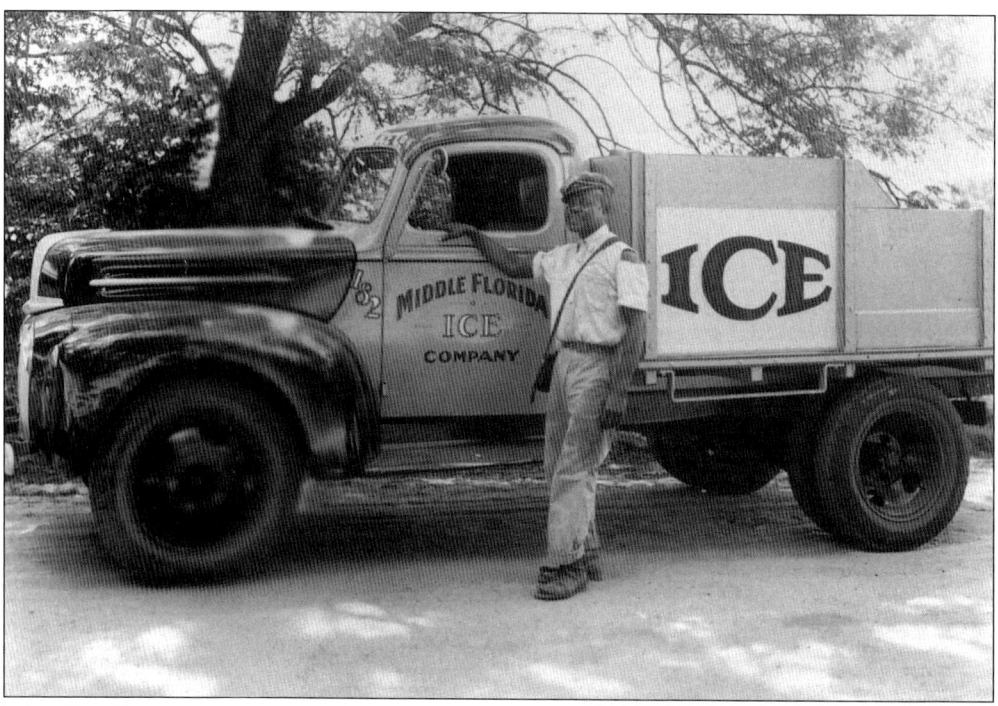

John "Buck" McKinney was a deliveryman for Middle Florida Ice Company during the 1940s. Most black homes received his services since there were no refrigerators. Blocks of ice were purchased and stored, sometimes underground, to preserve food until it was ready to be used. McKinney raised his family at 61 West Georgia Street.

Right: Joseph "Joe" Franklin owned and operated Modern Cleaners on Macomb Street in the historic Frenchtown community until the 1970s. The building is still standing, although the business is no longer in operation. Franklin's family originated 6 miles from Tallahassee on Highway 90 East.
Lower Left: Peaches Alease Twine Campbell poses in front of the family business, Twine's Cleaners and Laundry at 600 West Brevard Street, during the 1940s. For many years, Twine's was one of few such facilities available for use by African Americans. The building now houses NuDay Graphics, an African-American printing business owned and operated by Irving Holiday.
Lower Right: Rev. Cecil Sykes, a prominent AME religious leader, was also one of Tallahassee's early successful black businessmen. For many years, Reverend Sykes operated a shoe repair shop and store on West Virginia Street in the historic Frenchtown community.

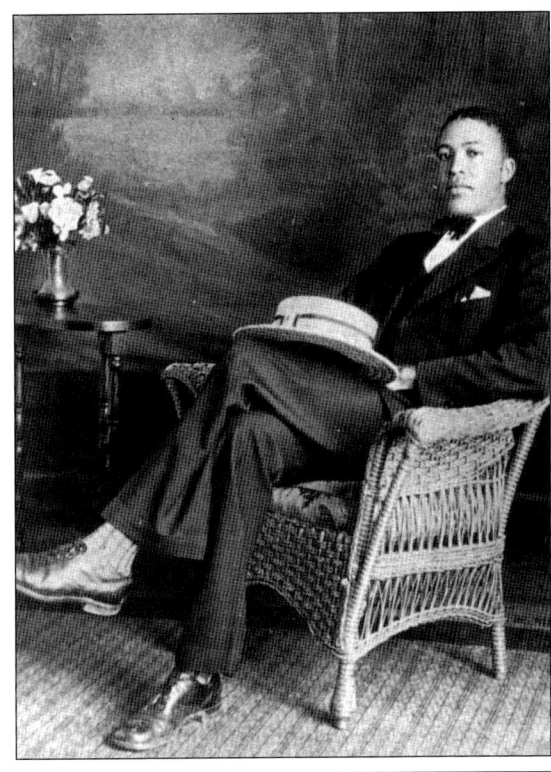

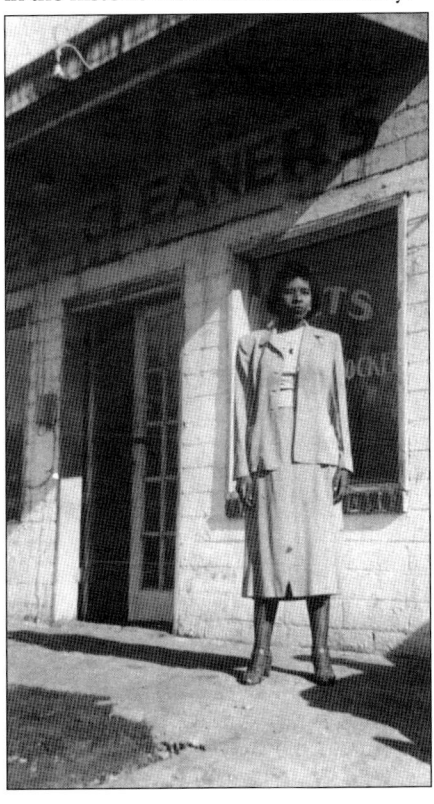

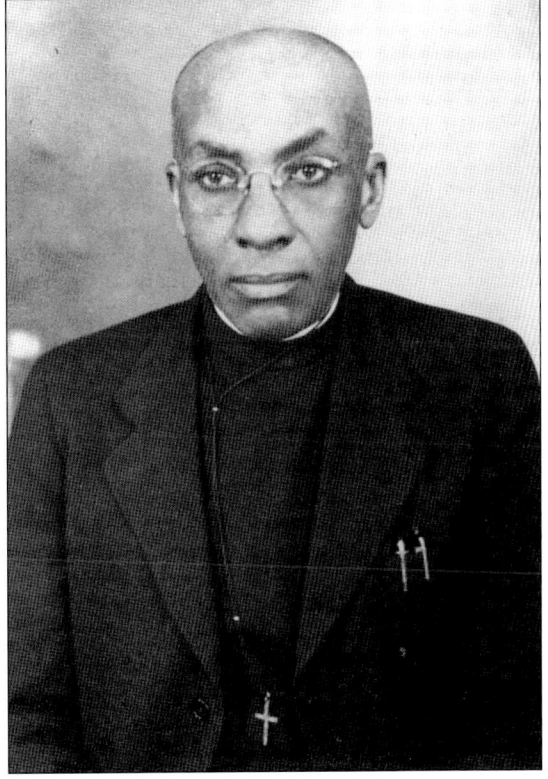

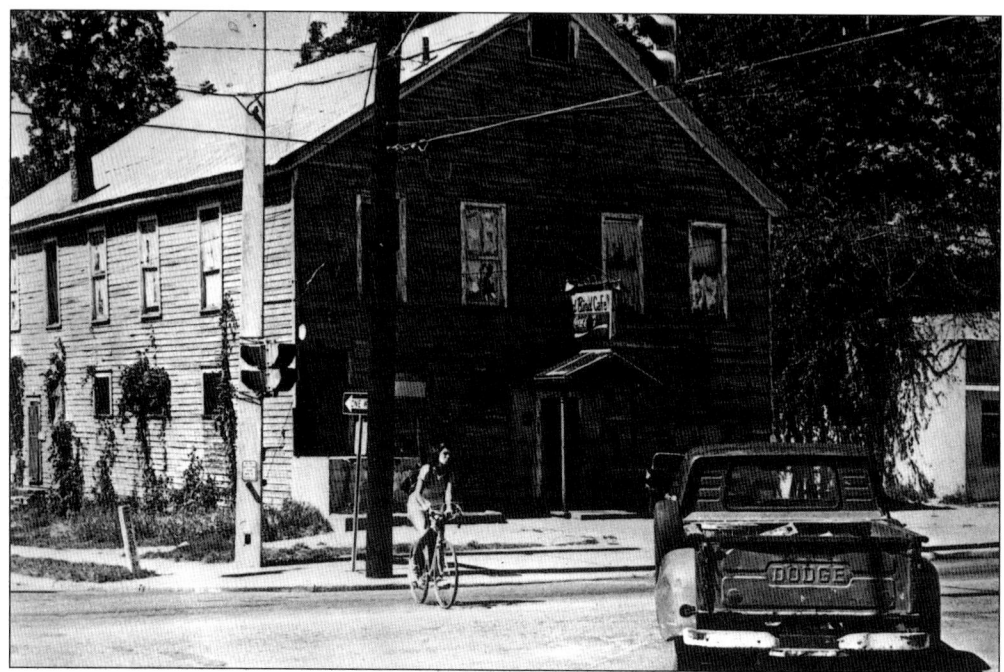

Knights of Pythias Hall, a late-night spot in the Frenchtown community, fell to the wrecking crew during the 1970s. Located at the corner of Virginia and Macomb Streets, it later became Red Bird Cafe. Along with other night spots such as Royal Palace, Cafe Deluxe, and Green Lantern, the Red Bird hosted famous musicians on the "chitterling circuit" including Al Green, Ray Charles, Bobby Blue Bland, and Little Richard.

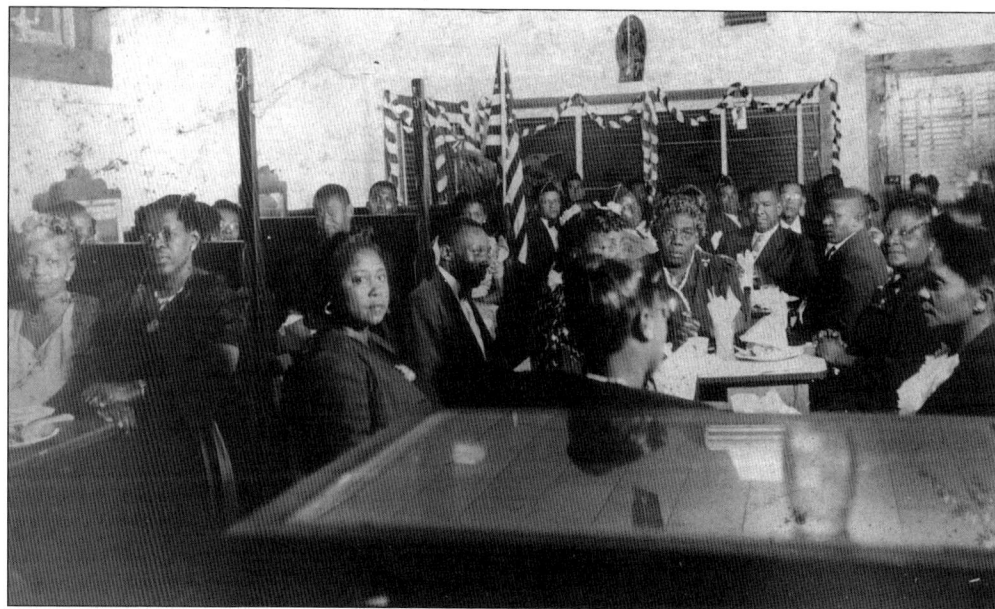

The Twilight Inn operated at 612 Madison Street from the 1920s through the 1960s. This photograph shows an American Legion holiday celebration held at the club, which catered to the middle-class black community. The business was owned and operated by Sallie Twine. Next door, at 614 Madison, was another family business—a boardinghouse and cafe.

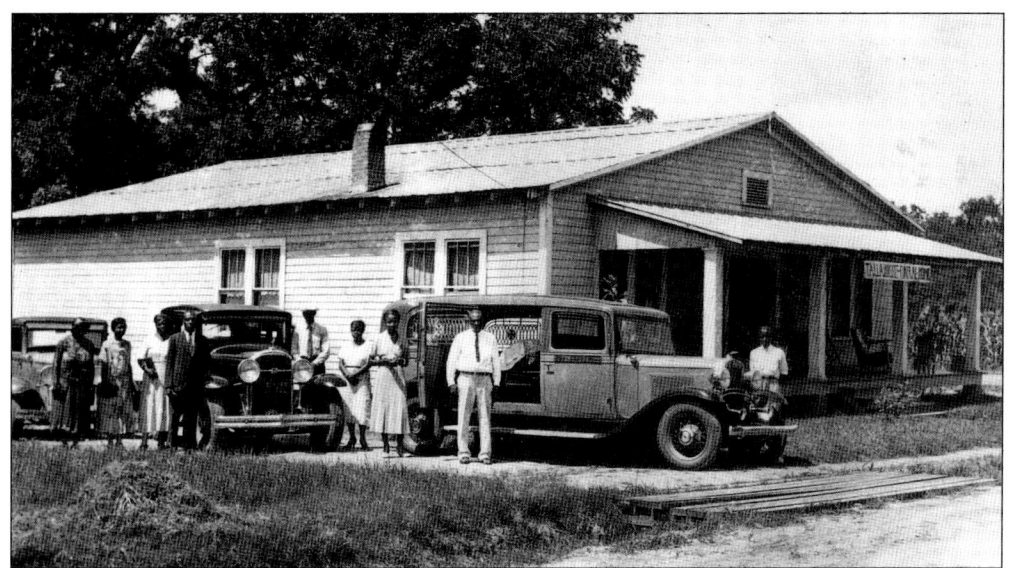

Thomas Strong purchased Mitchell Funeral Home (Tallahassee Funeral Home), located at 551 West Carolina Street, in the 1940s. Elbert W. Jones assisted in the business. Upon Strong's death in 1947, Jones became the new funeral director, purchasing half ownership and renaming the business Strong and Jones Funeral Home Incorporated. The business is currently operated by descendants of the founders, Linn Ann Jones Griffin and Darryl Lawrence.

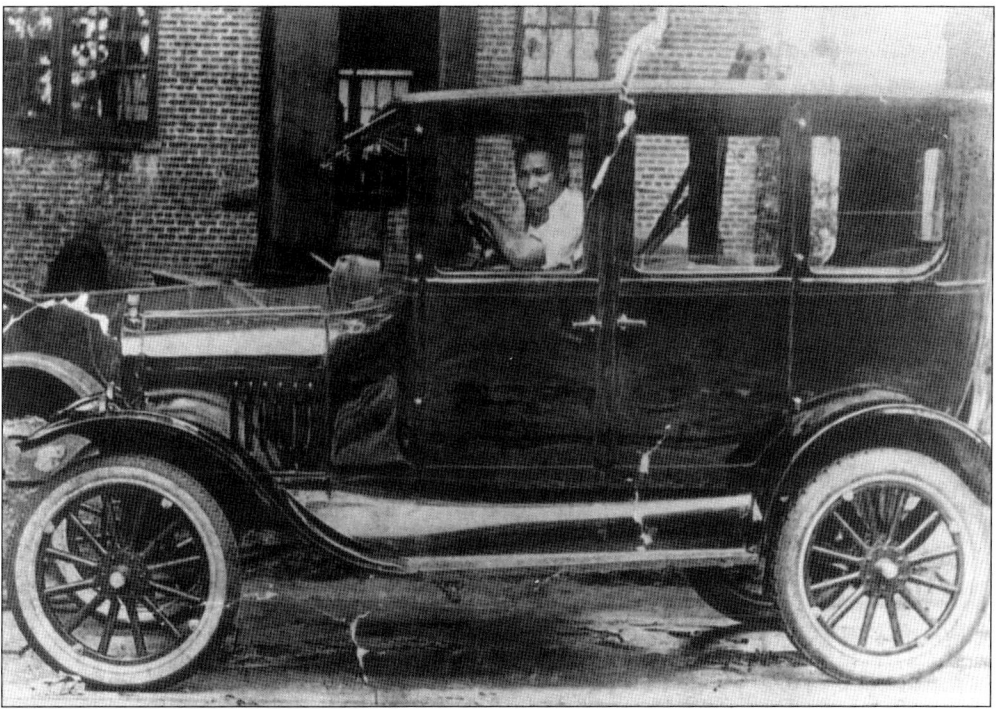

Paul Roberts (1889–1961), a farmer in the Rock Hill community, peddled fruits and vegetables within the city and sold them at the farmers' market (Curb Market), which was located in the vicinity of the old jail house on East Gaines Street. Additionally, he used his vehicle to transport people in order to supplement his income.

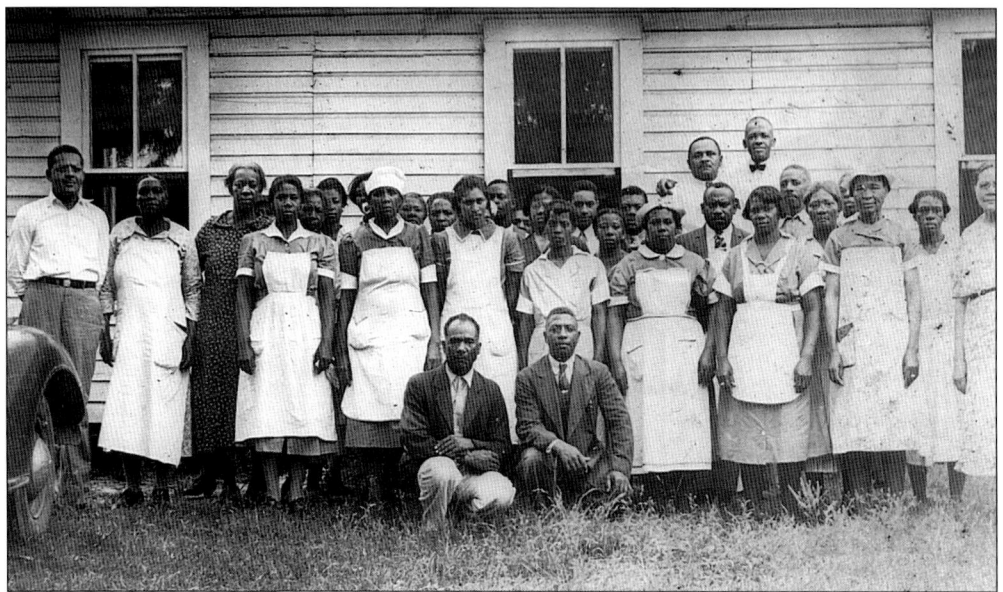

Black farmers, including Mary Speed (front row, standing, second from left) and Alberta McClendon (front row, standing, fifth from left), are pictured at the Curb Market located in the 300 block of East Gaines Street during the late 1940s. The site at that time was adjacent to the Leon County health department.

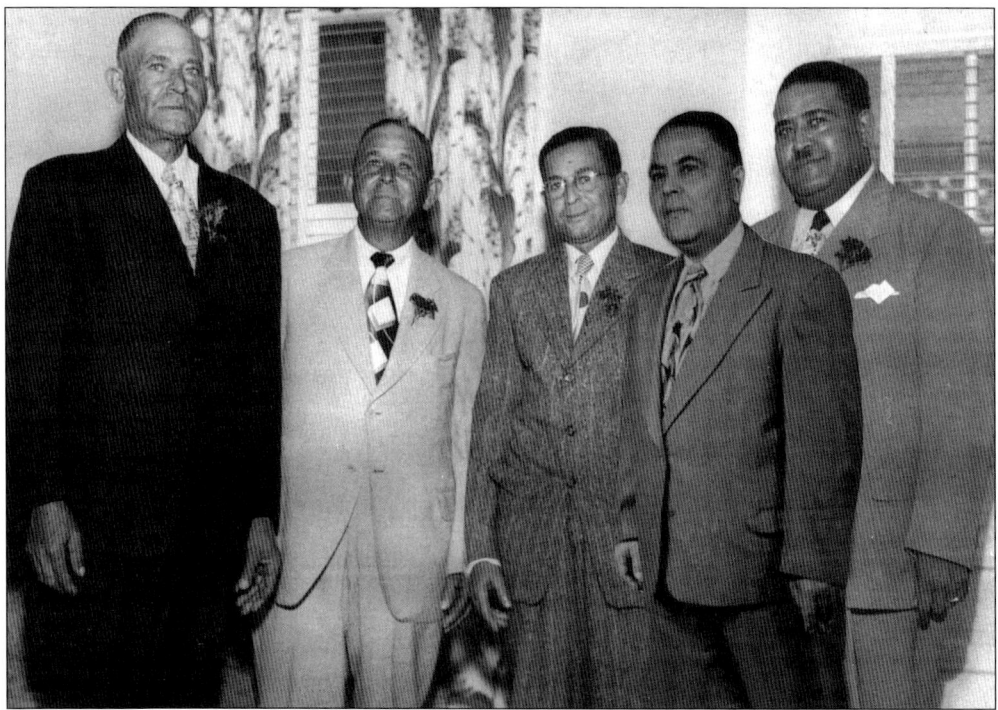

Mary and Harkless Hadley's five sons, who are, from left to right, Herbert, Hayward, Virgil, Ralph, and Tom, continued their family legacy by operating the family businesses on West Brevard Street. The businesses included two grocery stores, a filling station, and rental properties until the 1970s. The family homestead still stands at Brevard Street.

Three

CAREGIVERS

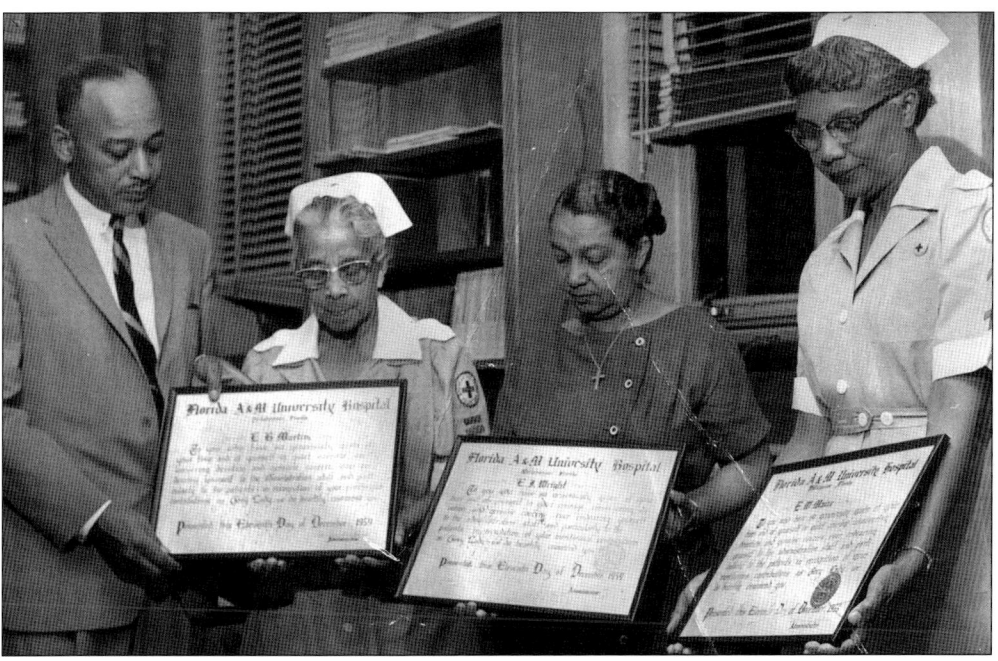

Elizabeth Hawkins Martin (second from the left), Eloise Wright (third from the left), and another volunteer Gray Lady at Florida A&M University Hospital receive certificates of appreciation from Millard Johnson, a hospital administrator, in the 1940s. Martin, a former schoolteacher, was an active member of the Gray Ladies of the American Red Cross and an active member of a local women's club which provided nursery care and special assistance for the elderly.

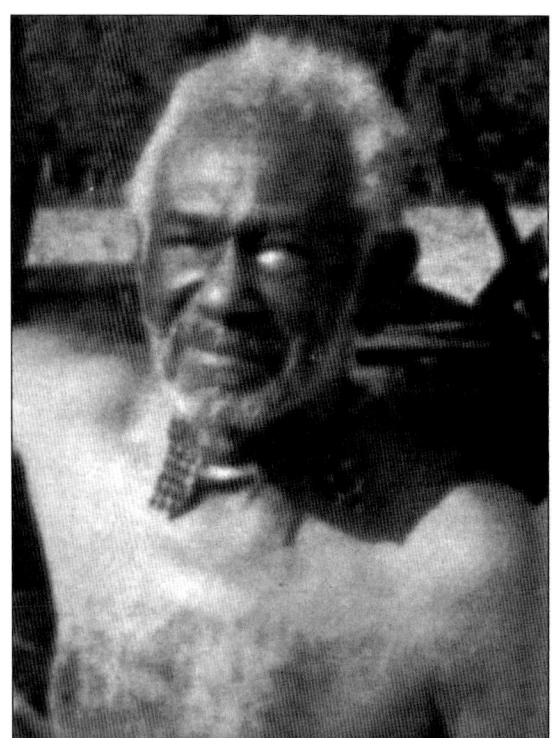

Grant Jackson's ancestors spent their early years among the Native Americans who shielded them from slave owners. Years later, Jackson acquired and farmed his own land in Miccosukee. A "medicine man," he was well known for his cures using herbs and roots. The copper around his neck was often worn to relieve arthritis. People would come from near and far to experience Jackson's healing potions.

Maggie Purcell, a practical nurse in Leon County, provided at-home care for many Tallahassee families, white and black, during the 1920s through the 1950s. She also made frequent trips to visit rural families and distribute articles of clothing. Her home was located on Pensacola Street, an African-American community that is now the location of the Tallahassee-Leon County Civic Center. "Mag" died in the 1960s.

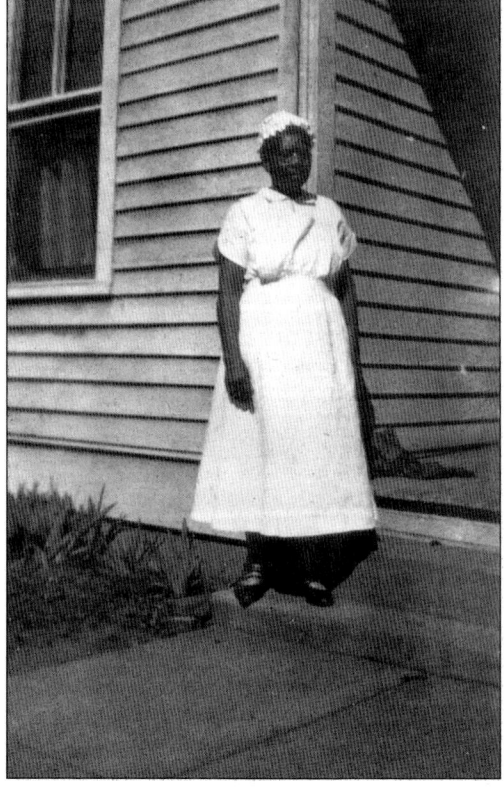

Dr. William J. Gunn (1855–1922) was one of the first black medical doctors in Florida. Mentored by Dr. Betton, a white physician who financed Gunn's schooling at Meharry Medical School, Gunn returned to Tallahassee and opened a practice on College Avenue. Upon his death, it was said that his was "a physicians' untiring service among his people, such service as was given without stint, modestly, with fortitude and courage."

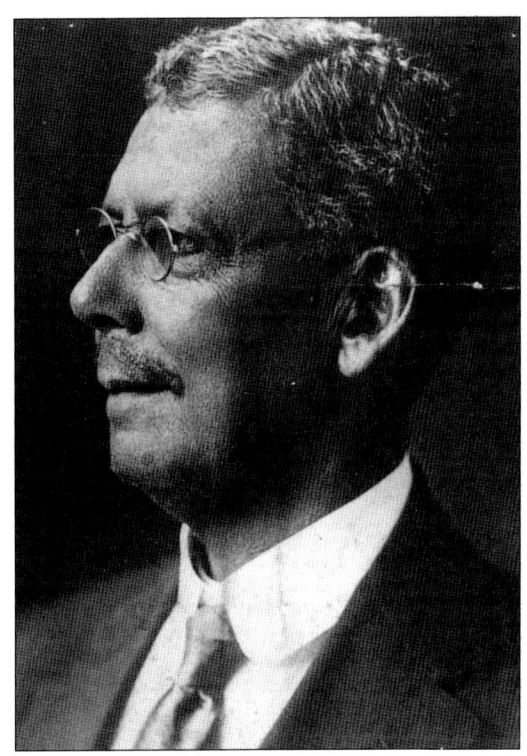

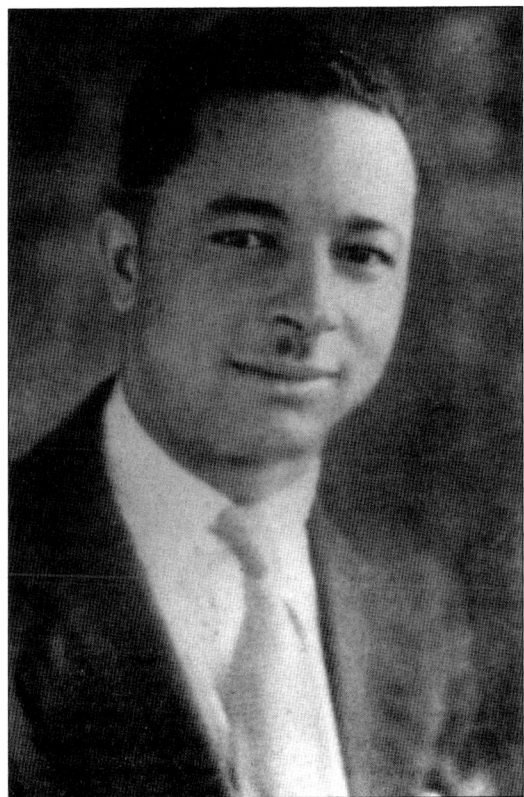

Dr. Leonard Hobson Buchannan (L.H.B.) Foote, a graduate of Howard University, served as the medical director at Florida A&M University and maintained a private practice at 1747 South Adams Street. Dr. Foote initiated the first Annual Medical Clinic on the campus. His former office has been restored and houses the practice of Dr. Bennie Thompkins, an African-American dentist.

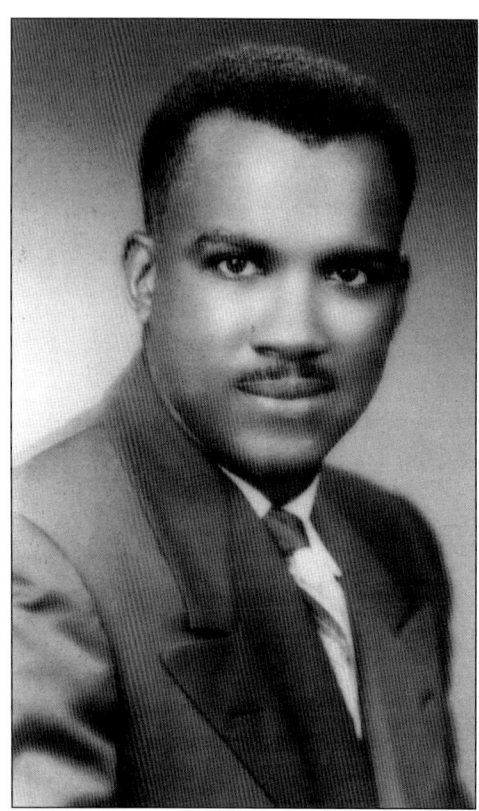

Dr. Charles Nathaniel Stevens (November 20, 1921–February 28, 1981) was photographed in August 1954 at Pike's Studio on College Avenue for a news article announcing the opening of his medical practice at 510 West Tennessee Street. Dr. Steven's office was located above Johnson's Furniture Company, next door to the Leon Theater, before he relocated it to West Georgia Street. The building on Georgia Street currently houses the dental practice of Dr. Freddie Martin, a descendant of Glover and Christine Martin.

Dr. Millard C. Williams, one of Tallahassee's first black dentists, began his medical practice on Tennessee Street and relocated to 501 West Georgia Street in a building owned by Dr. Charles N. Stevens. He was the secretary of the Inter-Civic Council and, thus, at the forefront of Tallahassee's Civil Rights Movement. Williams was the first black to serve as chairman of the Tallahassee Housing Authority.

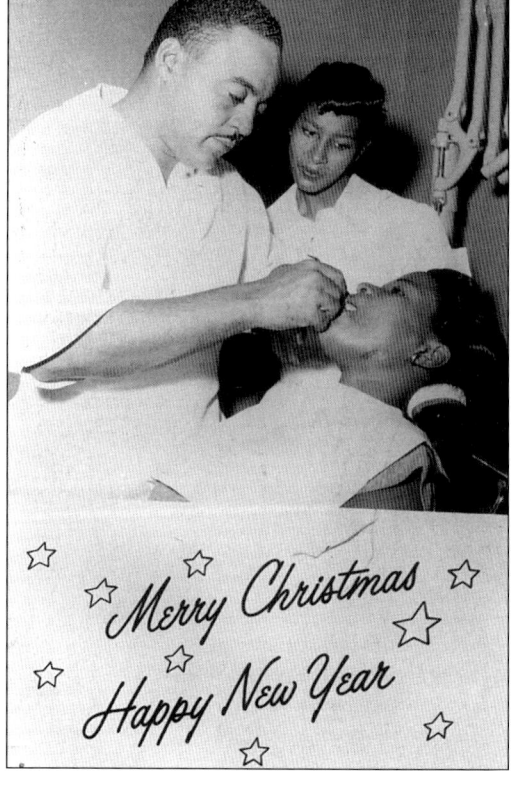

Many black families recall receiving medical care from Dr. James R. Bate, whose office was located at 219 1/2 Adams Street (telephone number 1082) from the 1930s to the 1950s. Dr. Bate, a physician and surgeon, lived at 442 West Pensacola Street (telephone number 1312). Members of the Bate family, including W.L. Bate of 221 Lincoln Street, still reside in Tallahassee.

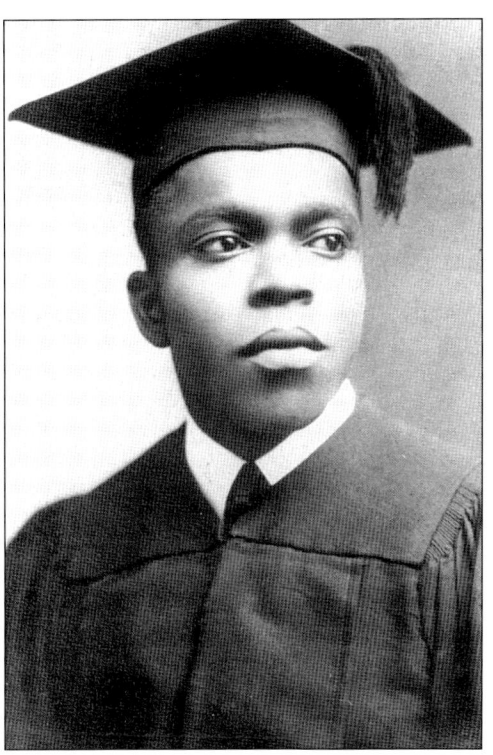

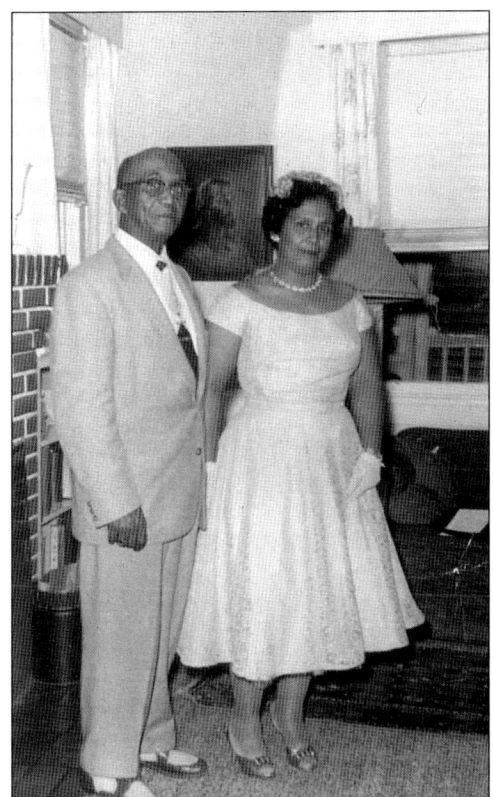

Dr. A.O. Campbell and his daughter Alpha are pictured here. Several streets in south Tallahassee, including Zillah, Omega, Alpha, and Laura, are named for Campbell family members. Dr. Campbell owned these and other large parcels of land in Tallahassee and rural Leon County. Bethel by the Lake, a Bethel AME Church recreation site, is located on previous Campbell-owned property.

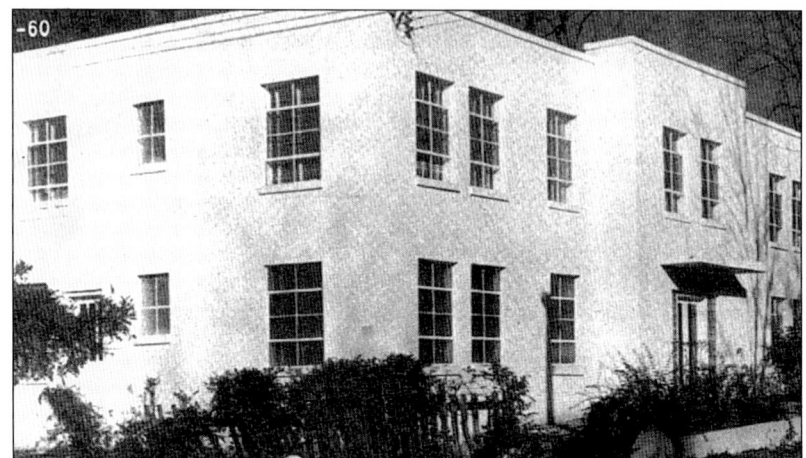

Laura Bell Memorial Hospital and Campbell Clinic, established by Dr. Alpha Omega Campbell, celebrated its grand opening in 1947. Campbell began practicing medicine in Leon County in 1913. The 2-story, 20-bed facility was located in the 300 block of Virginia Street. Property records show Campbell to be the owner of more than 150 pieces of land between 1947 and 1957. Dr. Campbell was known for never turning away a patient in distress.

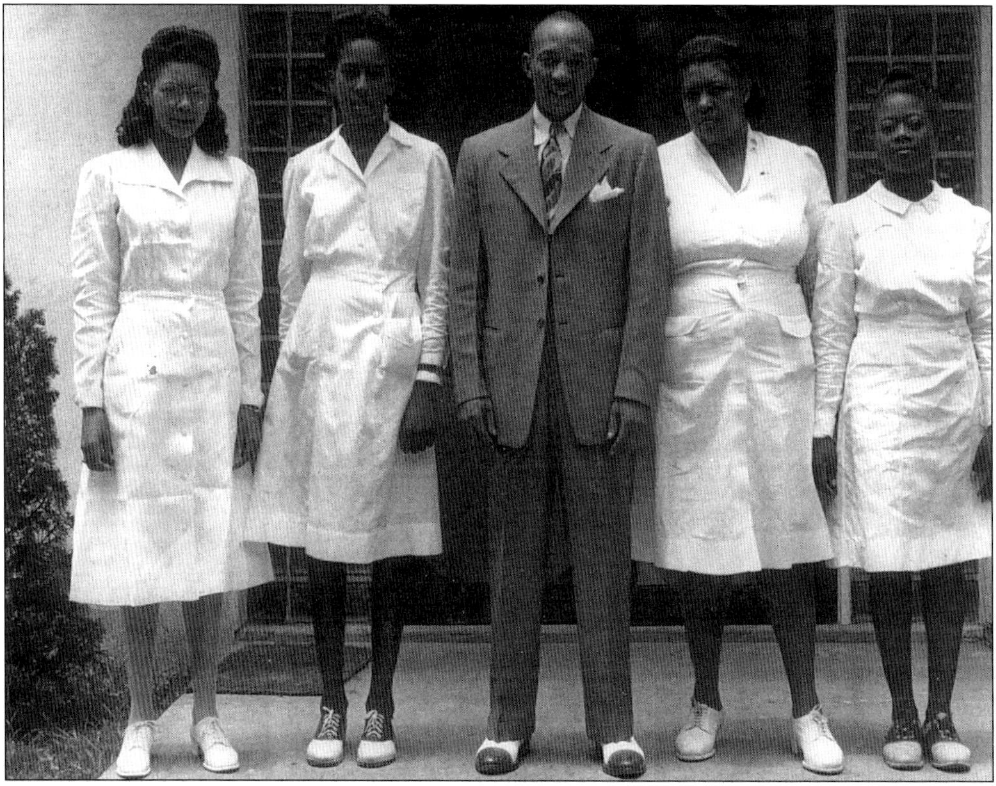

The medical staff at Laura Bell Campbell Hospital and Clinic pose in 1949 with a guest, Olympic gold medalist Jesse Owens. It was common for prominent individuals to provide accommodations for black visitors to the capital city since they were denied access to white-owned lodging due to Jim Crow laws. Flanking Owens are Hannah Duhart (left) and Maggie Maddox (right).

Henrietta Atkins, "Granny Atkins," was a lay midwife in Leon County. Born on March 12, 1865, Granny delivered over 3,000 babies before her death on March 12, 1967. She was one of few who accepted the challenge and trained for the certificate of midwifery during the 1930s. Granny Atkins received her certificate in 1934 from the Midwife Institute, which was housed at Florida A&M College (University).

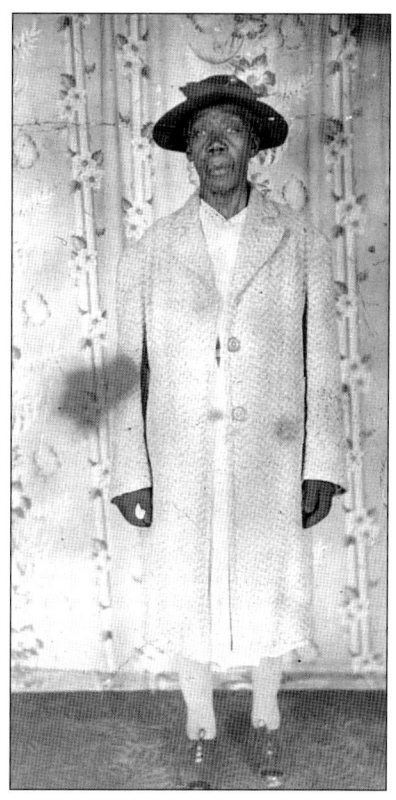

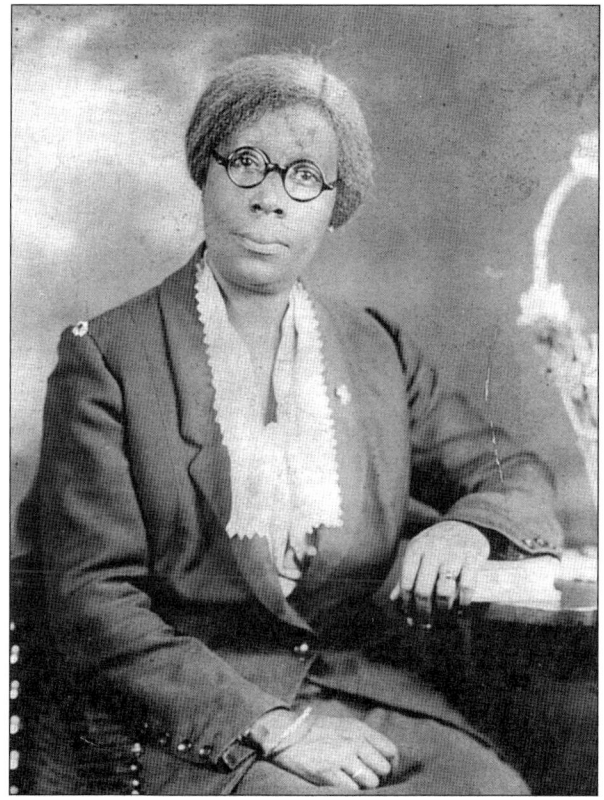

According to a September 1949 newspaper article, nurse Odell McGreen was the first "colored" nurse employed by Leon County. She served for 14 years and resigned in 1944 due to ill health. Credited with starting the first school for midwives, she also founded the Stay-Rite school of beauty and practical nursing. Mahoney Nurses' Association described her as "a moving force, promoting better health conditions for Negroes of Leon County."

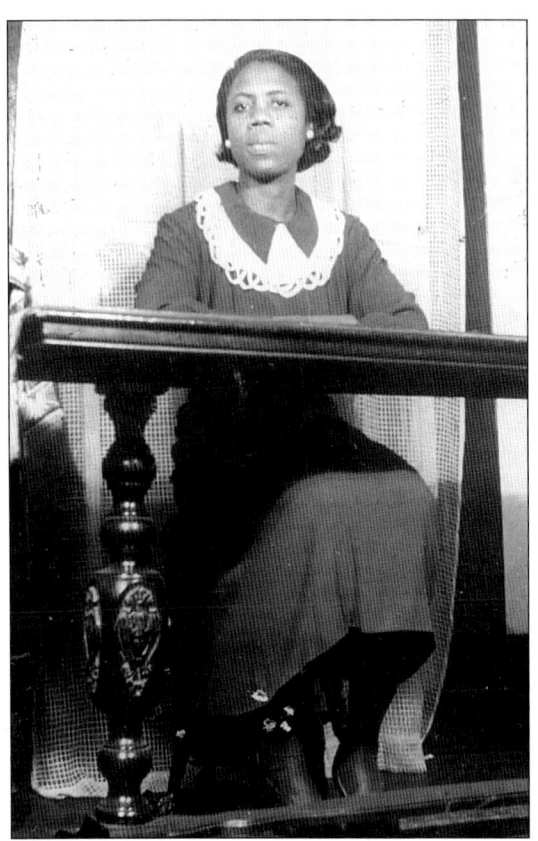

Ida Pemberton served from 1946 to 1961 as a home demonstration agent in Florida. As early as 1899, black agents attended land-grant institutes at State Normal College for Colored Students in Tallahassee, while white agents met in Gainesville, Florida. The purpose was to acquire important information related to improving the farm and home. A history is contained in *The Lamplighters, Black Demonstration Agents in Florida 1915–1965* by Barbara R. Cotton.

A Tallahassee 4-H Home Demonstration youth group tidies up after a camping excursion. This club and the Future Farmers of American (FFA) helped train Tallahassee's black youths in the areas of homemaking and gardening. Agents used activities such as these to enhance the living conditions for rural black Floridians during the period of 1915 to 1965.

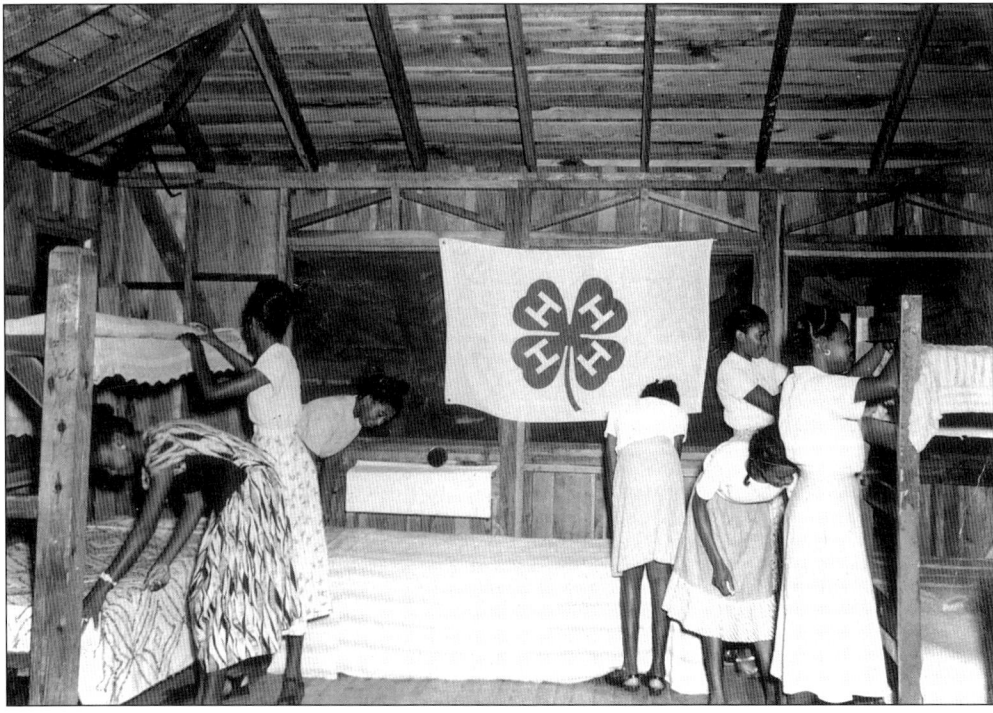

Four
THE CIVIL RIGHTS MOVEMENT

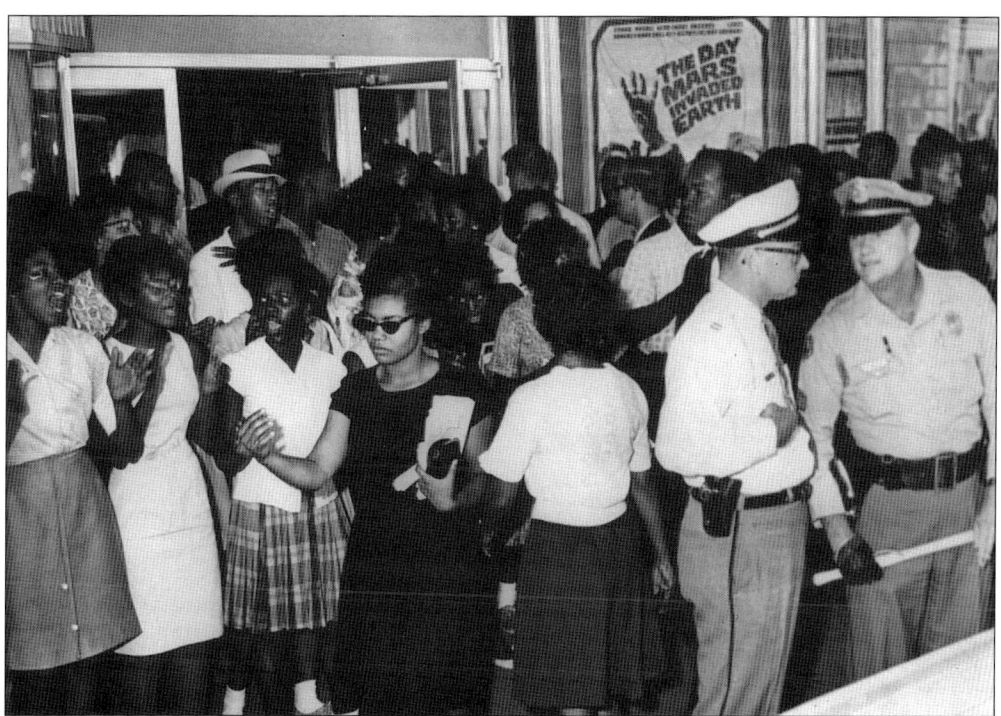

Students demonstrate in 1963 at a local downtown theater during the Civil Rights Movement in Tallahassee. The Florida A&M University student in front wearing a black dress and glasses is Patricia Stephens Due, president of the Congress on Racial Equality.

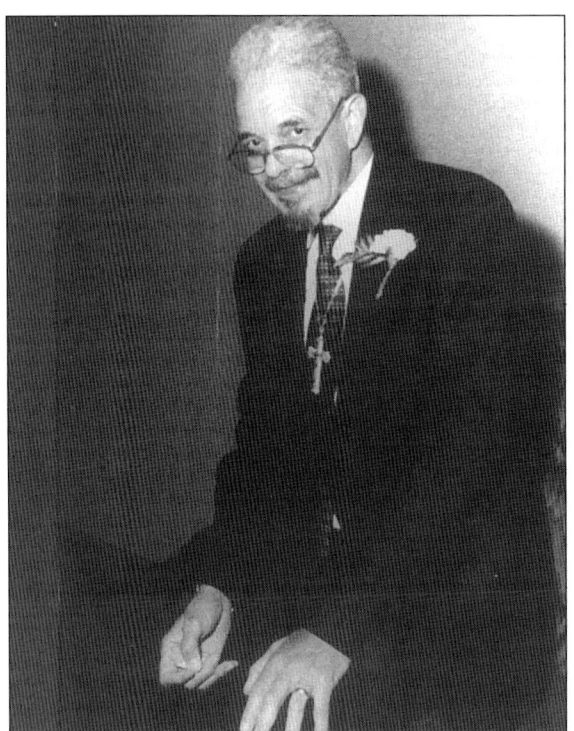

Rev. Metz Rollins stepped to the forefront when Florida A&M University students Wilhelmina Jakes and Carrie Patterson refused to give up their seats to white passengers on a city bus in 1956, beginning the Civil Rights Movement in Tallahassee. The pastor of Trinity Presbyterian Church, Rollins suffered criticism, ridicule, racial attacks, and hostility. Nevertheless, he persevered and was one of Tallahassee's leading civil rights activists.

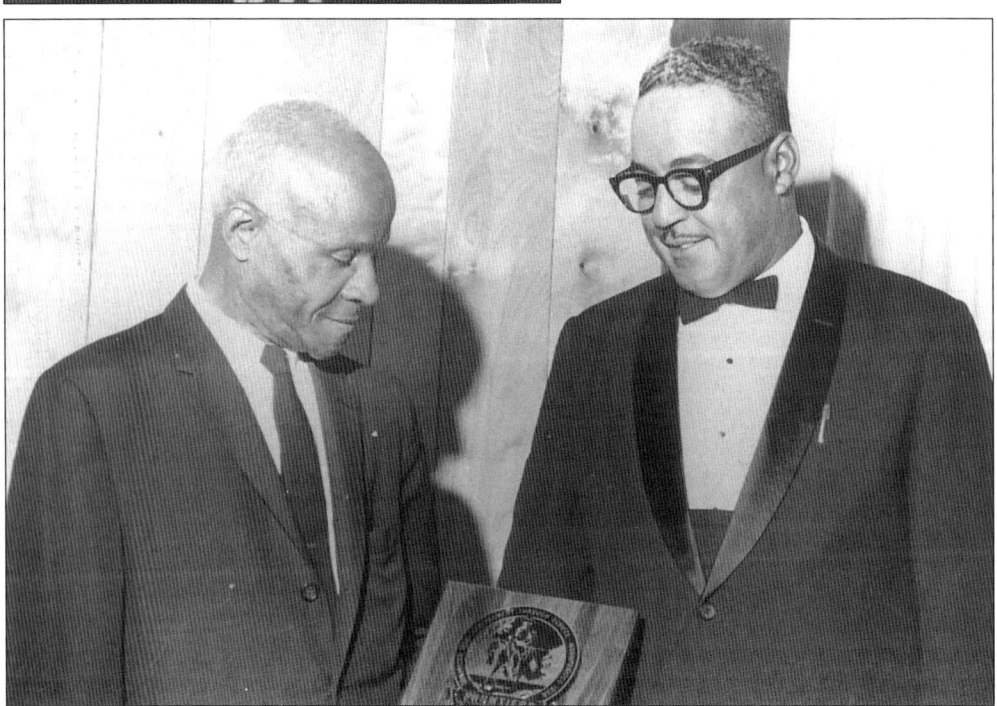

Dr. James Hudson, chaplain of the Inter-Civic Council and professor of religion and philosophy at FAMU, and Dr. Millicent C. Williams were stalwart in the Civil Rights Movement. They served faithfully, under the leadership of Rev. C.K. Steele and Rev. K.S. Dupont, the president and vice president, respectively.

The Reverend King Soloman Dupont, a respected civil rights and religious leader, died at the age of 80. A former pastor of Fountain Chapel AME Church, Dupont lived in Tallahassee for more than 30 years and was a charter member/vice president of the Inter-Civic Council. In 1957, he was the first African American to run for city commissioner, an act that required much courage and vision given the social climate.

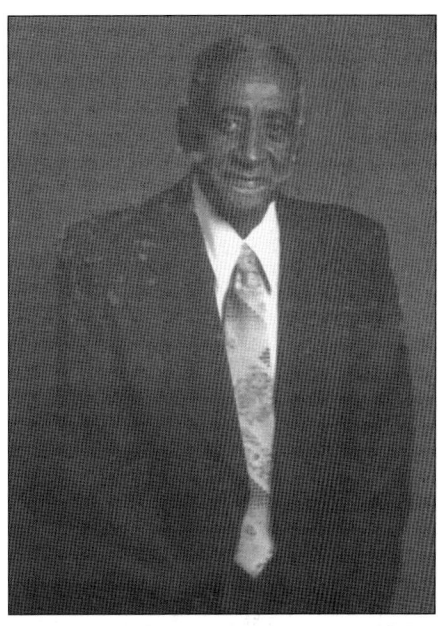

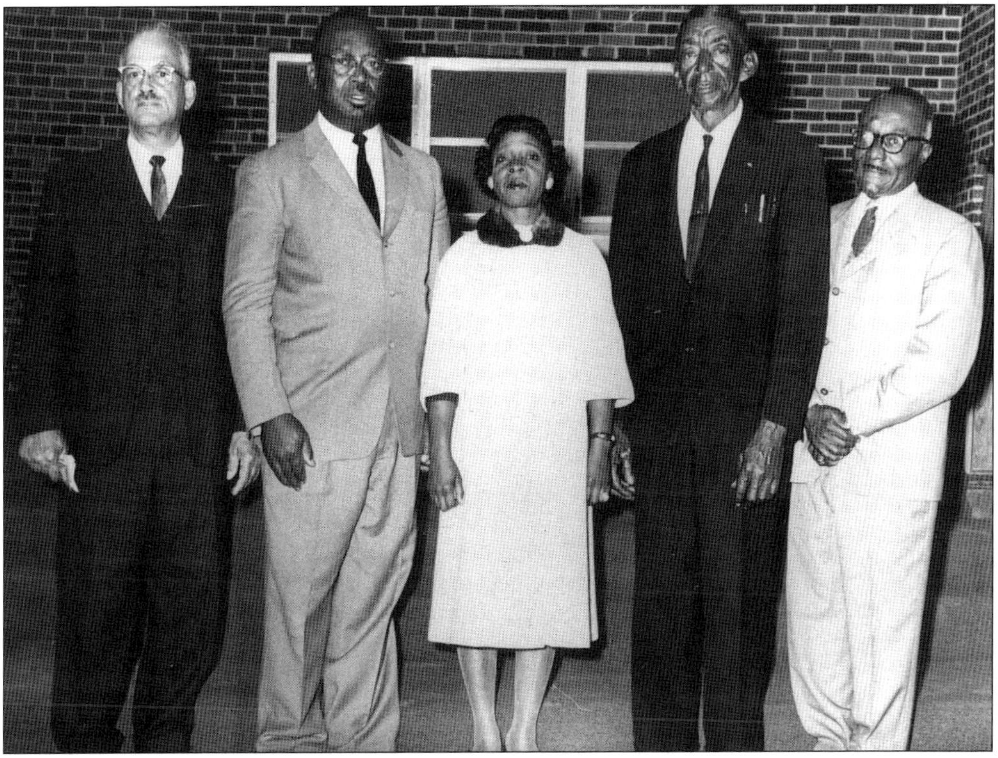

Civil rights activists Dr. Russell Anderson, Rev. Dan Speed, Daisy Young, O.J. Chestnut, and Rev. Milton Cox are seen here. According to testimony, Dr. Anderson, a local physician, provided significant financial support, including bail bonds for those arrested, and ran unsuccessfully for the school board in 1966 during the Civil Rights era. Though Anderson is now deceased, his family members still operate his medical practice, the Anderson Brickler Medical Clinic at 1705 South Adams Street.

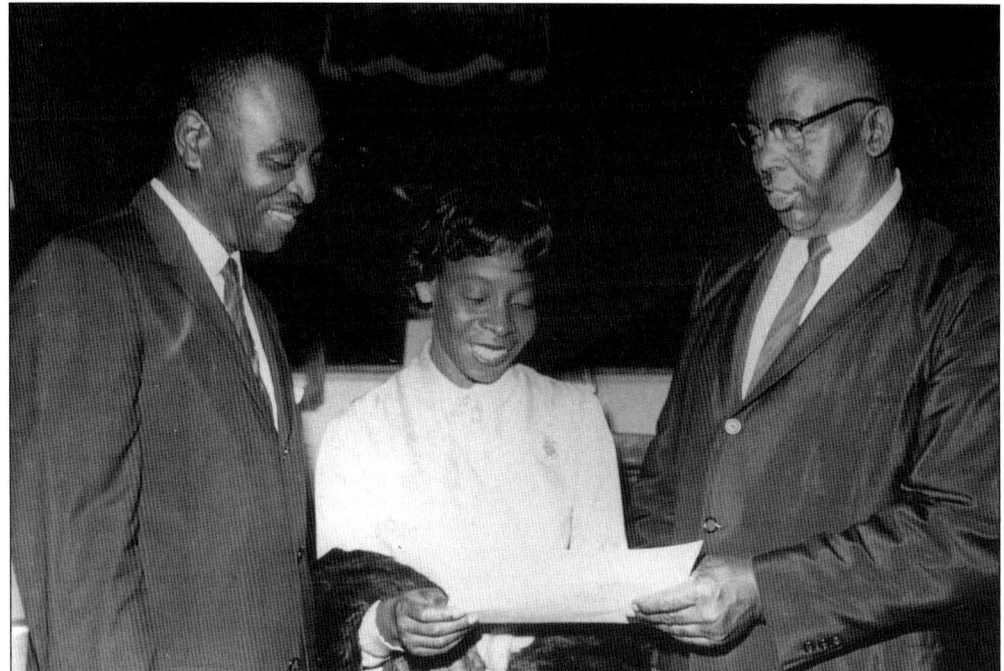

Dr. Sam Hunter, Daisy Young, and Rev. Dan Speed review a proclamation presented to Young in acknowledgment of her outstanding commitment to the National Association for the Advancement of Colored People, Tallahassee Branch. Dr. Hunter was a former principal and science teacher in Leon County schools, and Reverend Speed was president of the Tallahassee branch of the NAACP.

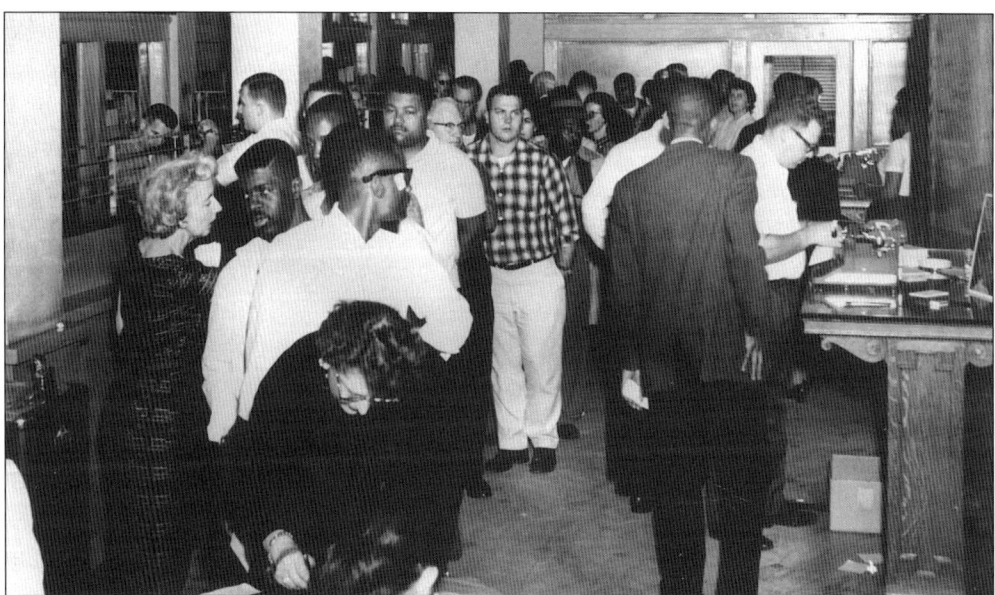

African Americans flooded the courthouse during the 1960s to register to vote in Leon County for the first time. Third in line is Riley Landers, a descendant of a pioneer Leon County family. Landers is a longtime employee of the United States Postal Service in Tallahassee. Currently, he is a claims and inquiry specialist with the U.S. Postal Service.

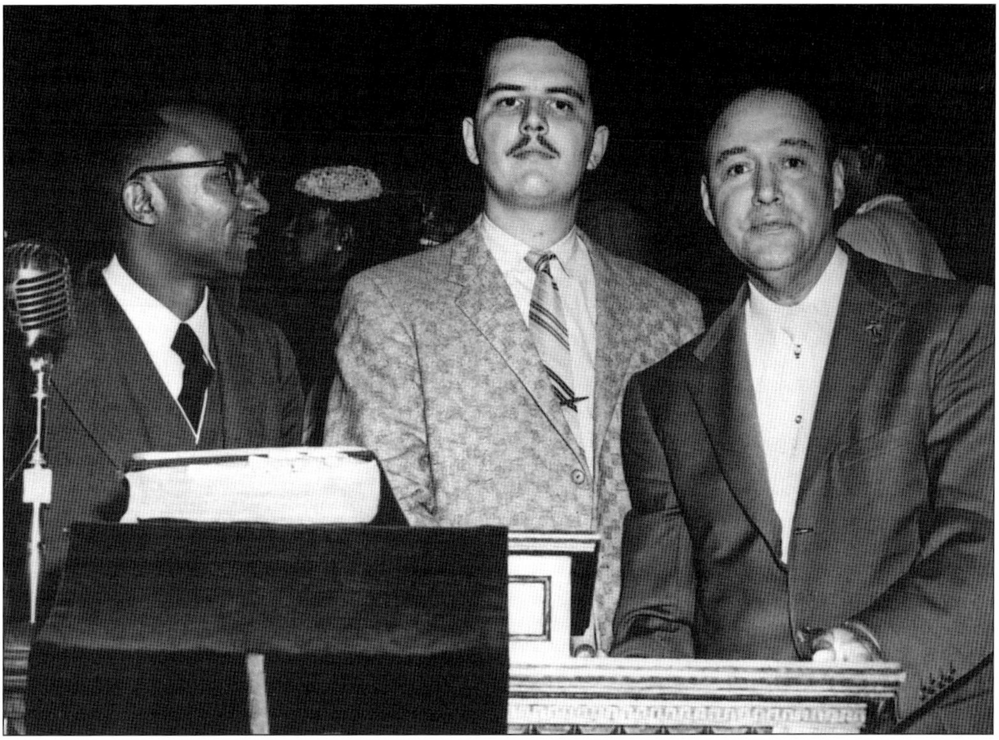

Rev. Charles K. Steele is photographed at Bethel Baptist Church with John Boardman and Rev. J. Raymond Henderson of California in the 1950s. Boardman, a white Florida State University doctoral student, was expelled because of his activities with the Inter-Civic Council. Steele continued the fight to integrate public facilities, such as hotels, restaurants, and schools, and to gain voting rights for blacks until his death from cancer.

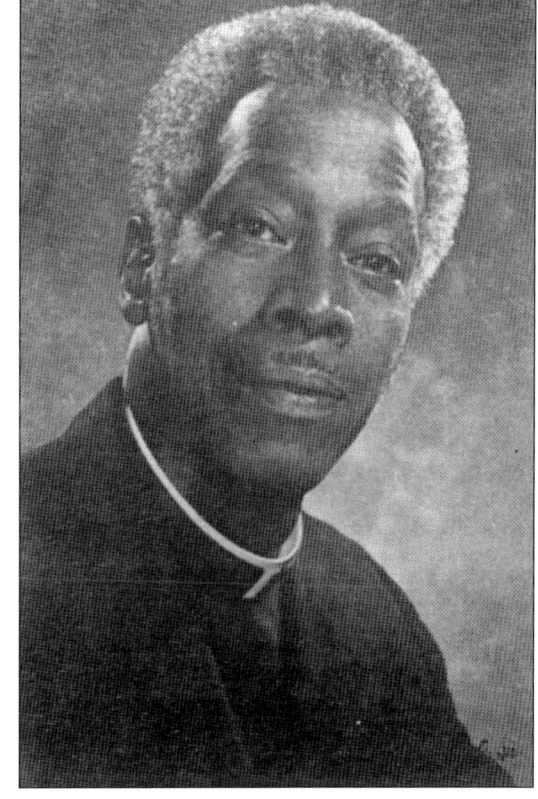

Fr. David Brooks came to Tallahassee in 1948 as the vicar of St. Michael's Episcopal Church and served until 1973. He devoted much of his time and attention during the 1950s and 1960s to civil rights activities. Imbued with deep desire to act as a spokesman for his people, he believed that "the real enemies of peace and progress are poverty, disease, ignorance, prejudice. They corrupt, corrode society, and breed unrest and hatred."

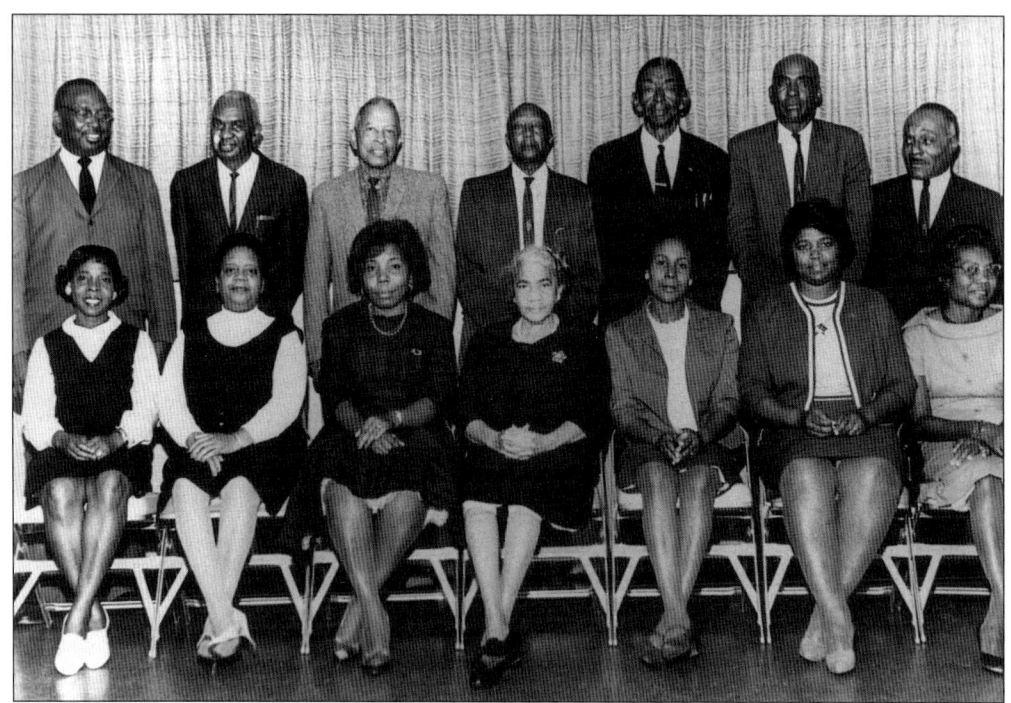

"Foot soldiers" in the movement included, from left to right, (front row) Daisy Young, E.M. Rackard, Inez Williams, Willie K. Perkins, Laura Dixie, Willie Mae Fisher, and Mary Ola Gaines; (back row) Rev. Dan Speed, Edwin Norwood Sr., Dr. Wilmoth Baker, William R. Perkins, O.J. Chestnut, Rev. Owen Smith, and Rev. Milton Cox. Baker, a physician, practiced at 217 1/2 Adams Street and later relocated to South Adams Street.

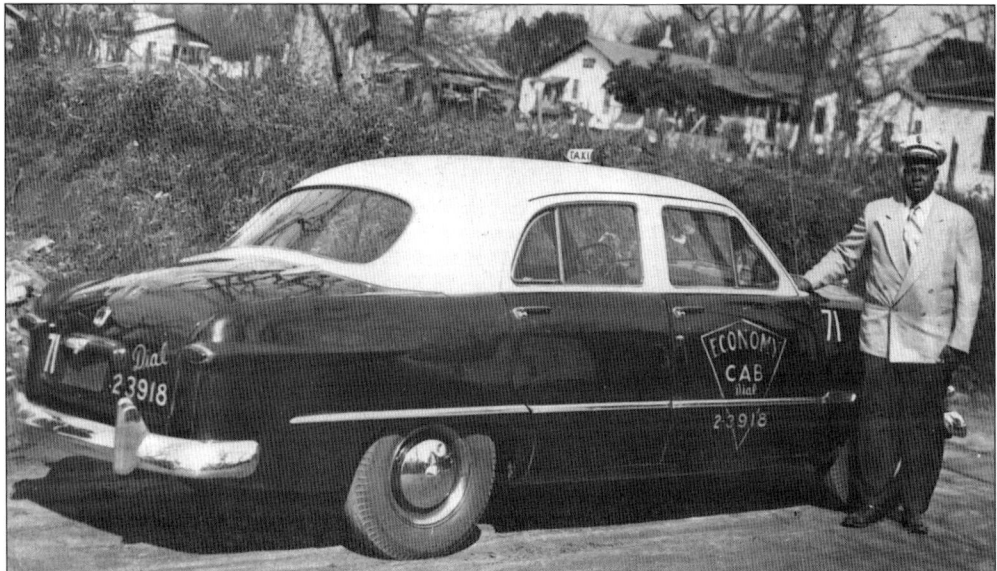

Seth Gaines drove an independent taxi in the 1940s and 1950s. In response to demands from civil rights activists during the bus boycott and Civil Rights Movement, he became one of the first African Americans to drive a bus for the Tallahassee City Transit on a regular route. Edgar Richardson was the first.

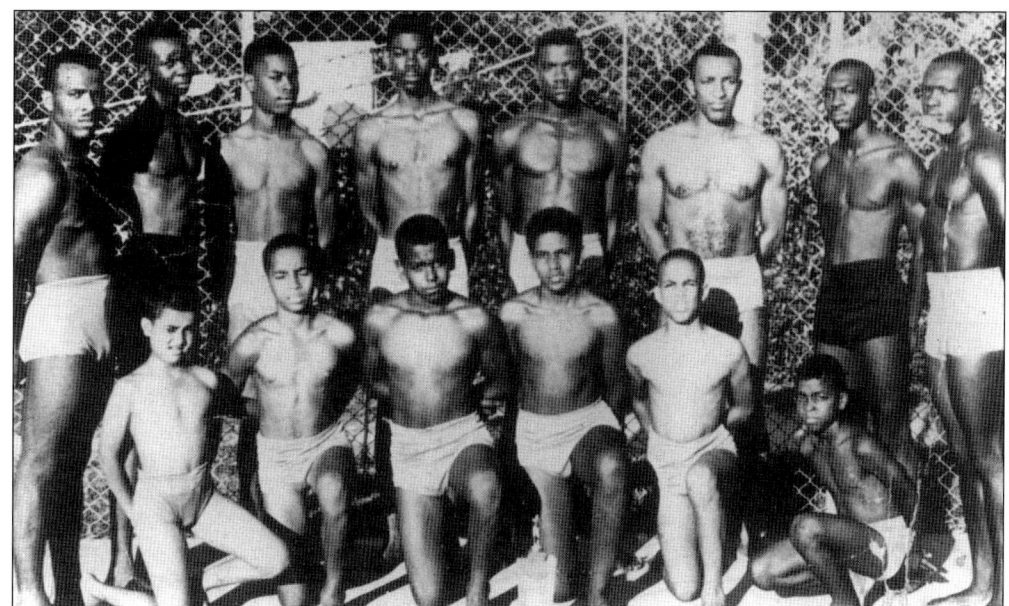

Robinson Trueblood Swimming Pool on Dade Street was built by the City of Tallahassee in response to wade-ins by African Americans at all-white pools. It was the only site where blacks could swim and train as lifeguards. The first swim team included, from left to right, (kneeling) Ricky Eubanks, Eugene Cromer, Ellis Carr, Hansel Tookes, M. Raines, and Raymond Williams; (standing) Roy Beard, Eddie Graham, Edward Holifield, Bishop Holifield, Charles Rambo, Manuel Rivas, Ulysees Pittman, and James Barnes.

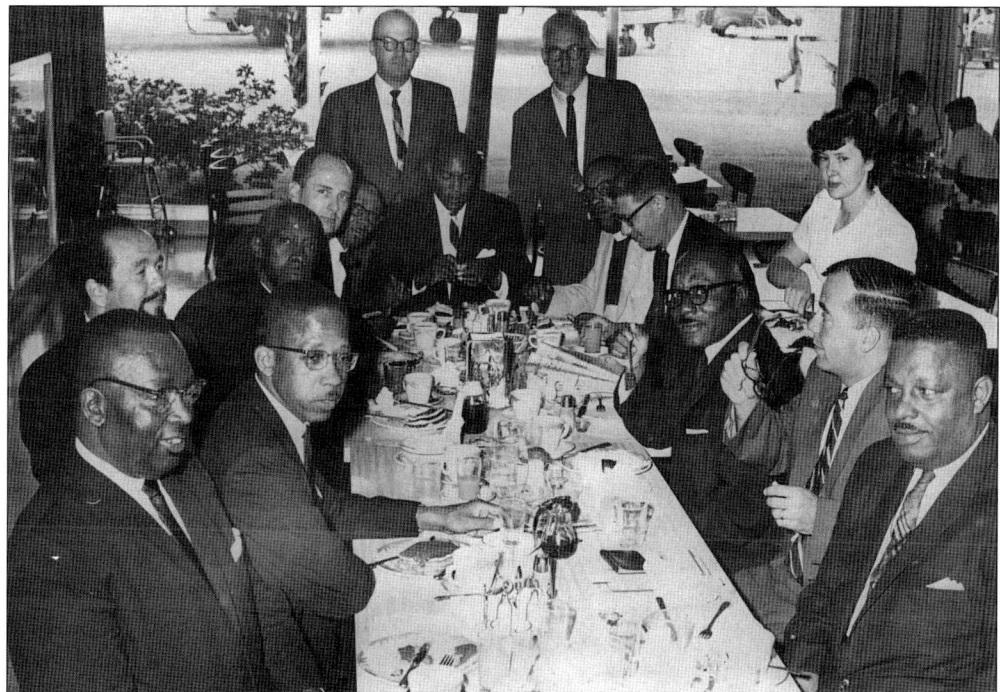

Civil rights leaders planning strategy at an airport include Rev. Dan Speed, Fr. David Brooks, Rev. Charles Kenzie Steele, Rev. Milton Cox, and Rev. Ira D. Hinson.

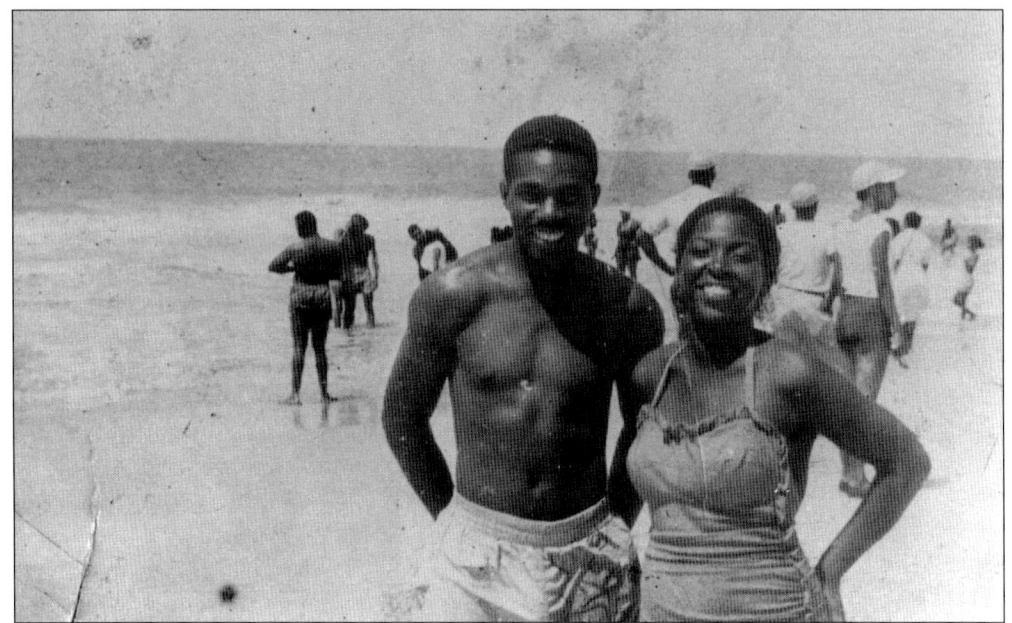

Leroy and Wilhemina Webster enjoy fun and sun at historic Money Bayou Beach in Port St. Joe during the 1950s. At this time, African Americans could not visit white beaches. As a result, some blacks purchased beach property for public use. Damon Peters Sr., Damon Peters Jr., Nathan Peters Sr., Raymond Driesbach, and Dr. F.M. Hall bought Money Bayou from Alfred P. Andreasen, a rich white Easterner, and operated it as a black beach until the 1980s.

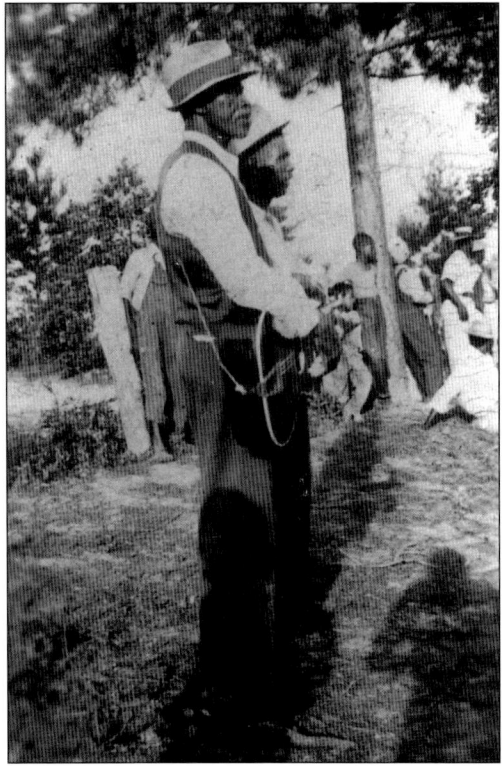

Henry White, the father of Hazel Fitz, plays guitar at the traditional 20th of May and Emancipation Proclamation Day Celebration.

Five
FACES AND PLACES

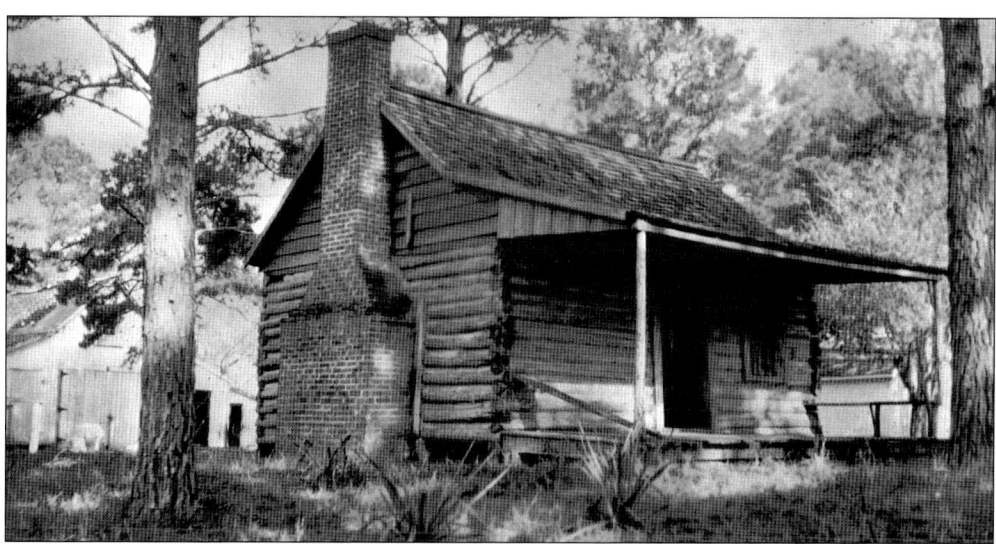

Pictured here are servant living quarters at Maclay, a hunting plantation, in the 1920s. Record books detailing the African-American families on Maclay, Overstreet, and Lake Hall properties from the 1920s–1940s include the following names: Sam Fitz, Peter Holliday, Robert Hadley, Seward Floyd, John Baker, William Spencer, Herbert Carr, Joe Dennis, Ike Gilliam, Rufus Hayes, Richmond Hiks, Joe Harris, Emma Sawyer, Charles Smith, Thomas Davis, Ed Jiles, and Mary Gallon. Tobias and Charlie Payne were among the black families who owned property in the area.

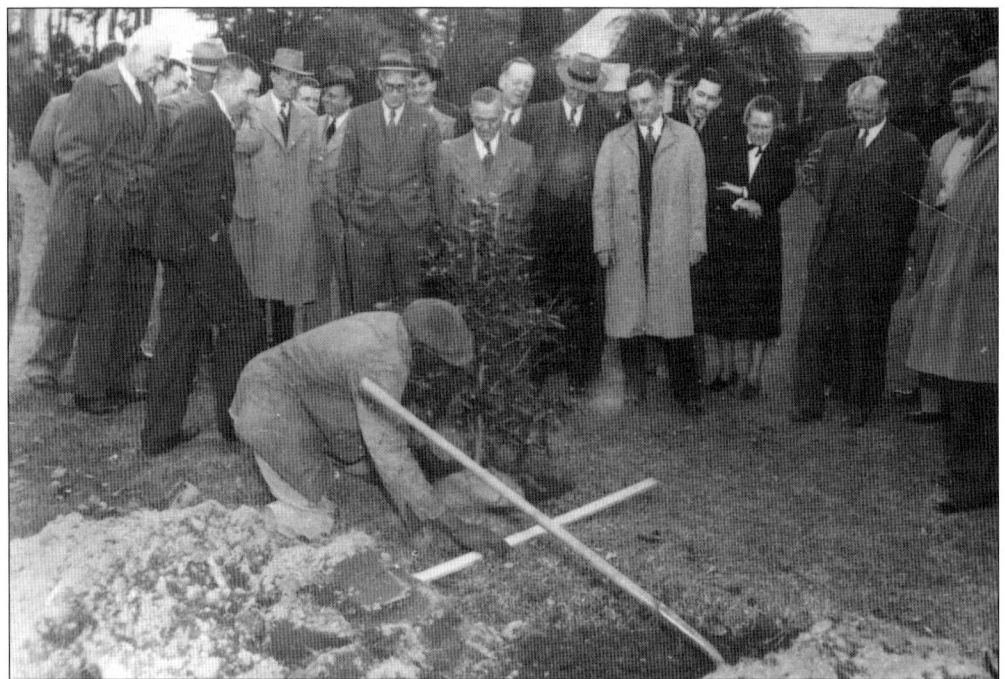

Depew Smith, a caretaker at Maclay, buries one of the owner's prize racehorses while dignitaries, including former governor Leroy Collins, look on in the 1950s. According to oral history, when the horses became too old to ride or race, the Maclays would have them put to sleep. This is indicative of the pride and personal attachment the owners had for their horses.

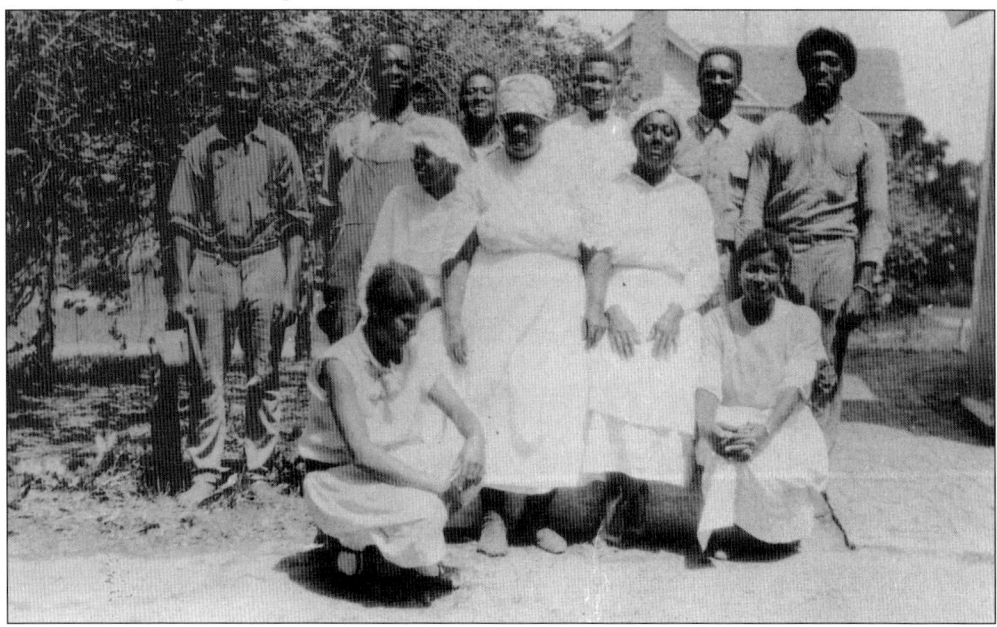

Maclay workers in the 1930s include cooks, caretakers, gardeners, and farm hands. Pictured are, from left to right, (front row, seated) Pinky Sawyer and Mutta Moo; (front row, standing) Annie Sawyer, Harriet Vernon, and Florence Edwards; (back row) Richmond Heights, Rufus Hayes, Jim Sawyer, Willie Gallon, Henry Sawyer, and Depew Smith.

These tenant farm women were photographed in the 1920s in rural Leon County.

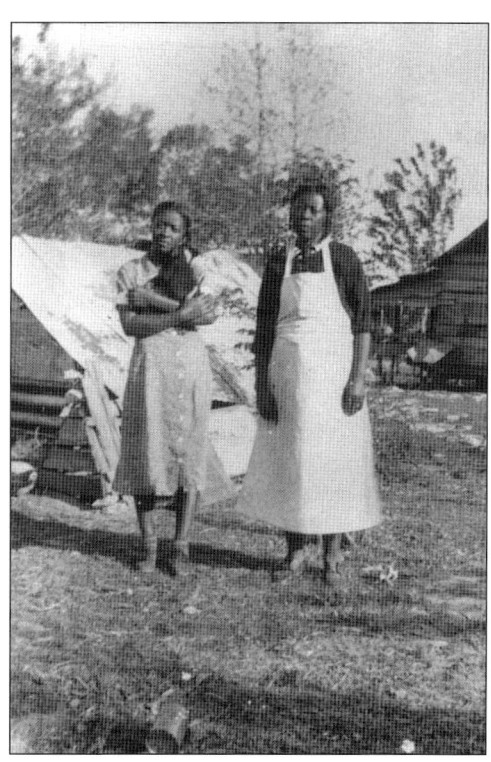

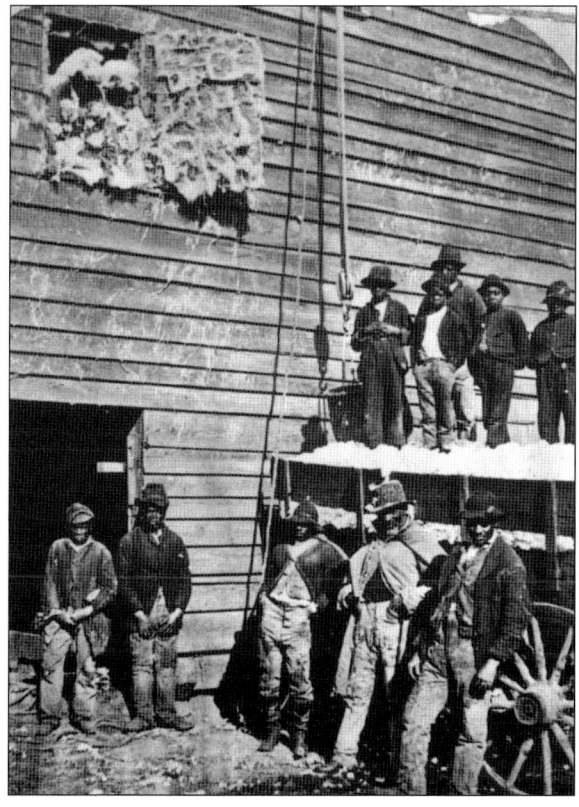

When the Civil War ended in 1865, the tenant and crop lien system of producing cotton became a way of life in the South, including Leon County. This 1879 photo depicts African-American farmers delivering cotton to a local gin. (Courtesy of the Florida State Archives.)

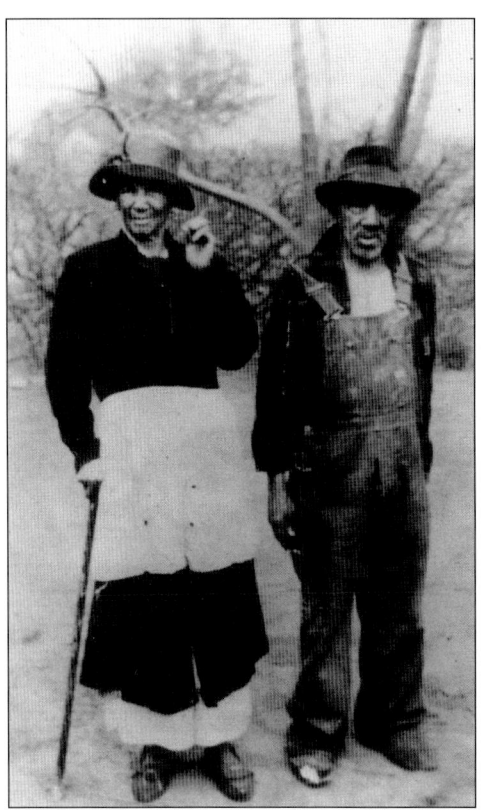

Luvenia and Ed Austin, pictured here in the 1940s, were sharecroppers on Welaunee Plantation.

Mary and Lucien Glenn, seen here in the 1930s, had become property owners at the turn of the century. A pioneer Leon County family, the Glenns supported their family by farming and peddling produce at markets in Leon and the surrounding counties.

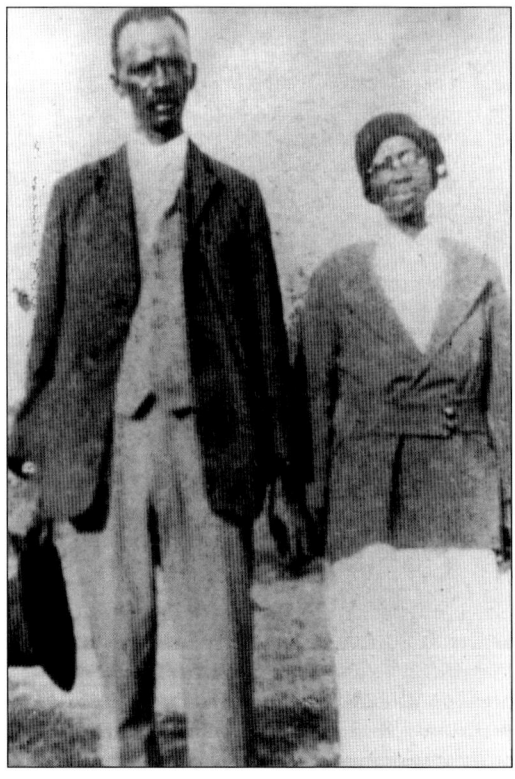

Willie Gardner Sr. was the son of George Madison "Mack" Gardner (1845–1919) and Annie Floyd Gardner (1857–1944), both of whom were former slaves. After slavery, the family migrated to Leon County, bought 40 acres on Meridian Road and property in the Frenchtown area, and opened a store. They later purchased 360 acres on Lake Jackson and rented to tenant farmers. Rent was paid in cotton, and cotton sales paid for the land.

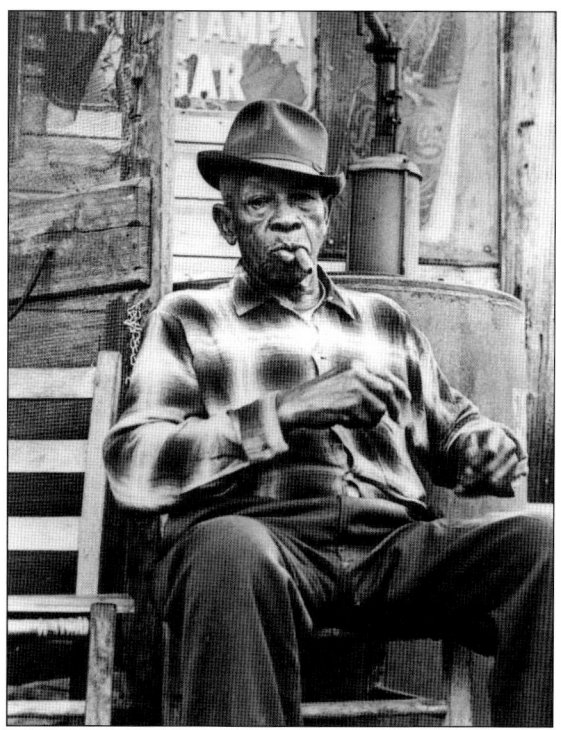

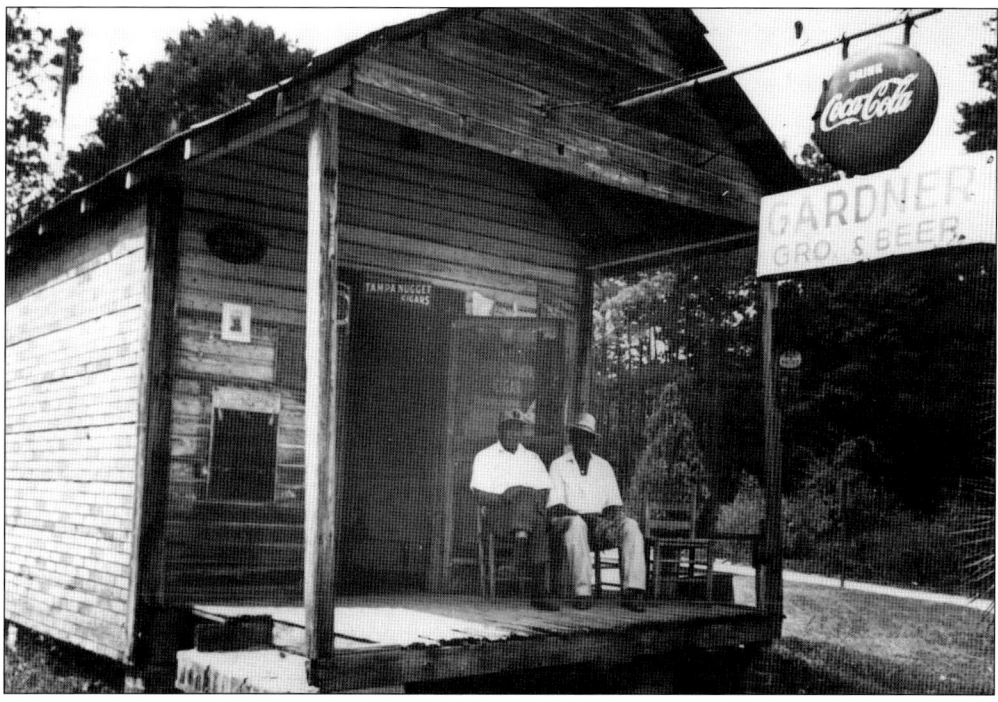

The Gardner legacy was continued by Willie, who became the proprietor of Gardner Store and the primary manager of the family property on Meridian Road. The store was operated well into the 1960s. Shown sitting on the store's porch are Willie and his son Mack. The store was demolished in 1995.

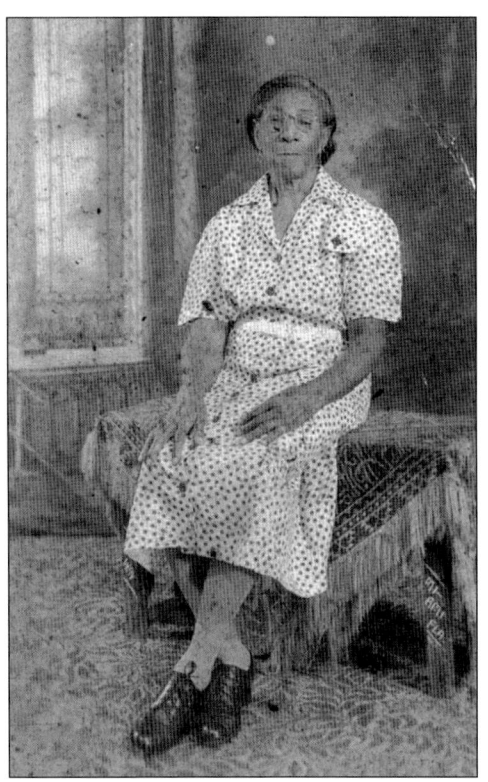

Celia Witherspoon, the wife of Rev. Willie Witherspoon, lived to be 105 years of age. After slavery, the Witherspoons purchased 140 acres on North Thomasville Road. The Witherspoon family donated the land for Horseshoe School, which still stands and is on the site of the Bradfordville Baptist Church. The Witherspoons' daughter Iola, who is now 97 years old, lives on Dunn Street in Tallahassee's historic Springfield community.

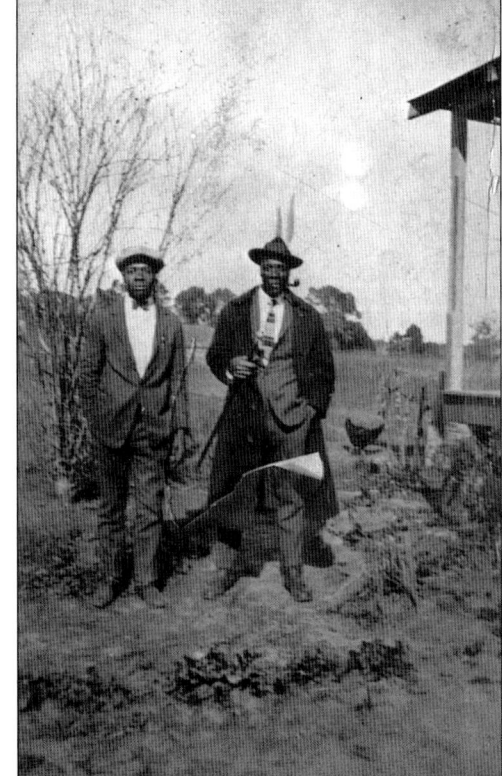

Photographed in the 1930s, James Larkins and Walter Brown are on the old Winthrop Place. Formerly part of rural Leon County, the area is currently the location of the predominantly white Betton Hills community.

Elizabeth "Bettie" Lane Dickey was a descendent of a slave family who lived on Orchard Pond, one of two plantations owned by Gen. Richard Keith Call, the third and fifth civil governor of the Territory of Florida. The Dickey family is still piecing together its history.

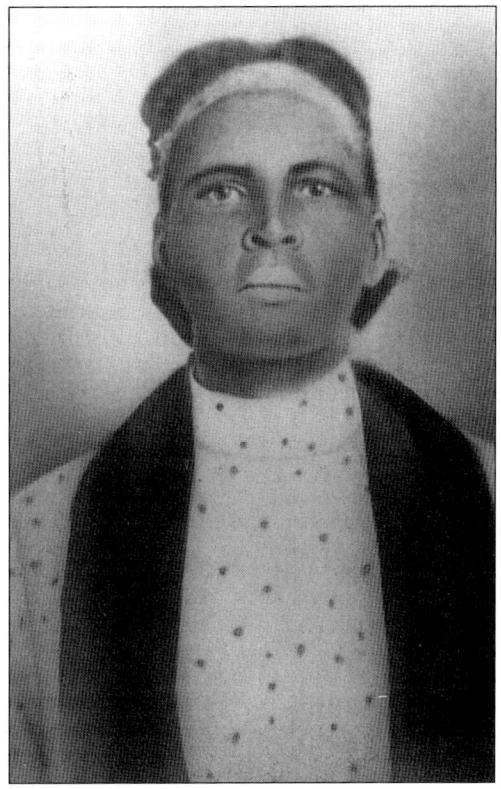

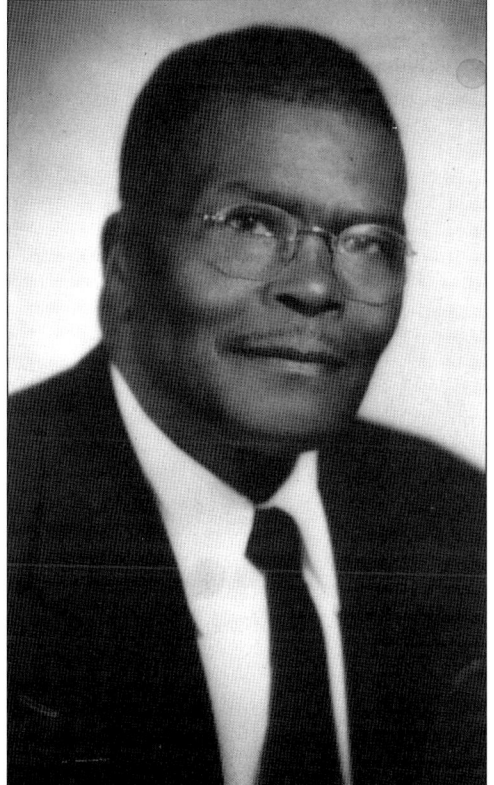

Cornelius Speed Sr. (1890–1961) was a descendant of a pioneer Leon County family. He was a resourceful farmer and an outstanding businessman; along with his brother Dennis, he established and operated Speed's Groceries on Boulevard Street for many years. Cornelius was an active community leader and a member of many fraternal and civic groups. The Speeds were faithful members of Rock Hill Missionary Baptist Church, which was founded by Speed's father in 1897.

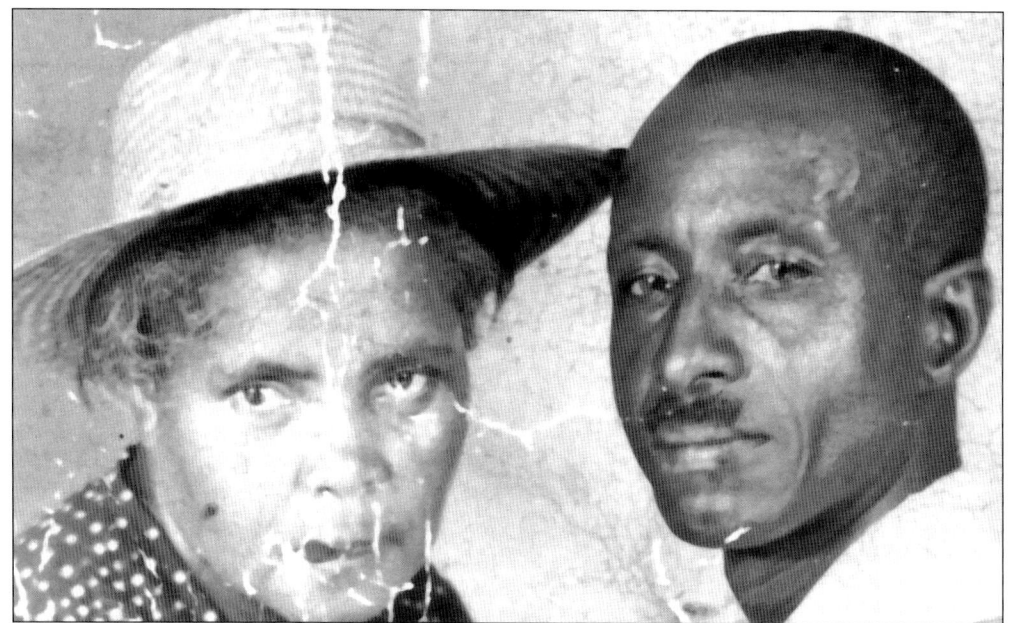

Mary and Essex Barnes, descendants of slaves, were married, lived, and raised their family on Welaunee Plantation. They were one of the last African-American families to live on Welaunee, residing in the old home place headed by Oliver Barnes. After leaving Welaunee in the late 1940s, the Barnes family purchased property across the Miccosukee highway and became independent farmers.

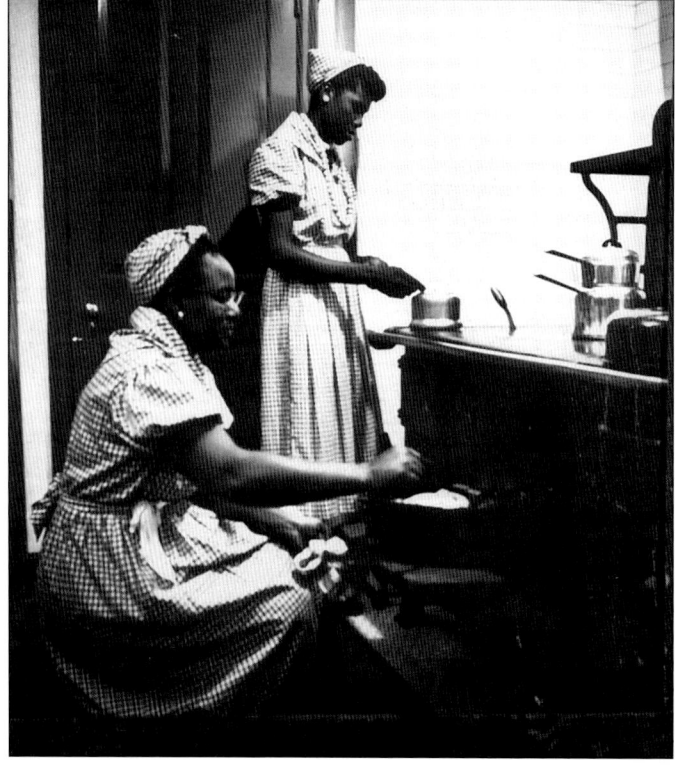

Flora Hunter (left) and a co-worker cook on Horseshoe Plantation in the 1930s.

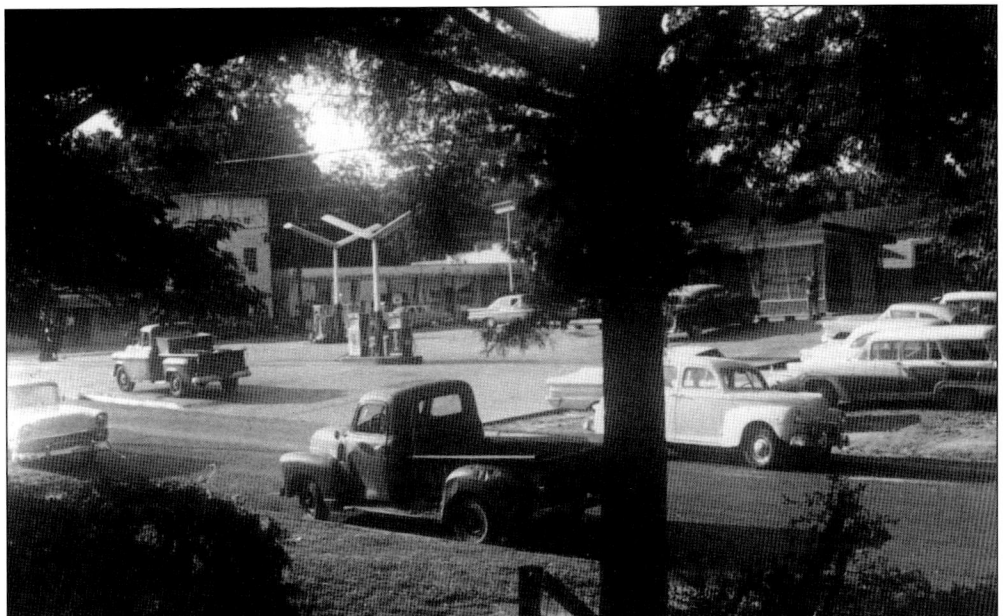

This is a 1950s view of the historic black community of Frenchtown, looking south from Carolina Street, the location of numerous black-owned commercial establishments. Most of these buildings, as well as several historic homes and structures, were demolished as part of the city's revitalization and redevelopment projects.

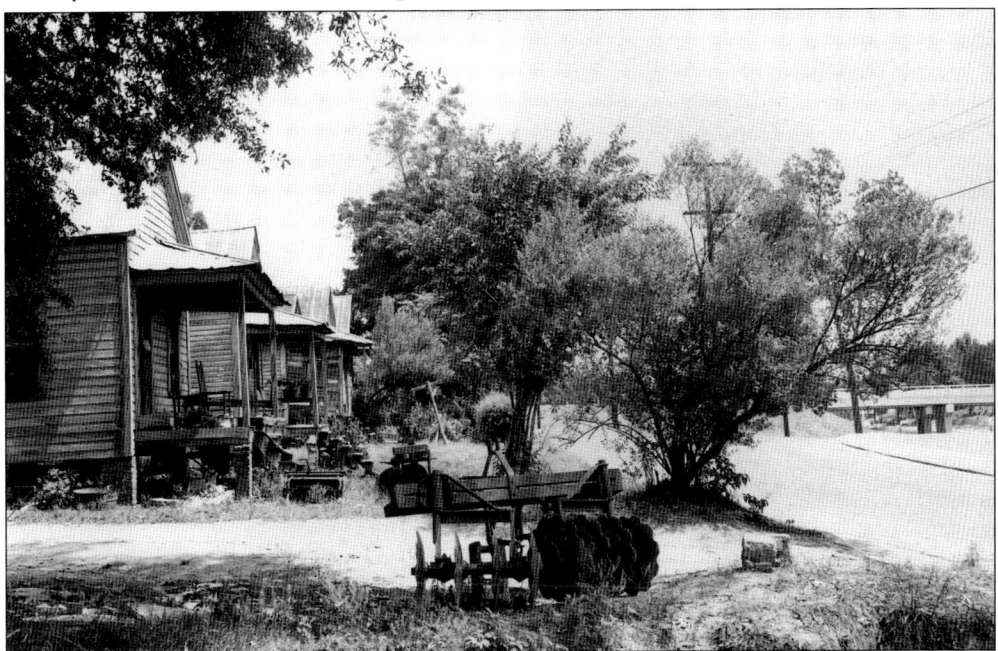

Smokey Hollow, a historic African-American community, was established in the late 1800s. Most of the housing was demolished to accommodate urban renewal. Former residents include Lucille Brown, Leon County's first black public librarian; Famous Amos, the "Cookie Man," Jessie Adderley, the mother of Julian and Cannonball Adderley; and Charlie Ash, the fourth black officer hired by the Leon County Sheriff's Department.

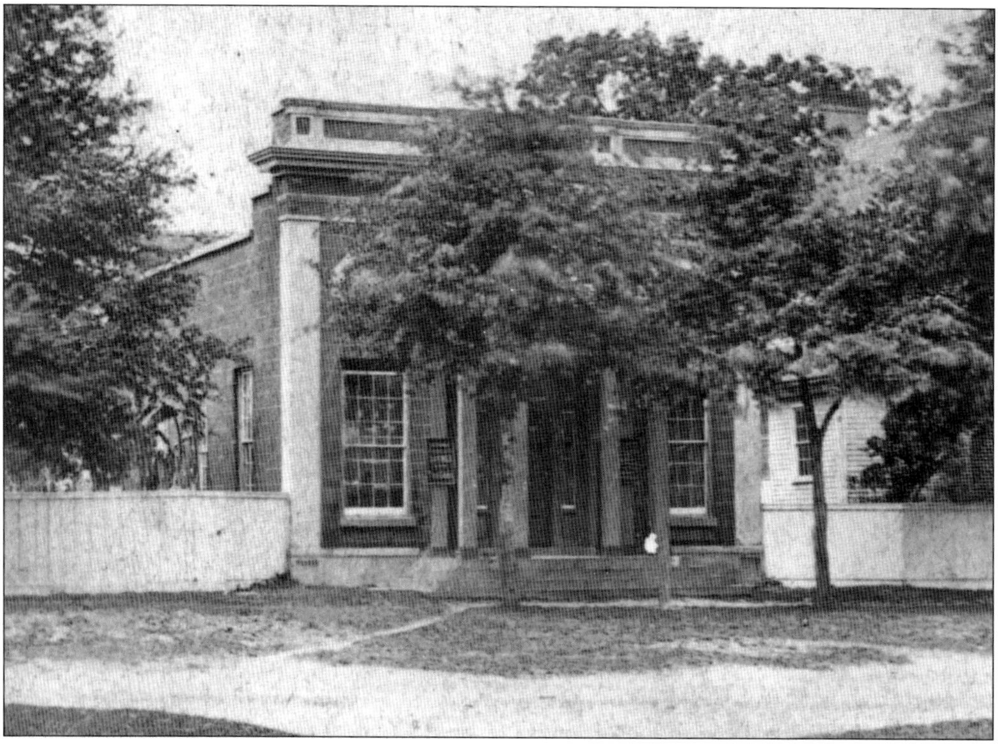

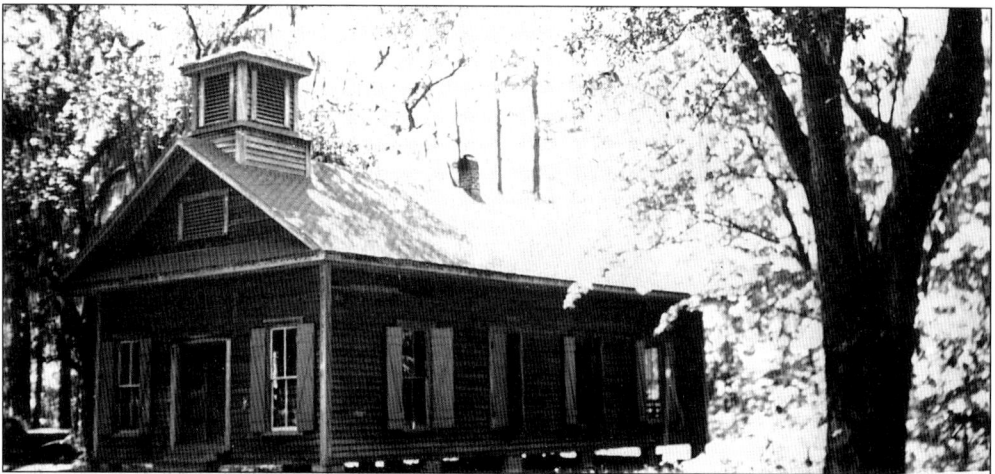

Union Bank Building, chartered as a land-mortgage bank for plantation owners, was completed with the help of slave labor in 1841. Planters borrowed more than they could repay; bankers had based the loan amounts on misinformation regarding the number of slaves owned by the planters. The bank failed, but was later reopened as the Freedmen's Savings and Trust Company (1866–1874), a place where former slaves could open savings accounts and secure loans for farms and businesses. The building currently houses the FAMU Black Archives.

Horseshoe School began on the North Thomasville Road property of Rev. Willie Witherspoon, a black landowner. The one-room schoolhouse was for children in grades one through eight. After the building was destroyed by fire, classes were held in Horseshoe Church until the nearby Lake McBride School was built. The church was eventually sold and moved to its current location on the Bradfordville Baptist Church site.

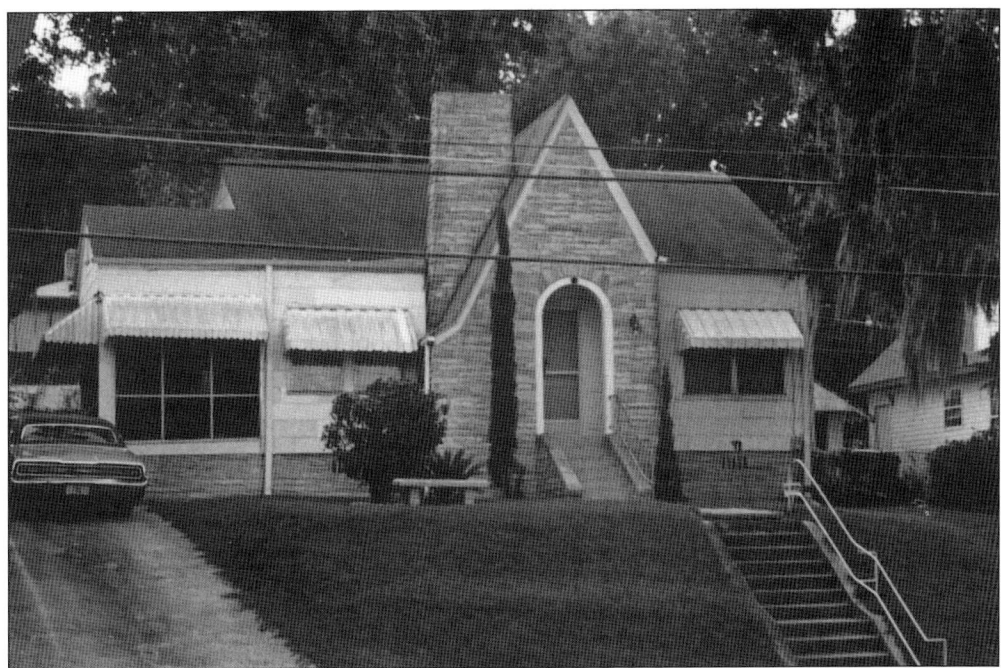

Tuskegee Airman Roy Spencer still lives in his family home at 1536 South Adams Street, next to the historic Ship Ahoy Restaurant building. He frequently shares with the community and news media his experiences as a black pilot at a time when it was extremely difficult for a person of his race to have such an opportunity.

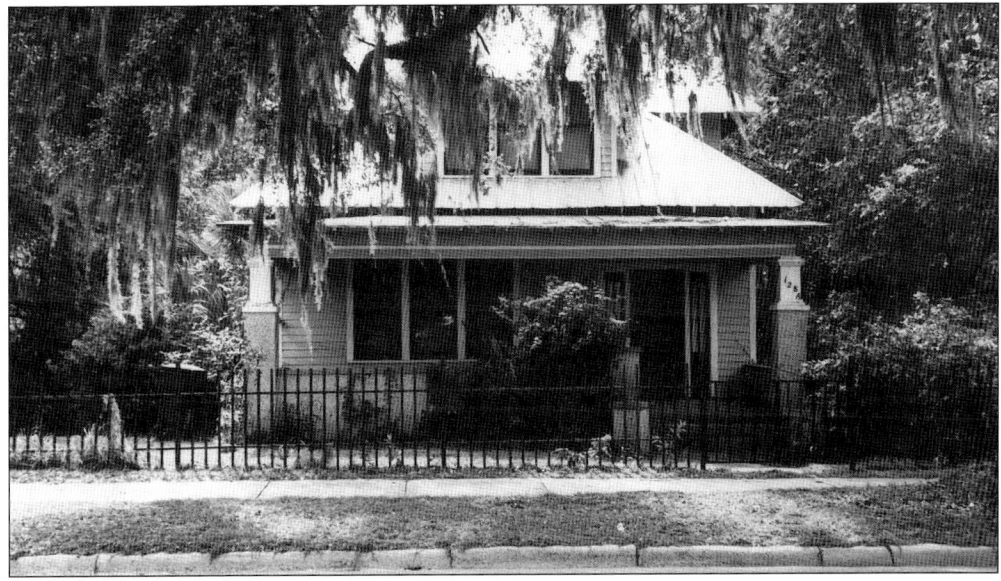

On South Bronough Street, the Nims-Ford House, adjacent to the main Leon County Public Library, was the home of one of Tallahassee's most prominent and prosperous African-American families, John and Louise Nims. John was a wealthy businessman with substantial land holdings. Louise was a schoolteacher and the daughter of Reconstruction-era sheriff Capt. W.H. Ford. Captain Ford served with honors and was also active in politics, participating in State Convention committees.

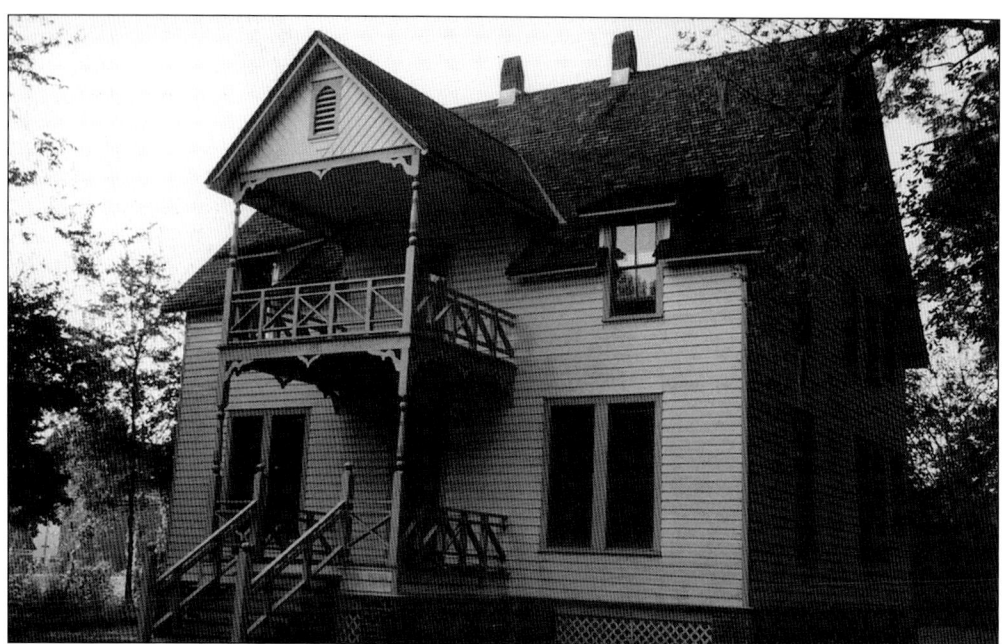

Gibbs Cottage was built around 1892 and is the oldest and last remaining wooden structure on the FAMU campus. It was the home of Thomas Van Renssalaer Gibbs, an African-American legislator credited with writing the legislation that created FAMU. Gibbs was also secretary of state from 1868 to 1873, the superintendent of public instruction from 1873 to 1884, and a FAMU professor. He died in 1898, leaving a wife and ten children.

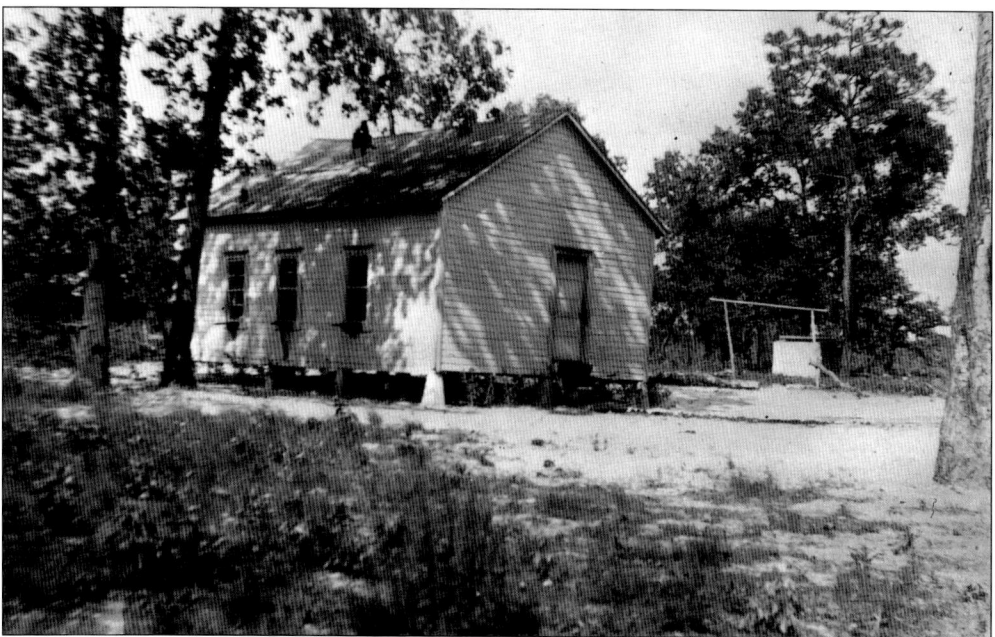

St. Peters School, a one-room schoolhouse for African Americans, was located in the historic black community of St. Peters. This community, located north on Centerville Road, was once a densely populated tenant farming, sharecropping, and landowning community with many black families. The school was noted in school board minutes as early as 1893.

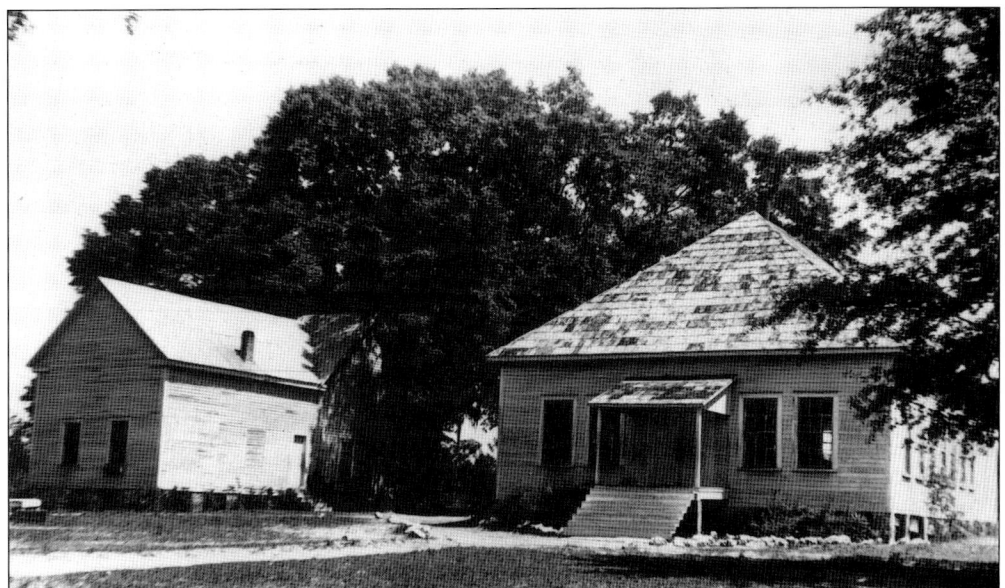

This one-room schoolhouse for African-American children, Station I School, formerly known as Chaires School, is recorded in the Leon County School Board minutes as early as the 1870s and was located about 9 miles east of Tallahassee in rural Leon County. Shown here is one of two buildings that housed the school, which carried grades one through ten, and later grades one through six. The school closed in 1967 as a result of desegregation.

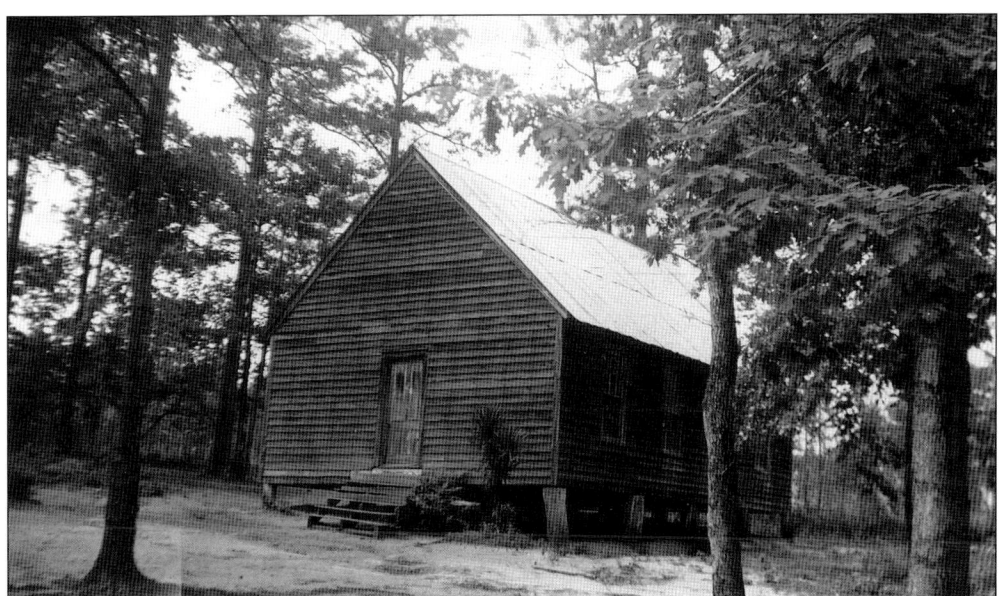

Bell School was another one-room schoolhouse built during Reconstruction to provide an education for newly freed slaves and their descendants. It was located on the west side of Meridian Road, close to the Florida-Georgia line, and it was one of many schools, including the Hammock, Poplar Springs, Sheppherd, and Cotton Schools, that served the children of African-American tenant farmers and sharecroppers.

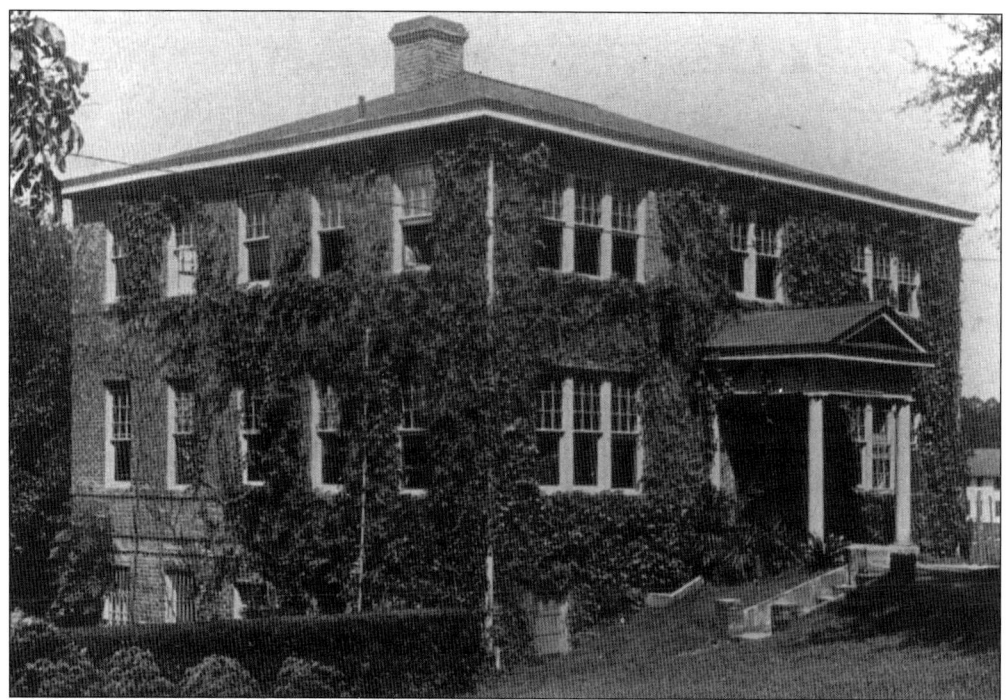

This photo of the "Old" Agricultural Building at Florida A&M University is a nostalgic reminder of yesterday's FAMU. The structure housed agriculture and home economics and was renovated during Pres. George W. Gore's tenure. The new building was named in honor of Dean B.L. Perry Sr., who served as the dean of the Division of Agriculture from 1928 to 1947, and Miss Ellen O. Paige, a dedicated home economics teacher who served the institution from 1899 to 1942.

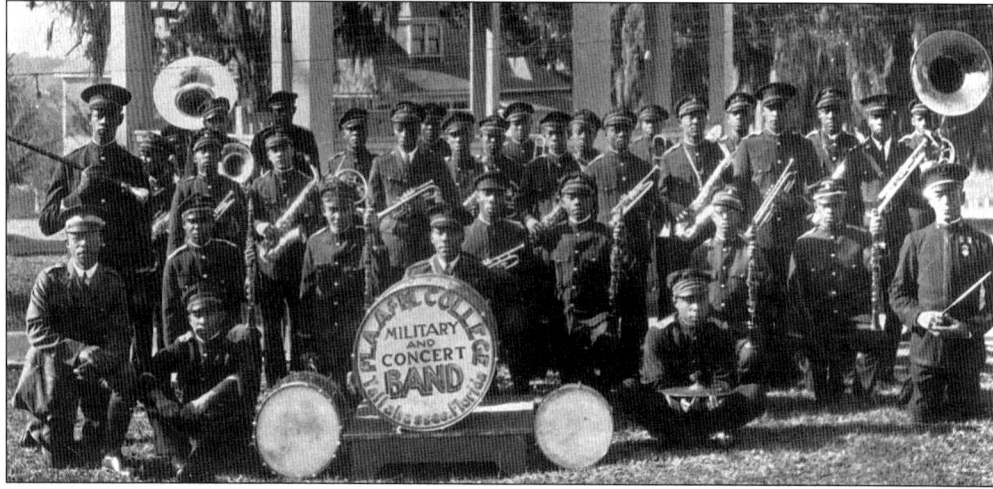

Since April 15, 1887, when the Florida legislature established a permanent state normal school, later Florida A&M College (University), the school has led the nation as a center of excellence in higher education. This 1929 photograph of the FAMU Military and Concert Band, which became the Marching 100 under the direction of Dr. William P. Foster, is indicative of the growth that led to the university's designation as "College of the Year" for 1997–1998 by the *Time Magazine/Princeton Review*.

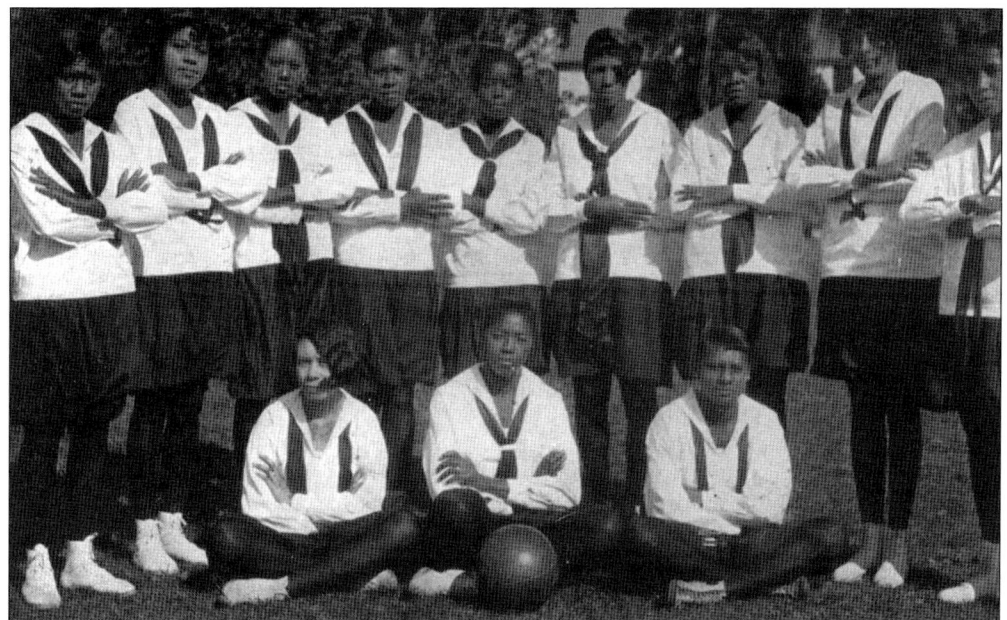

Pictured is the 1929 girls basketball team at Florida A&M University. The university has produced outstanding athletes in all sports, including native Tallahasseans such as Leroy Gibson, Tommy Lee Mitchell, and Robert Paramore. The school has an early history of providing opportunities to participate for both males and females. Much growth in women's sports occurred under the leadership of Sarah Hill, the first intercollegiate athletics coordinator for women.

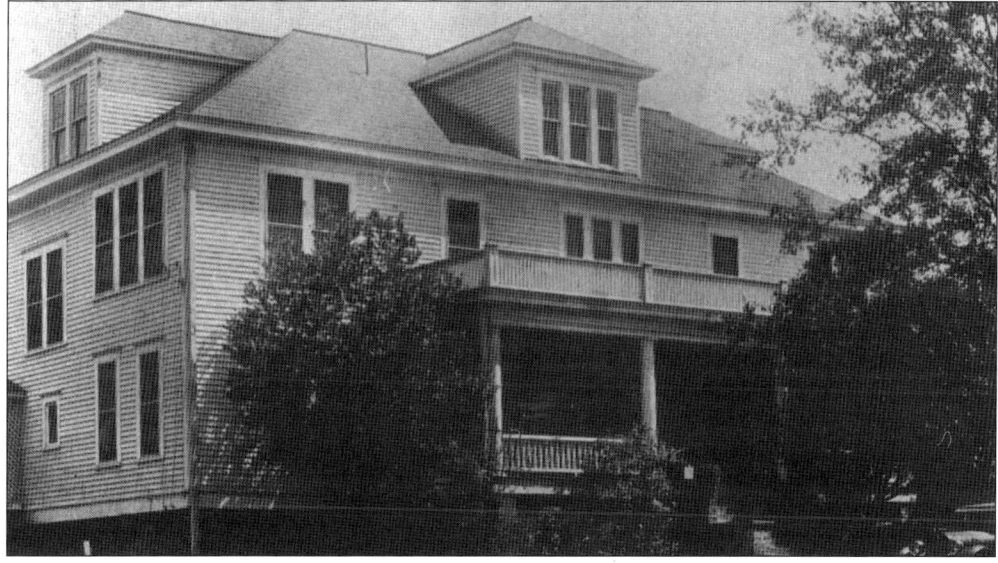

Pictured here in 1929, the Florida A&M University Hospital, a vernacular frame structure, was established in 1911 with 19 beds. Improvements were made over the years, including an enlarged brick building and accreditation. For years, the hospital was the only public facility that provided Tallahassee's African-American population with in-patient care. The hospital closed in 1971 as a result of desegregation. The patients and staff were transferred to the then all-white Tallahassee Memorial.

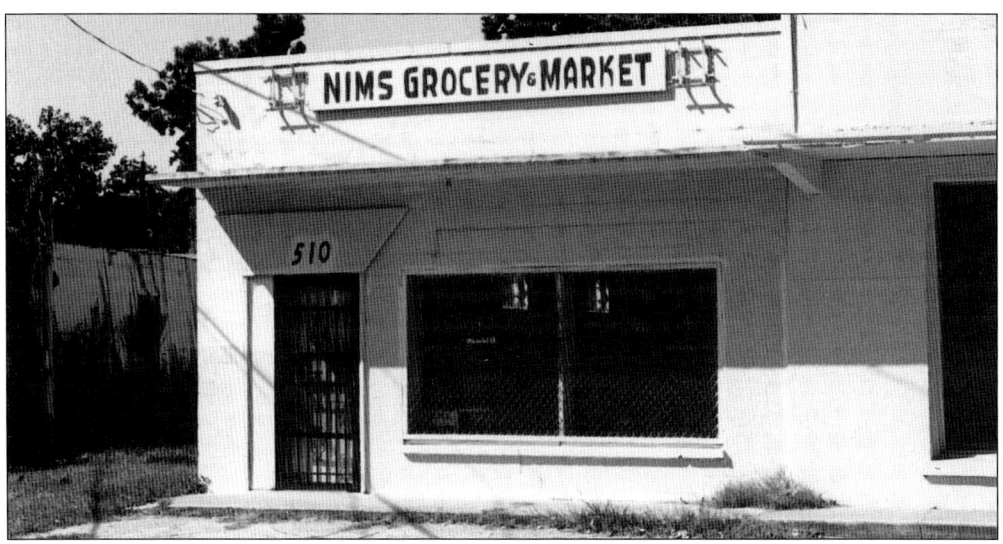

This small grocery store located at Macomb and Brevard is the last vestige of the legend of one of Tallahassee's prominent families, the Nims. The family owned and operated grocery and meat markets in Quincy, in Tallahassee at the site of the current Department of Transportation Building, and in downtown Tallahassee on Adams Street. Joe Nims, who lived to be 107, carried on the tradition from this location until his death. His widow, Mamie, still lives in Tallahassee.

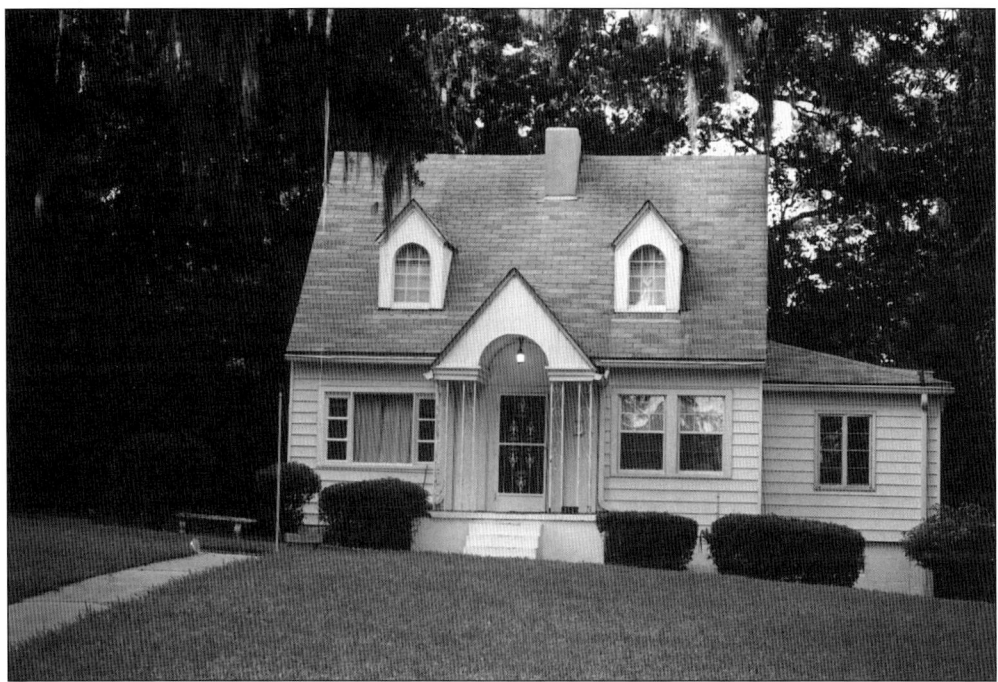

This is the former home of Dr. Gilbert L. Porter at 212 Barbourville Drive. Dr. Porter was the principal of Lincoln High School. He received a Ph.D. and served as the executive secretary of the Florida State Teachers Association. Relocating to Miami, Florida, in 1965 to help with school desegregation, Porter became the first Dade County African-American assistant superintendent. Porter Elementary School of Discovery, Dade County, is named in his honor.

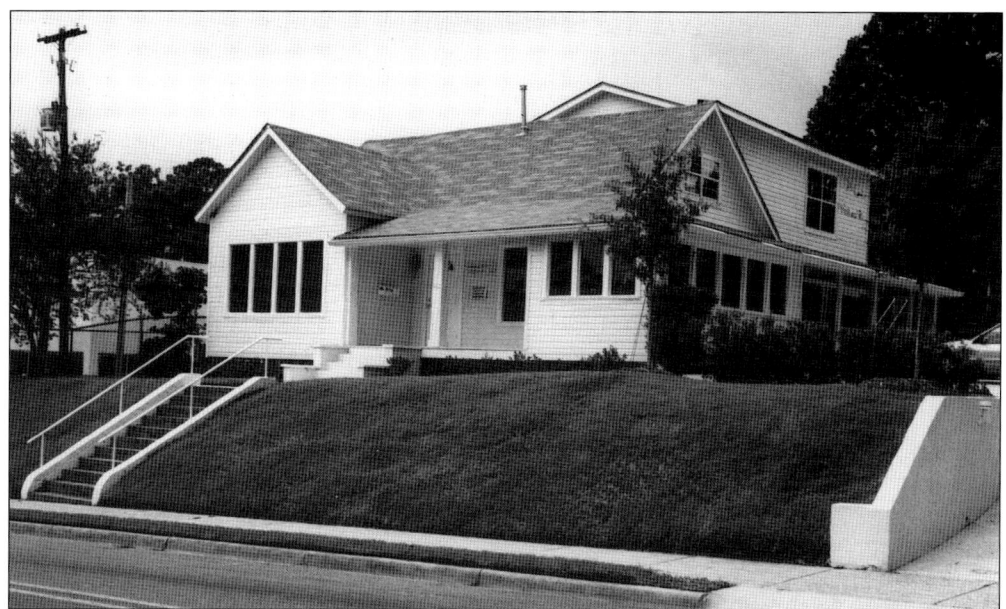

Shown here is the former home of Presiding Elder Daniels of the AME church and his wife, C.B.N. Daniels. The house is located in Frenchtown at 462 West Brevard Street. Two other families lived in the home before it was remodeled in 1998 to house the law practice of three black female attorneys: Carolyn Cummings, Angel Wallace Davis, and Barbara Kay Hobbs.

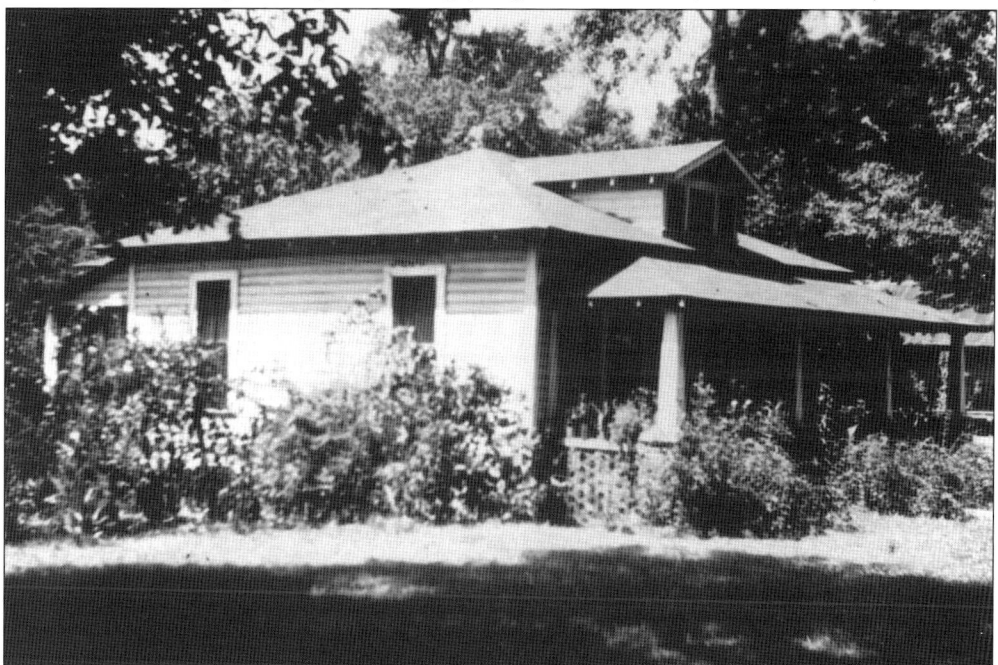

Shown in this 1990 photograph is the homestead of the John Swilley family on East St. Augustine Street. Swilley was a master bricklayer and helped construct many of the buildings in Tallahassee, including the Exchange building in the downtown area. He was the second African American hired at the federal prison in Tallahassee, where he taught bricklaying. He also served as a worshipful master of Mt. Olive Lodge.

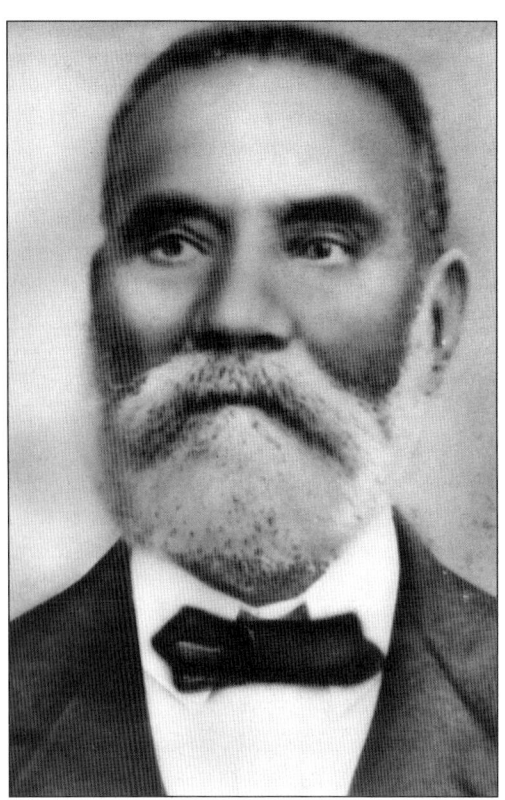

Charles Rollins lived with his family at 1210 Old Bainbridge Road in a home he built in the mid-1800s. A third structure, built in 1915, is still standing. Rollins and his wife, Mary, a midwife, farmed several acres of land and operated a dairy farm. The Rollins family still owns extensive acreage on Lake Jackson in rural Leon County.

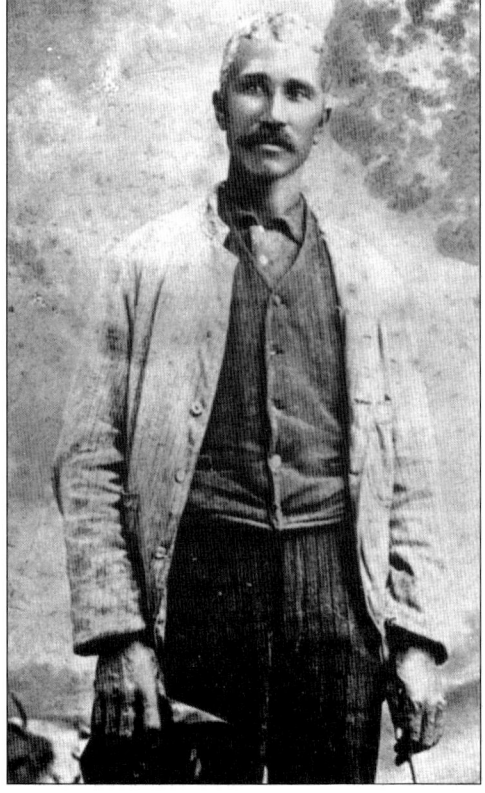

After slavery, Henry Watson (1815–1904) purchased property on North Thomasville Road. The property was later sold by his family and is currently the location of the Thomasville Road Mall and Miracle Theater. Watson is buried in the historic Betton Hill Cemetery. A historic marker was erected at the cemetery in 1999.

Six
Matriarchs and Patriarchs

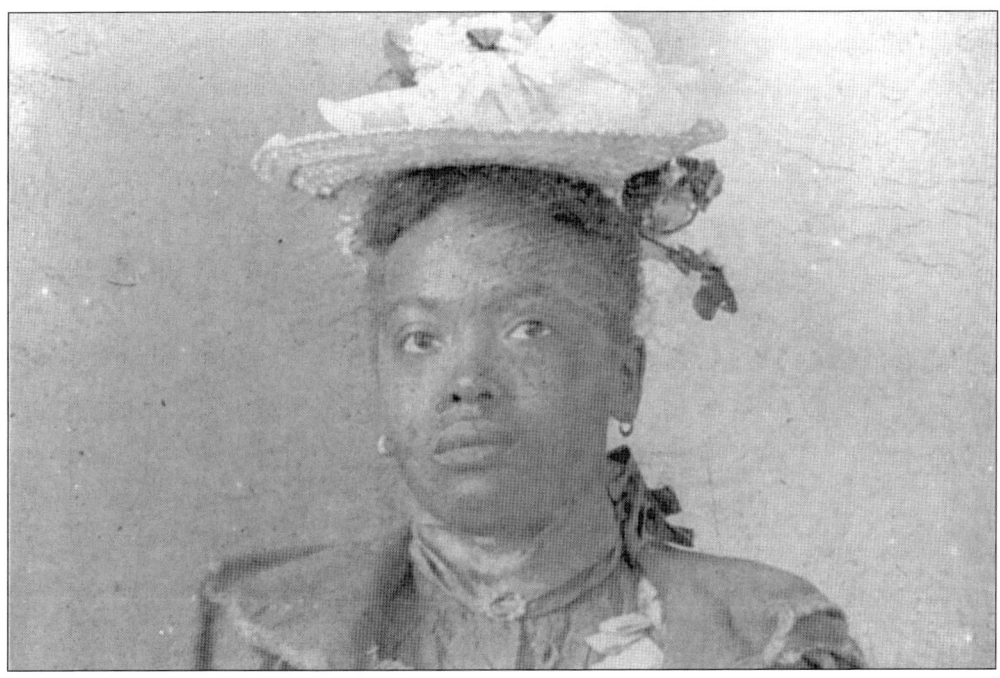

Cherrye L. Turner Spencer, born in Leon County on December 24, 1879, was the sixth child of Washington and Cherrye Turner. She and her husband, Jack, raised seven children: Roberta, Cora, Samuel, Frances, Annie Lee, James, and Cherrye. They farmed until all of their children were grown, then sold their possessions and moved to Tallahassee. Their son Samuel owned a wood yard on Dunn Street and a laundry on Disston Street.

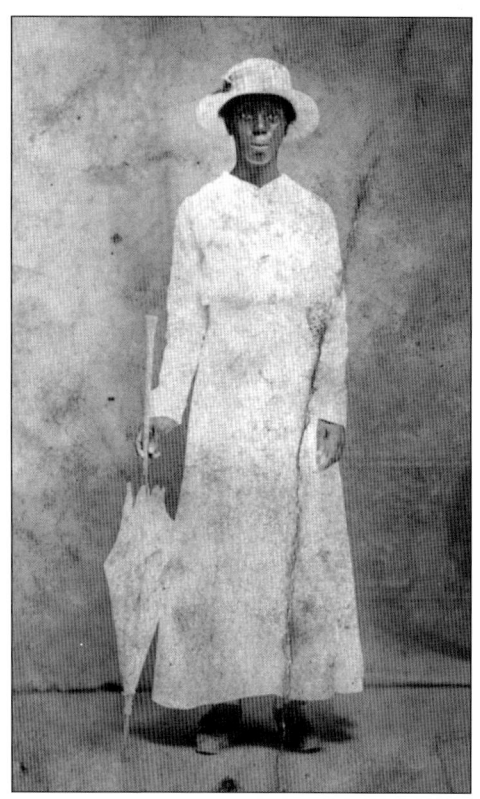

Emma Edwards Reed, a domestic worker, was born in the late 1800s and lived in the Lake Hall community. A custodian at the original Lincoln High School, Reed was absent from work only one day, the day she had a stroke that resulted in her death. Her dress is indicative of the distinctive styles worn by rural African-American women during the early 20th century.

Lillie Franklin Davis, along with her husband, Lonnie, was the owner of Davis Grocery. The store provided a valuable resource for families in the historic African-American community of Springfield. Before availability and open access to large grocery chains, families made most of their dry and household goods purchases from stores such as Davis Grocery, which was located next to the Davis family's private home on Abraham Street in Tallahassee.

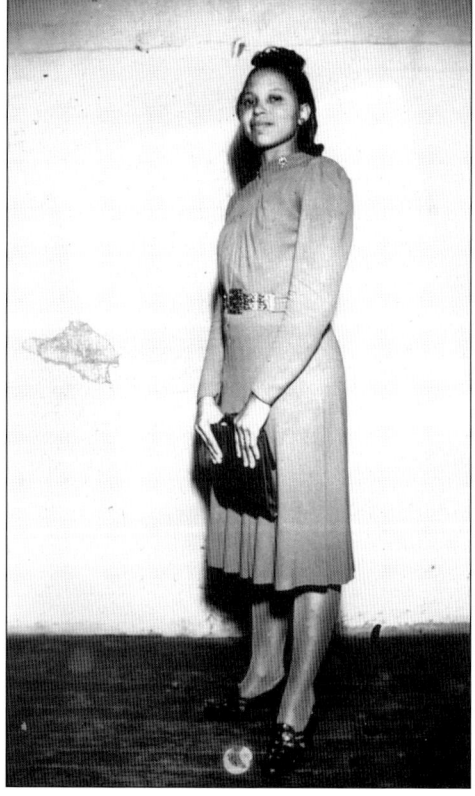

Pictured here is Lucinda Roberts, the wife of Turner Roberts. Standing beside her is her son Paul, who, as an adult, drove a taxi and farmed. He made frequent trips to town to sell his produce.

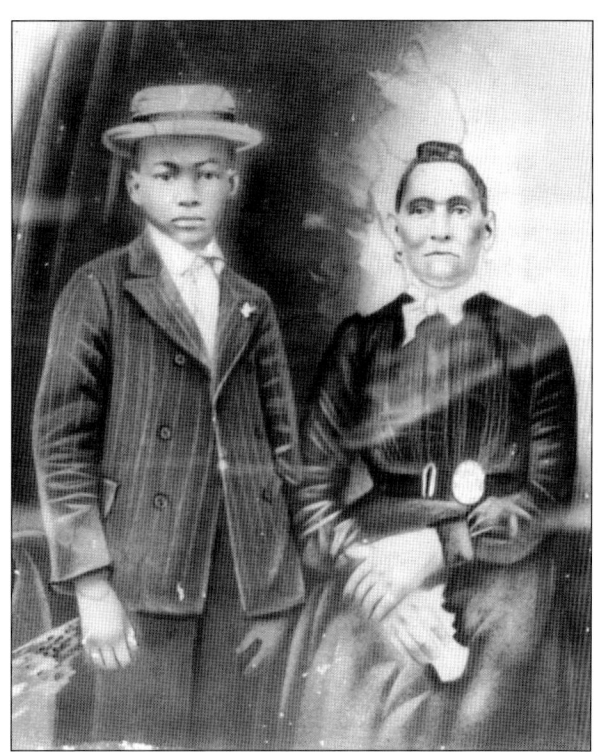

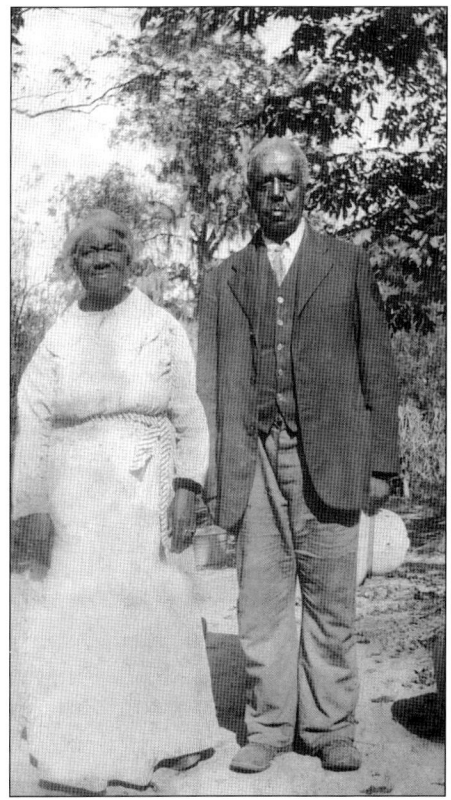

Charlie and Mary Payne, seen here in the 1930s, married and raised their children in the Lake Hall area. The Paynes were entrepreneurs—they owned two stores, rented fishing boats, and also farmed their own land.

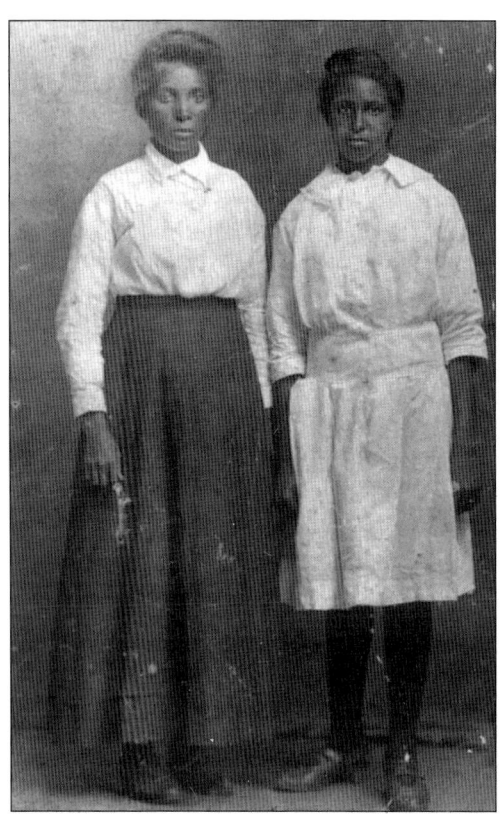

Annie Franklin and her daughter Naomi were photographed in the 1930s. The family moved from their farm in rural Leon County and established and operated a community store and service station in Springfield and a cleaners in Frenchtown. Naomi's other siblings were Joe (the owner of Modern Cleaners), Benjamin, Lillie (the owner of Davis Groceries), Franklin, Hazel, Mary, and Annie.

Photographed during the 1800s is the woman who headed the Osborne family, Rachael Osborne. Her son Leroy and his wife, Cornelia, lived for many years in the historic Frenchtown community at 714 Macomb Street. Rachel's granddaughter Bennie Mae Osborne Moseley, an educator, retired from Leon County schools in 1988.

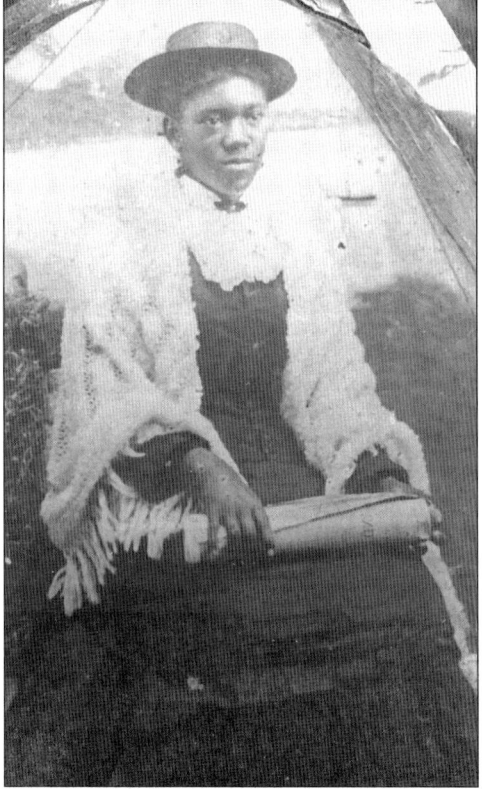

Susan Lucus Cauley, seen here in the 1920s, was the oldest daughter of James and Lavina Lucas, landowners and farmers, who came to Tallahassee from North Carolina and Virginia in 1860. Susan married George Washington "Pink" Cauley and raised her family around the Tram and the Old Midyette Roads, now Capital Circle South East.

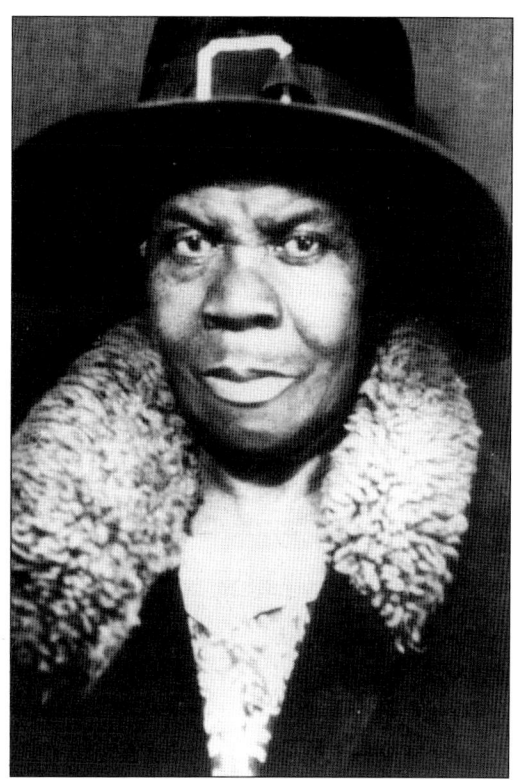

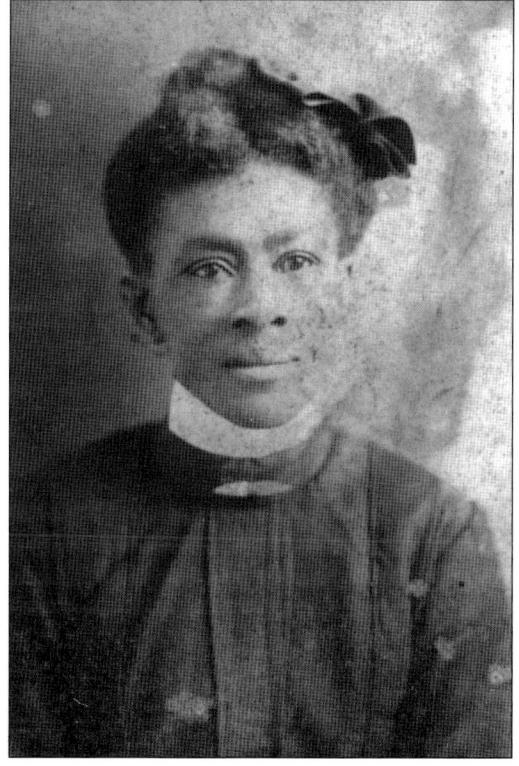

Elnora Hunter, the sister of Lucy Hunter and the mother of Margaret Yellowhair, was married to Edward H. Yellowhair. E.H. ran for the position of tax assessor and received the highest number of votes, 216, according to the council minutes of February 18, 1885. In 1976, Mrs. Pete Birdie Grant Roberts, in an oral history interview, shared testimony to the life of Mrs. Yellowhair.

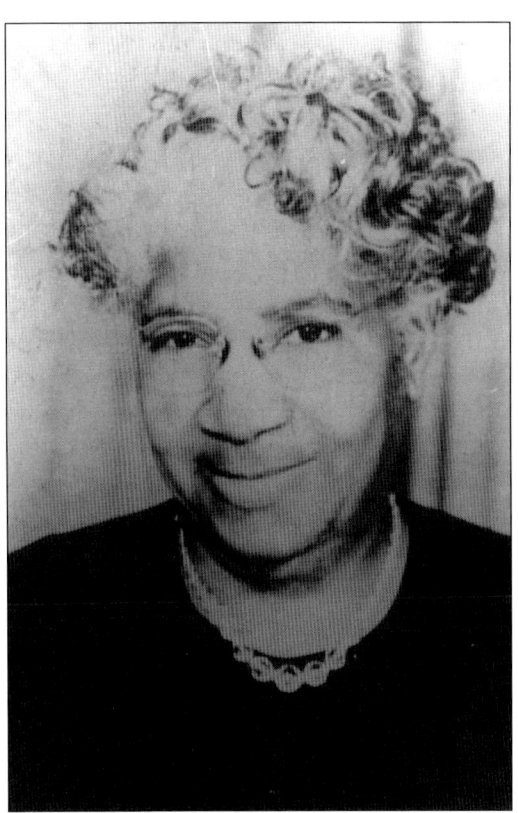

During her lifetime, Catherine Ross, a former educator and principal at St. Stephens School, a one-room African-American schoolhouse, owned 66 acres of land on what is now Lake Bradford Road. Much of the property remains in the family today. A road, Catherine Ross Court, was named in her memory.

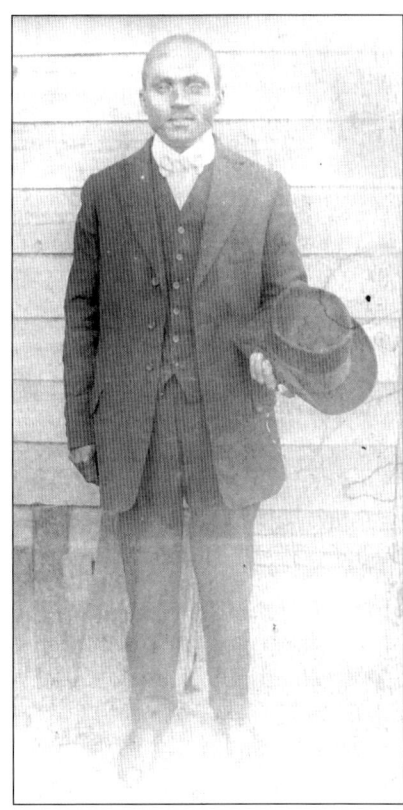

Thornton S. Ross, photographed here in the 1930s, was the husband of Catherine Ross.

Ruby Hunter James, the mother of Annie Mae Oliver, was born in rural Leon County on the Griscom Plantation. In her adult life, James worked for Senator William C. Hodges as a cook at Goodwood Plantation. The plantation, which is located behind Tallahassee Memorial Regional Medical Center, was recently restored as a museum.

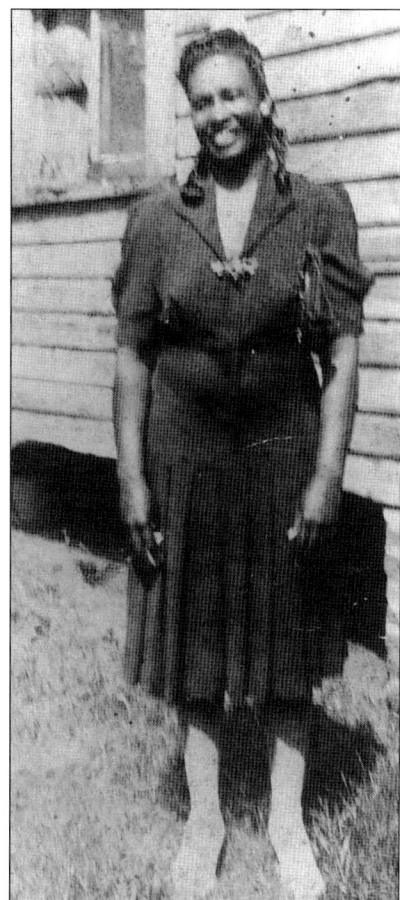

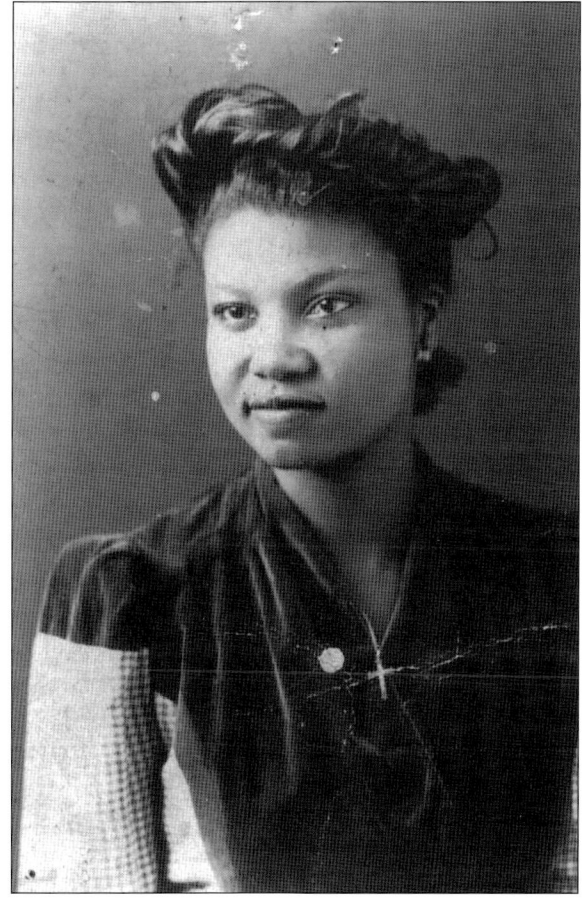

Edith Reid West, pictured here in the 1930s, raised her family on West Georgia Street in the historic Frenchtown neighborhood. From there, she nurtured many of Tallahassee's children. Some of her family members still live in the family home. West's father was a surrey driver at the turn of the 20th century.

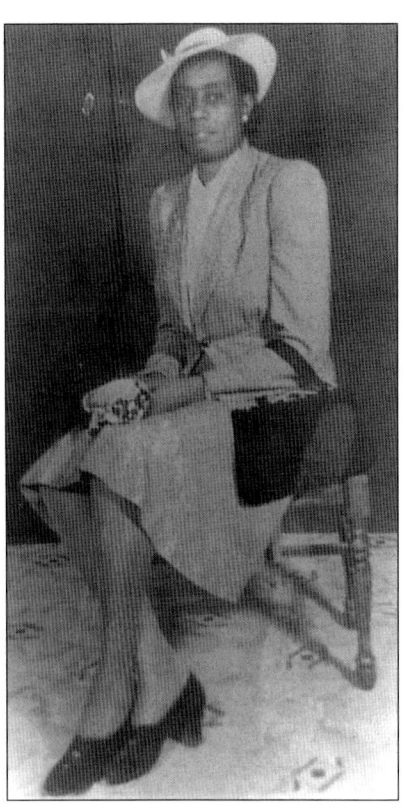

Photographed in the 1920s, Cornelia Roberts Osborne, a longtime resident of the Frenchtown community, raised her family there and operated a snack shop next to her McComb Street home. The building that housed the snack shop and Osborne's home are still standing at their original locations.

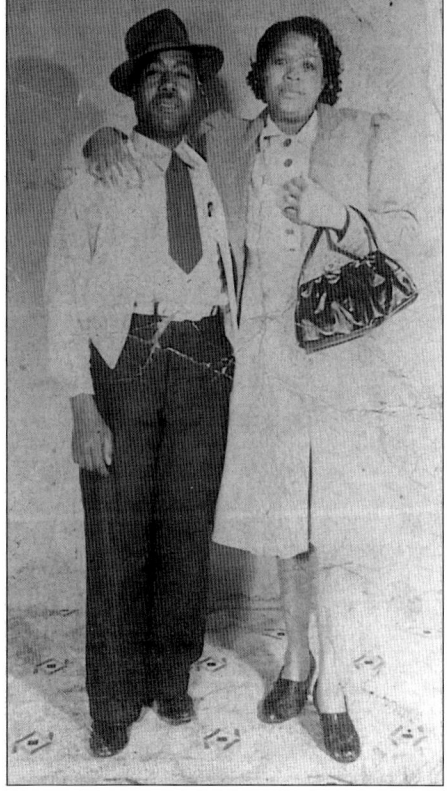

Tobias McKinley Payne and his wife, Beatrice Young Payne, owned extensive property in the Lake Hall area and raised their family there. They farmed and rented boats to fisherman, both black and white, from the 1930s through the 1960s.

Seen here in 1939, Samantha and Ellis McGhee resided on Georgia Street in the historic Frenchtown community, where they raised 11 children. One of their sons, Alphonso, was the first graduate of the Florida A&M University Law School.

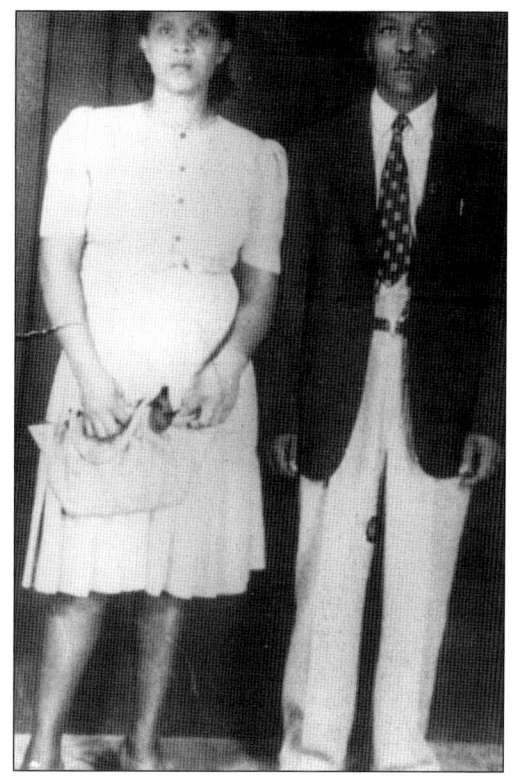

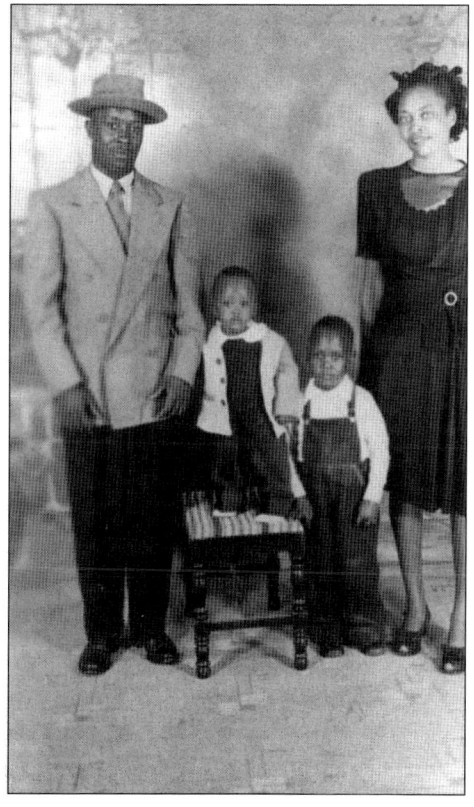

Dr. Devurn Glenn, his wife, Allie Mae, and the couple's sons Ronald and Devurn Jr. are pictured here. Dr. Glenn was the first principal at Nims Middle School and the first African American to work in the Leon County School Board administrative office, where he served as assistant superintendent.

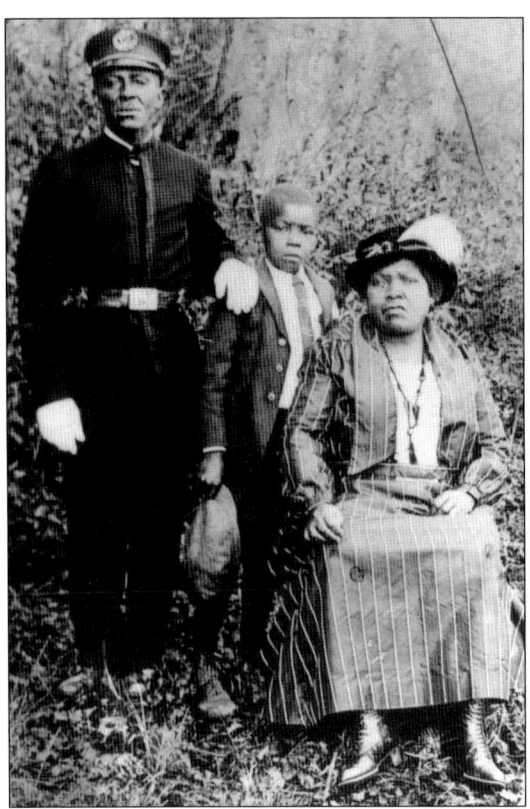

Photographed in the 1920s are Philip J. Nelson (center) and his grandparents, Nancey Adams, a painter, and Florida Adams. Nelson's father, Philip John Nelson Sr., owned and operated a fish market on Adams Street at the current location of Tallahassee's city hall, while Nelson's mother, Maggie Nelson Sampson, was a housewife.

In 1969, Philip John "P.J." Nelson desegregated Rickards High School by becoming its first African-American principal. He retired in 1979. He is also a charter member of Frontiers International and Kappa Alpha Psi Fraternity. Nelson was a former assistant principal at the original Lincoln High School and a teacher/principal at Bell, a one-room African-American schoolhouse.

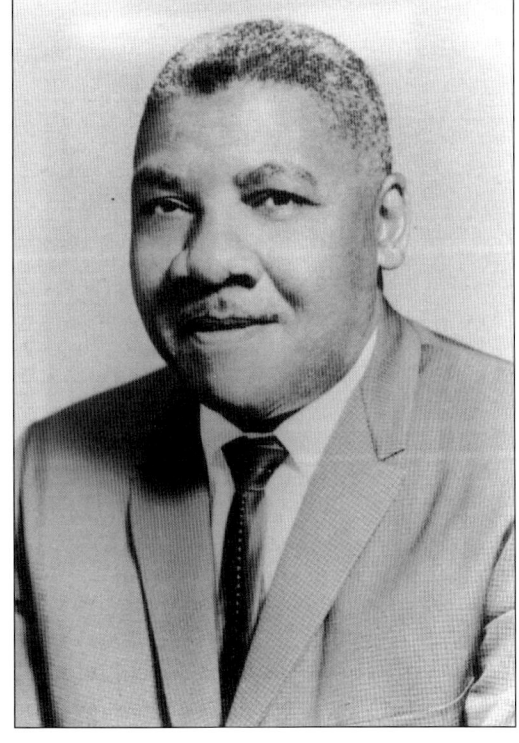

Alberta Oliver, the mother of James "Billy" Oliver and the grandmother of Gwendolyn Oliver Parker, is pictured here during the 1930s. Oliver raised her family in the historic African-American community of Carroll Quarters, a community named after her mother, Annie Carroll. As entrepreneurs, the family owned extensive property and a store located on North Thomasville Road, behind the Miracle Plaza Mall.

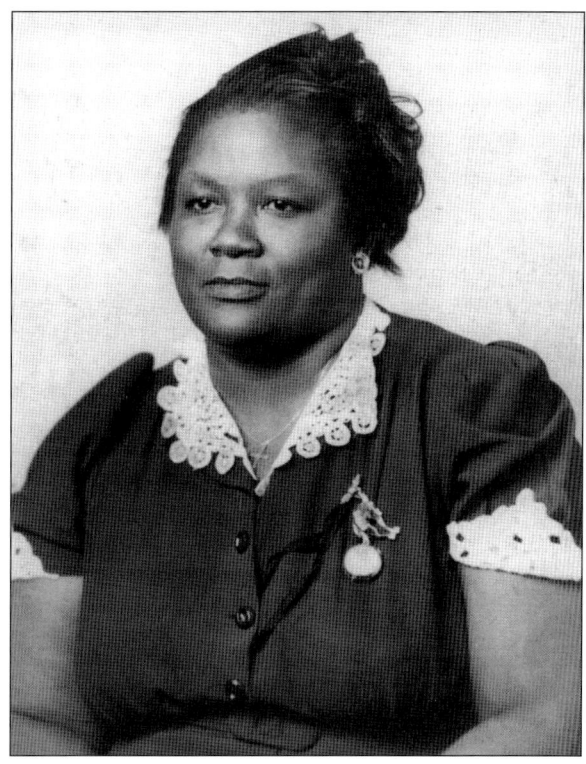

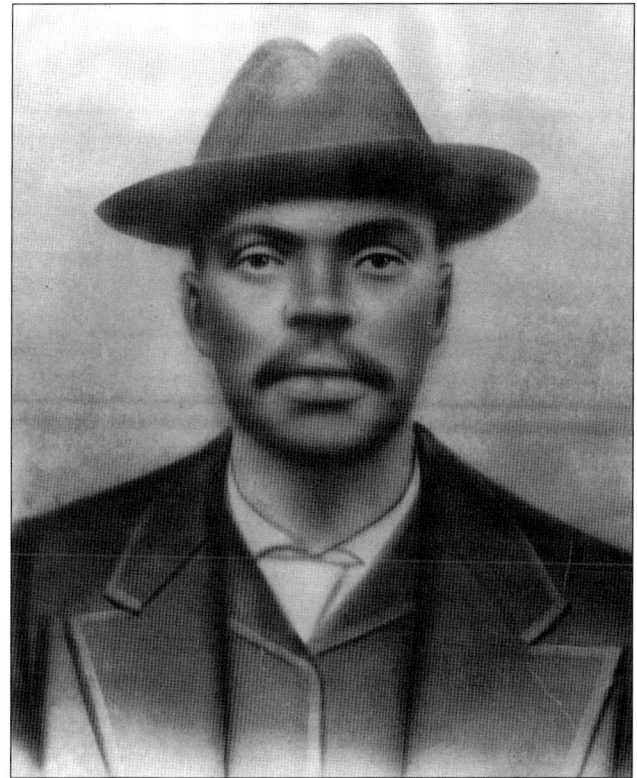

David Thompson Sr. (b. June 1842) and his wife, Sibbie (b. 1848), were married in 1864. After slavery, they came into possession of 240 acres in the Chaires community. A $1,500 loan for a mule and seeds to plant was obtained, but a subsequent terrible crop year resulted in default. The remaining acres were saved by their son Israel and family friends J.R.D. Laster, E.A. Pottsdamer, and John Swilley. The last payment was made to Laster in 1952.

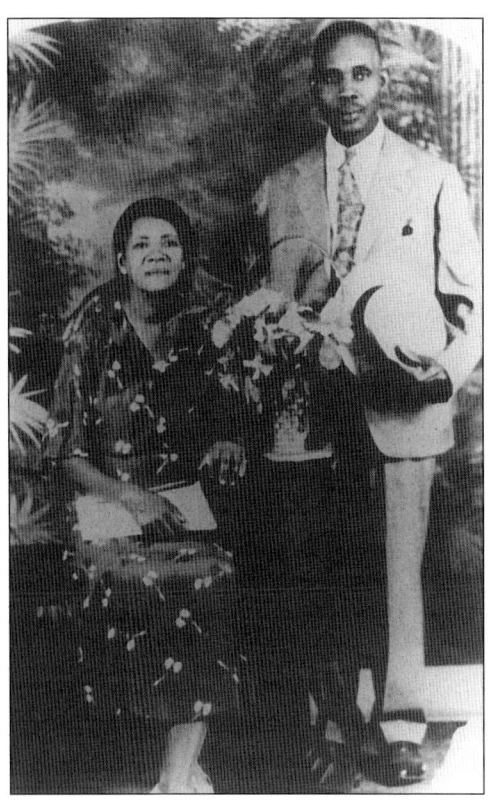

Ike and Ida Young, photographed in the 1920s, raised their family on Waverly Place on North Meridian Road in Tallahassee, Florida. As was typical of many rural couples, they had several children: Mattie, Elia, Bessie, Lena Mae, Alice, Edith, Louise, Lettie, Ike, Arthur, David, Willie, Annie, Isaac, Johnny, Frank, and Ida.

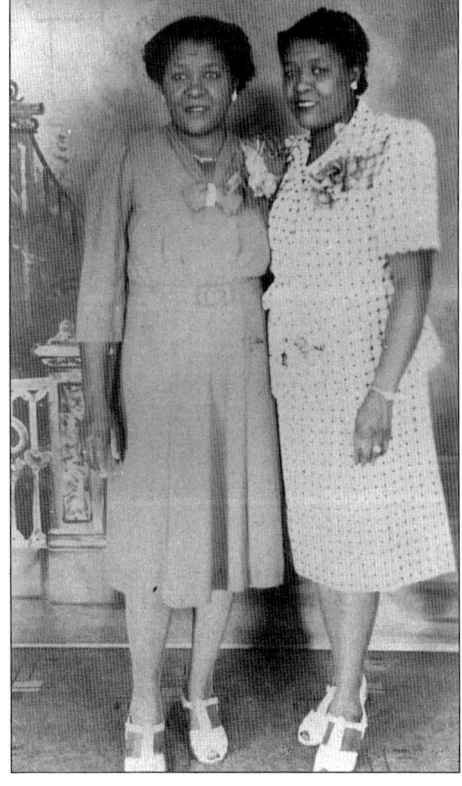

Twins Louise and Lucy Turner, born in 1901, are shown photographed at the age of 62. Now 98, they live in Tallahassee at 315 West Call Street. Lucy taught piano lessons until her retirement; she learned the piano from a Mrs. Gadsden on Copeland Street many years ago. The twins recall other African-American families who used to live in their community, including Shirley Brown, the Dilworths, "Mama" Sheppherd, and the Mamie VanBrunt Blake family.

Pauline Brim and Cleotha Willis grew up on Welaunee Plantation on Miccosukee Road. Willis's parents were Malachi and Ellen Willis. Both came from pioneer Leon County farm families. They married and later moved to the historic black Tallahassee community of Springfield where they raised three boys and one girl.

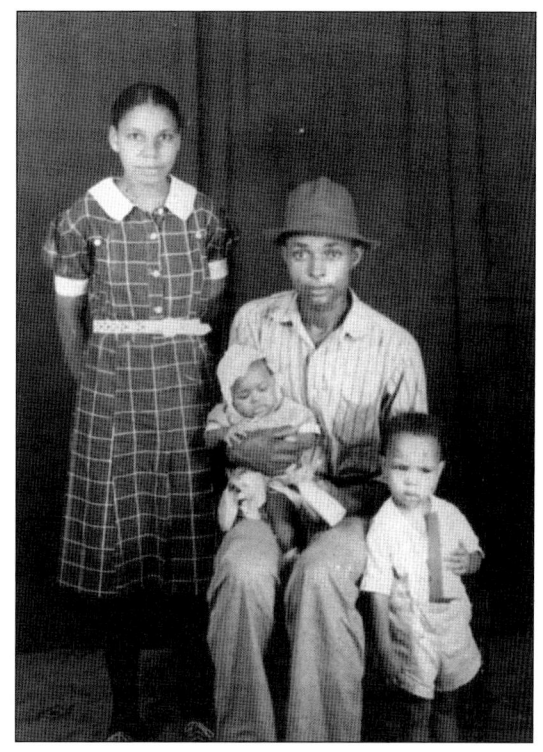

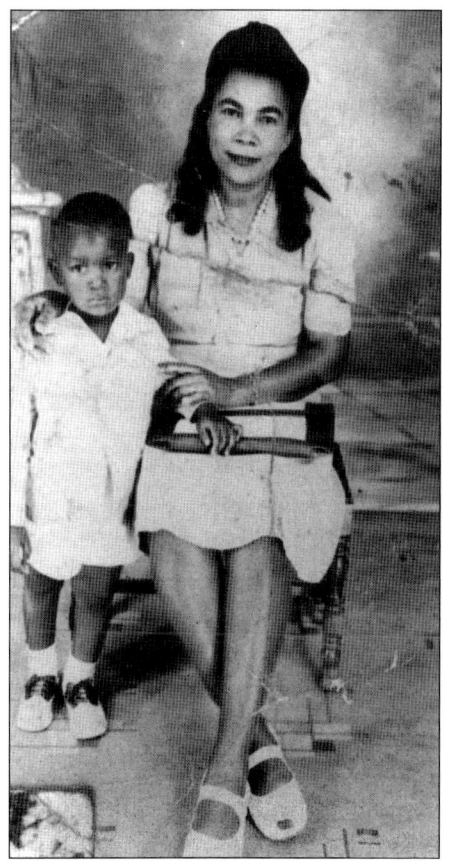

Katherine Speights is pictured in the 1950s with her grandson. Speights, at age 94 in 1997, provided valuable and significant oral history information pertaining to Tallahassee and Leon County to Riley Museum staff. She grew up in the Buck Lake and Chaires community and attended Greenhowe, a black one-room schoolhouse on Old St. Augustine Road.

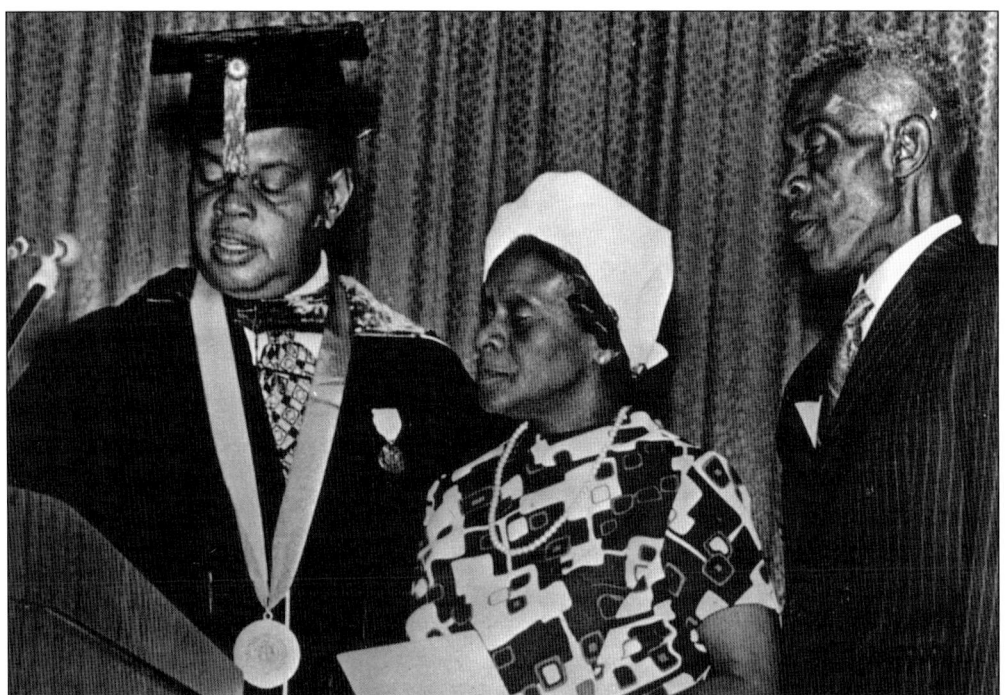

Mary and Mose Pemberton, photographed with President Benjamin Perry Jr., celebrated one of many family graduations. They were recipients of the Presidential Award from Florida A&M University in 1971. The couple, who did domestic and custodial work, was honored for having graduated seven children from the university as well as several grandchildren.

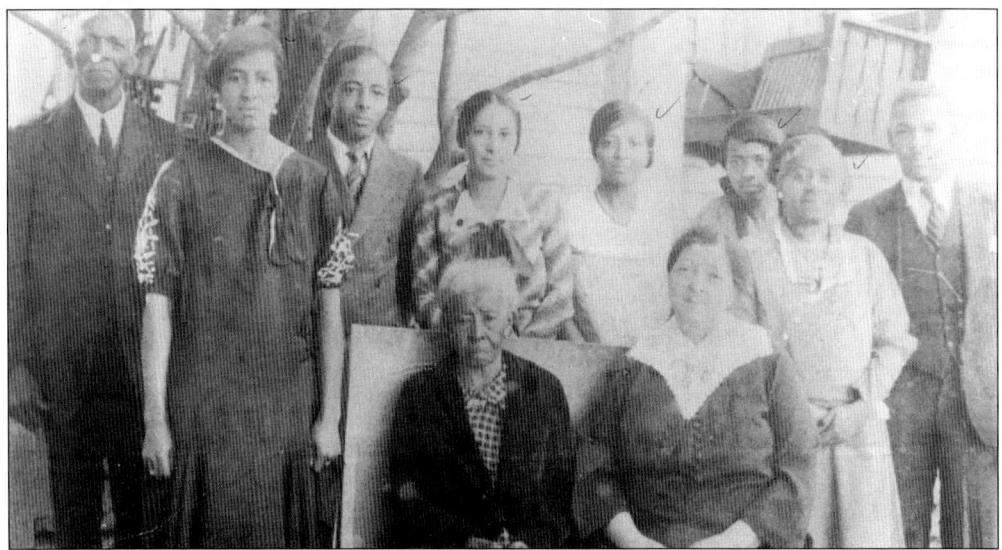

Paralee Webb (sixth from left, standing) taught at Testerina, a one-room African-American schoolhouse in Leon County on Miccosukee Road, before accepting positions at Griffin and Lincoln. Seen here with her are the following, from left to right: (seated) "Grandma" Elizabeth Anthony Jefferson, a former slave, and Annie Sheppard; (standing) family members Henry Jefferson, Lenora McCrary, Herbert Jefferson, Levetta Collins, Elouise Williams, Webb, Pearly Lee, and Mary White Oliver. Paralee lived with the Sheppards at 175 North Bronough.

Seven
EVENTS AND CELEBRATIONS

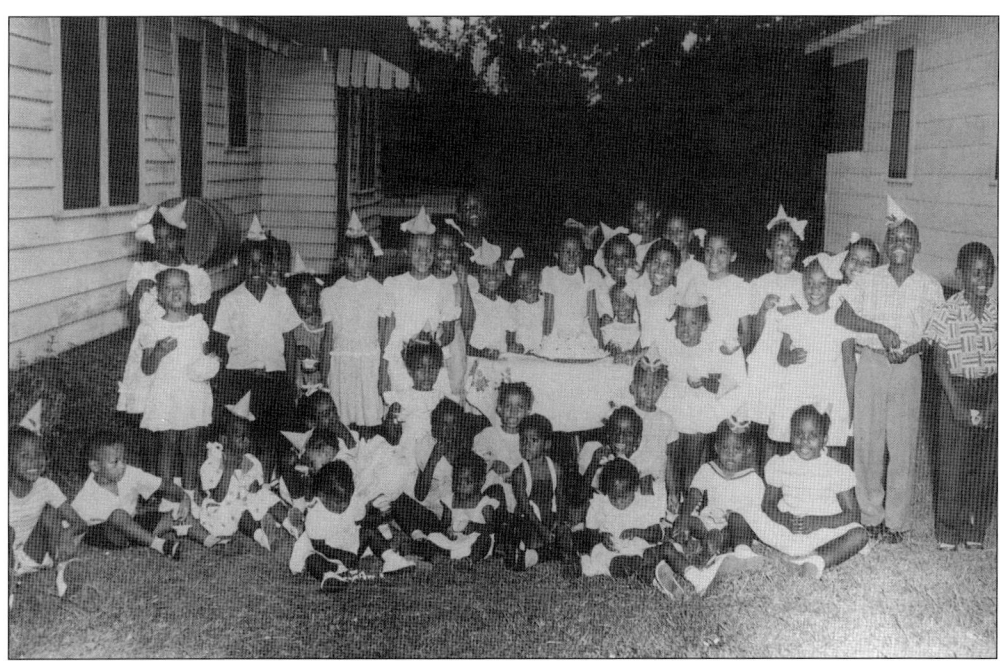

Playmates celebrate at the birthday party of Janice McCloud (Bryant) in the 1940s. Pictured in this group are Gerald and Sandra Cooper; Josie Weaver; Jonella Reid; Myra, Gloria, and Joyce Smith; Francis Allen; Peggy McGhee; Sonja and Carmen Howell; Gloria Gilliam; Ralph and Francis Allen; Carol, Ann, and Barrie Roberts; Jean and Jeannette Mannings; Ricky Pope; and Howard Jackson.

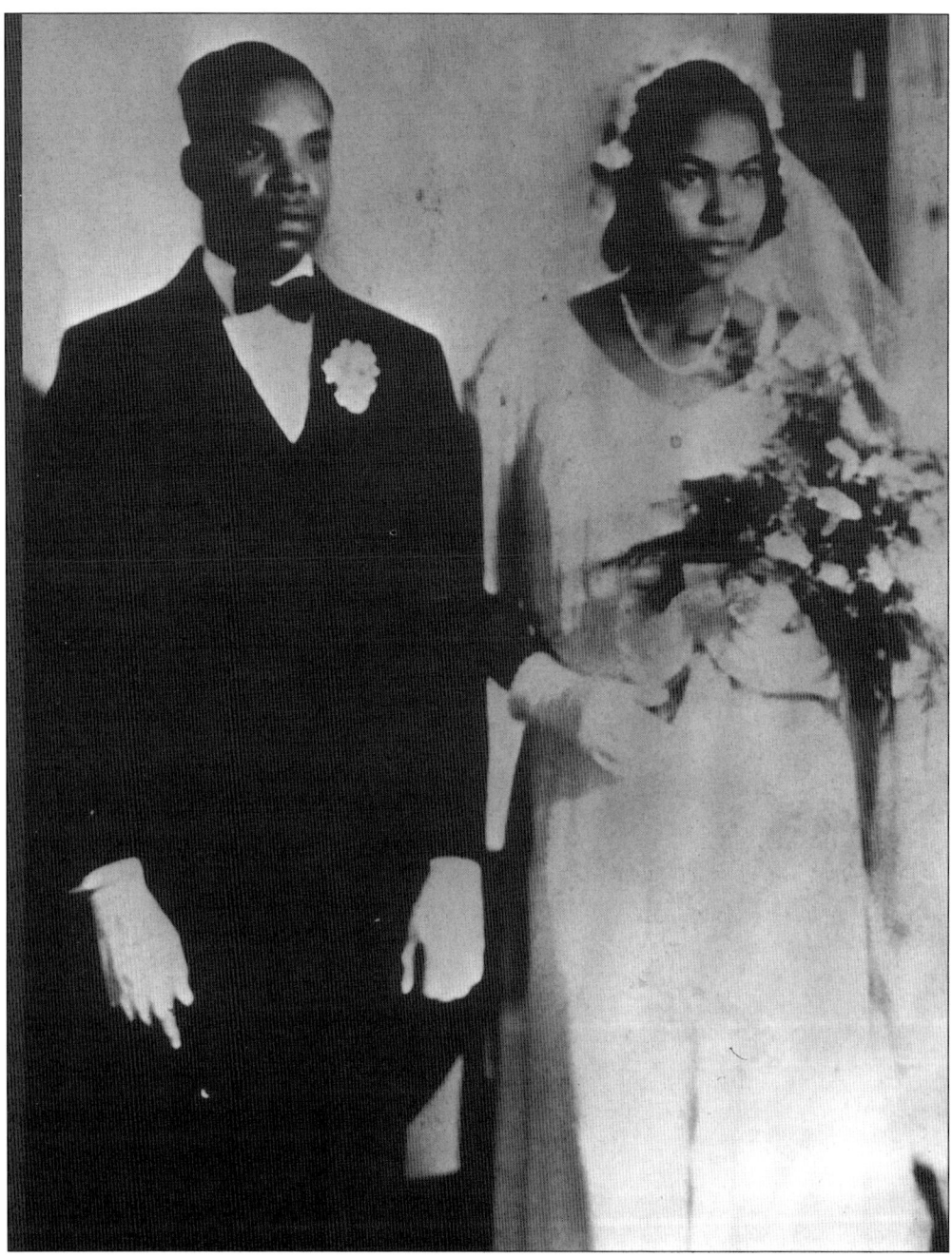

Flora Mae and Peter Hunter were wed on March 9, 1933. The Hunters purchased property on North Thomasville Road where Mrs. Hunter still resides. She authored a recipe book, *Born in the Kitchen, Plain and Fancy Plantation Fixins*, in 1979, for which she received the 1988 Florida Heritage Award. She attributes her famous Southern dishes to years of cooking on Sunnyhill, Foshalee, and Horseshoe Plantations.

Rev. Divillow Crawford (March 22, 1887–June 10, 1968) and Victoria Twine Crawford (August 13, 1898–December 21, 1979) were married for 48 years. Victoria lovingly referred to her husband as "Mr. Crawford." They lived at 624 Madison Street. The Crawford children are Robert, Patricia, Phyllis, Richard, Wilhelmina, Carl, Eva, and George.

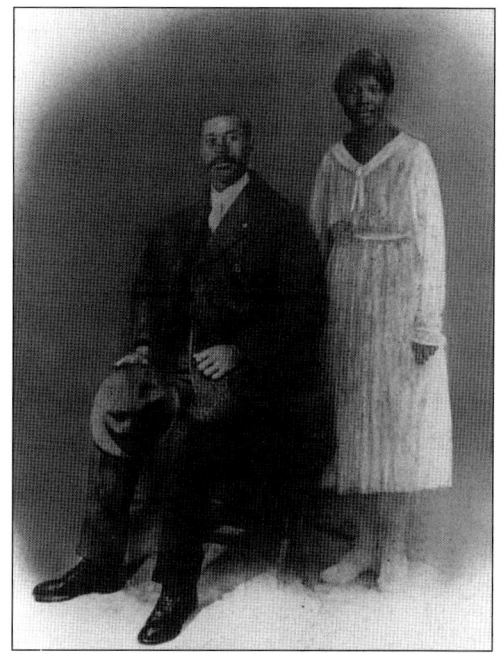

The love letter below was written by Divillow Crawford during World War I to his future bride, Victoria Twine.

Nov. 10, 1918
Pvt. Divillow H. Crawford
Co. D 877 P Inf.
A. E. F. N.Y.

Dear Victoria,

I am far from you but however my mind holds you tight in memory. I often wish for that happy day when we shall meet again and be as we have often wished. I will someday meet my dear heart again when the war is over and we all go marching home. I hope to see you just as sweet as I left you.

I can't write you often as I desire for I am here where I step in shell holes everyday so you may know I don't have much time to write. It is Sunday night now and I have a little time to write. The guns are not sounding so loud while I am writing to you, for now.

I think of you kindly. Remember me to mother (yours-mine) and Mrs. Ruffins. Write me often. Maybe I will get your letters after while. I am traveling so fast until I haven't got any of your letters since I left Camp Evens, Mass. which is more than two months.

Darling, keep writing me. Maybe I will get some of your letters after while. It is Nov. the 10th and I haven't heard from you since August. I am looking for a letter from you every day but I move so fast until the mail cannot find me for some time.

I am deep down in the trenches; so deep until a rifle ball can't find me. Then you know it will be hard for me to get my mail. But I guess it will find me. By the time you get this letter - wish it could express with words my wishes to see you darling. I look at this photo. I haven't missed a time of sipping the sweetness from the lips of it. Just s I write a loud shell fired and my little candle sitting on the bottom of my drinking cup is almost gone out. I was afraid I could not finish this.

I wonder what you are doing tonight when it is seven o'clock out here. It is noonday over there in Tallahassee. Love to all for me. Go to the mirror and get a kiss for me.

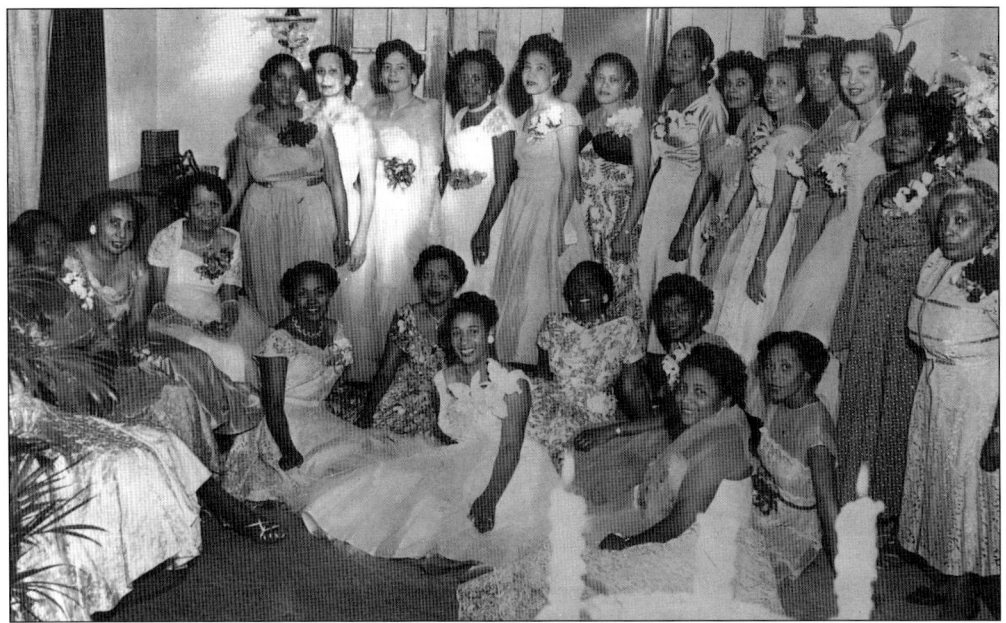

The following people, from left to right, attended an elegant affair hosted by FAMU president George Gore and his wife, Pearl: (seated) Marjorie Campbell, Marian Hadley, Marie McMillian King, Pearl Gore, Inez Jones, Mai Norwood, Claudia Batey Silas, Polly Fears, Genevieve Lowe, Augusta Ford Nims, and Archie Engram; (standing) Amerique Breckenridge Briggs, Pilar Rhaney, Willie Pearl Porter, Nickie Perry, Audrey Kelker, Beatrice Clarke, Edna Calhoun, Jacquelyn Thomas, Sue Russell, Lola Stewart, M. Lucian James, Julia Lewis, and Lollie Fleming.

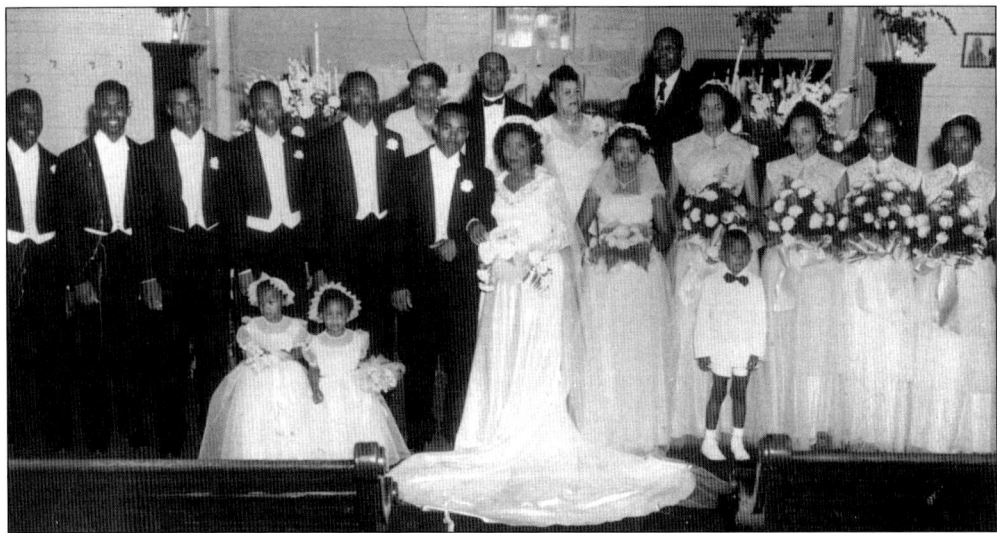

The 1952 wedding of Wilhemina "Brown Baby" Crawford and Leroy Wester was held at St. Mary's Church on Call Street. The groomsmen are John Dukes, Carl Crawford, Salem Pope, George Crawford, and Timothy Gainous. The bridesmaids are Eva Crawford, Carol Blow, Verda Gavin Rollins, Queen Hargrett Bruton, and Lula Mae Young. Bobby Joe Dean is the ring bearer, and Rita Gail Dean and Cynthia ? are the flower girls. Standing behind the wedding party are the bride's parents, Victoria and Divillow Crawford; the wedding coordinator, Emily Stephens; and Rev. M.G. Miles, who performed the ceremony.

Jean and James Brewington, an educator and businessman, respectively, are pictured here on their wedding day. James owns one of the last pieces of private commercial property in the historic Frenchtown community.

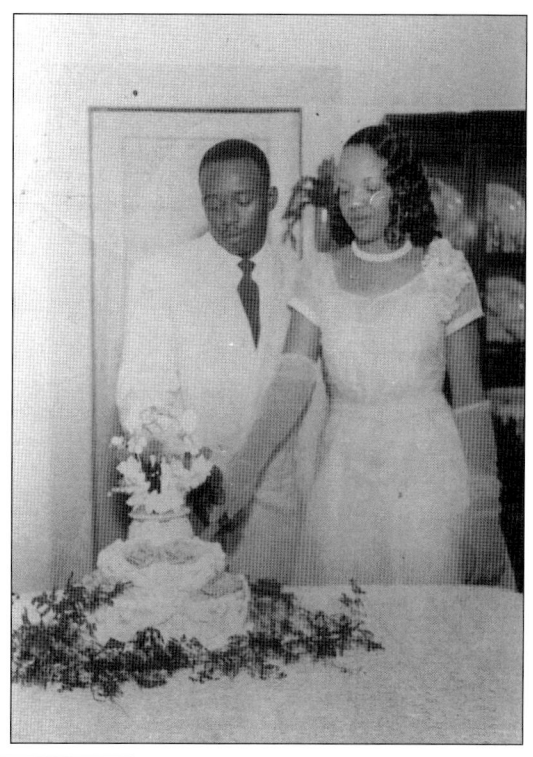

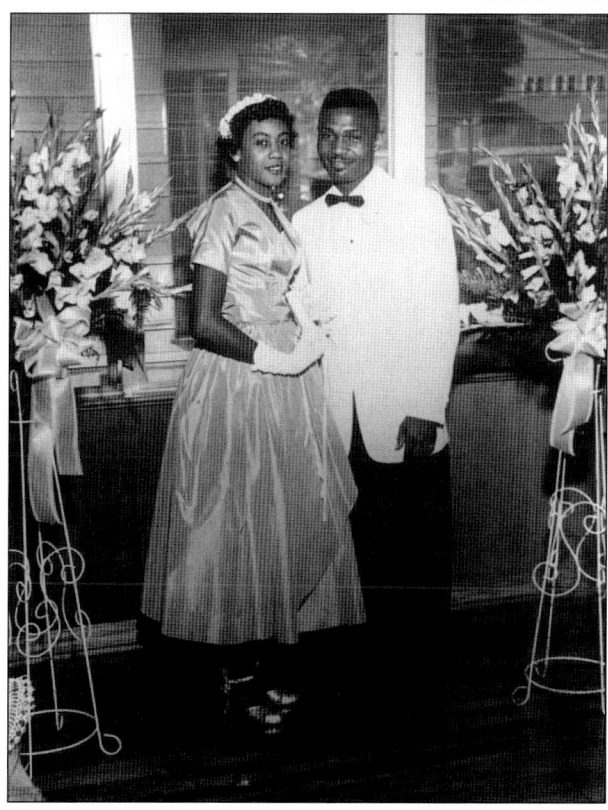

Bennie Osborne and Moses Moseley pose on their wedding day in 1954.

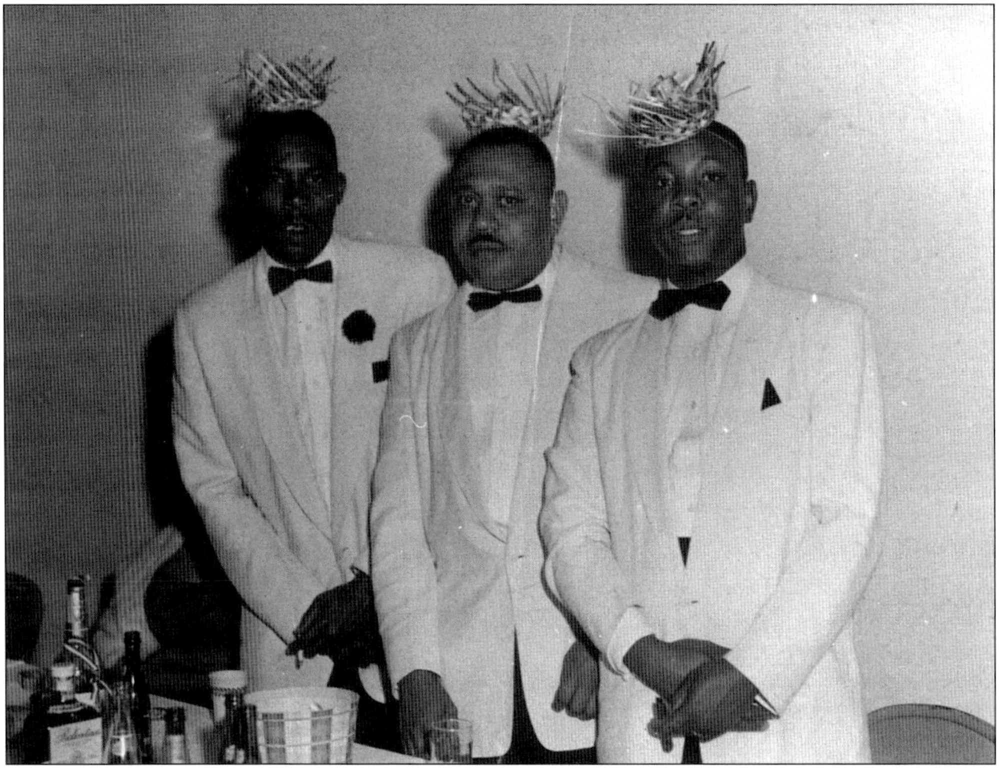

James "Billy" Oliver, George "Rabbit" Holiday, and Samuel Gilliam celebrate at a New Year's Eve party. Each is a descendent of a Leon County pioneer family, having roots in Tallahassee, Leon County, at the beginning of the 20th century.

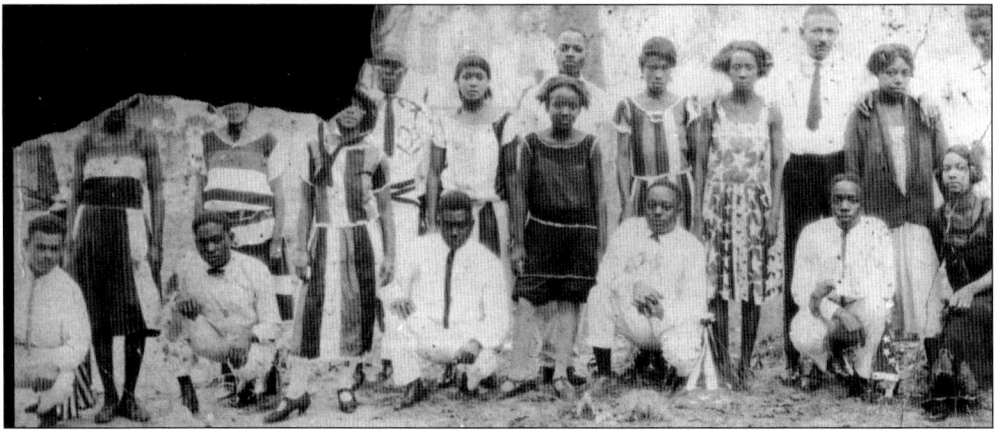

This African-American dance group had the distinction of participating in Tallahassee's first centennial celebration in 1924. Some of the group's members are Charlie Holiday, "Nonie" Williams, Florence Smith, Joe Ford, Beatrice McPherson, Charlie Yellowhair, Earl Pope, William Miller, Bob Wilson, Lucy Turner, Beatrice Golf, Walter Whitaker, Bob Jones, and "Big B" Jones. Charlie Yellowhair was the son of E.H. Yellowhair, tax assessor in 1885. Lucy Turner, now 98 years old, still lives in Tallahassee.

The Lawyer Smith Combo provided entertainment in the area during the 1930s up through the 1970s. Smith, the leader of the band, is on guitar, Curtis King is on drums, and ? Hammond is on keyboard. Many young men, such as King and Hammond, earned their way through college at Florida A&M University by playing with the Lawyer Smith Band. Smith was married to Daisy Twine, the daughter of a pioneer Tallahassee family.

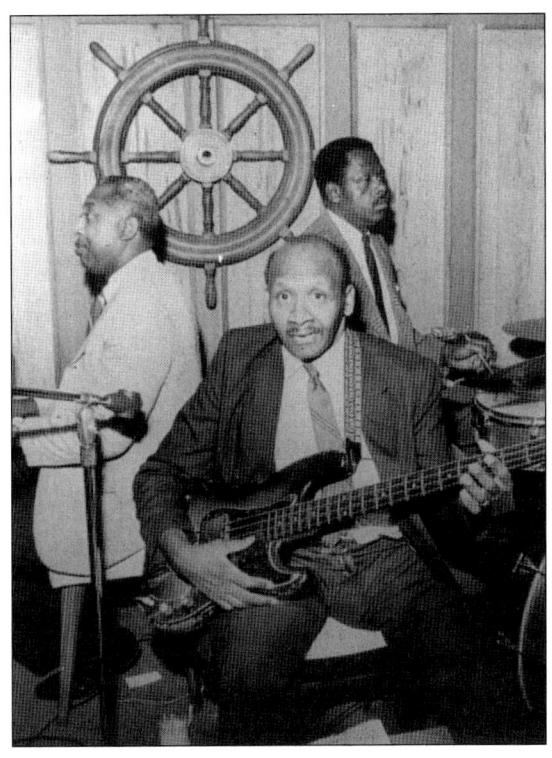

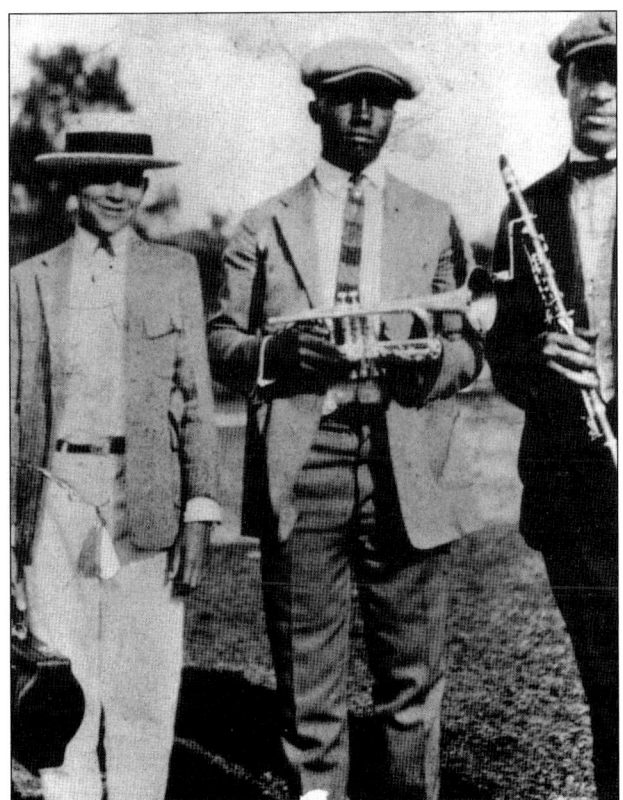

The Tallahassee Band provided entertainment in the 1930s. Shown are Frank Nims (left), an unidentified man (center), and Aurelio Casanas (right), the father of Lucille Alexander and Aquilina Howell.

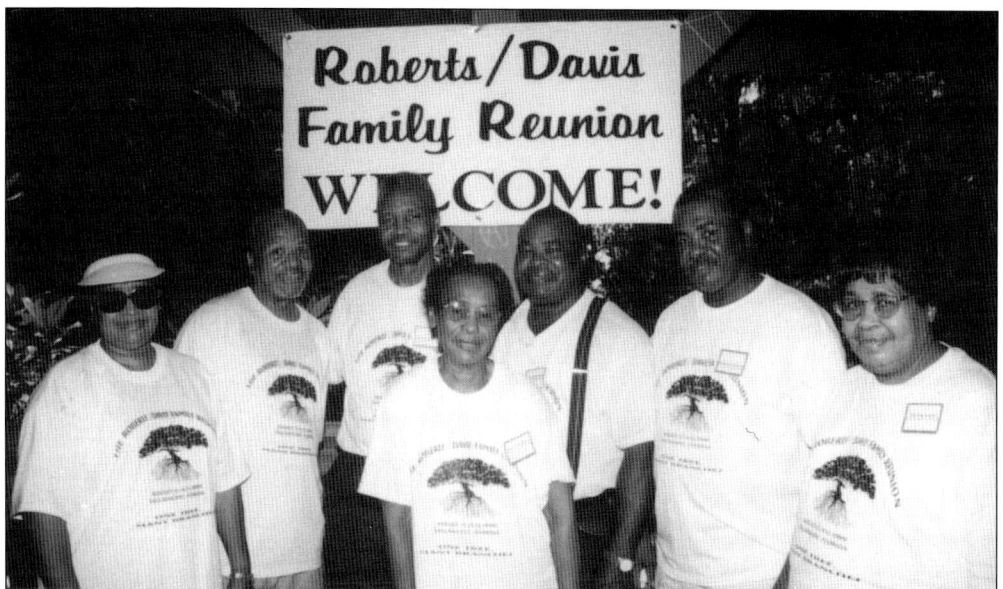

Annual reunions bring family members together to share their history and renew family ties. The Paul Roberts and Rosena Davis family held a reunion in August 1999. The families originated in the Rock Hill and Dawkins Pond communities. Shown here, from left to right, are family members Lillie Smith, Harry and Paul Roberts, Bennie Higgs (front center), and Raymond, Mathew, and Martha Jones. Other participants in the celebration were Dorothy and Frank Sloan and Harry and Hazella Brown, representing the Davis side.

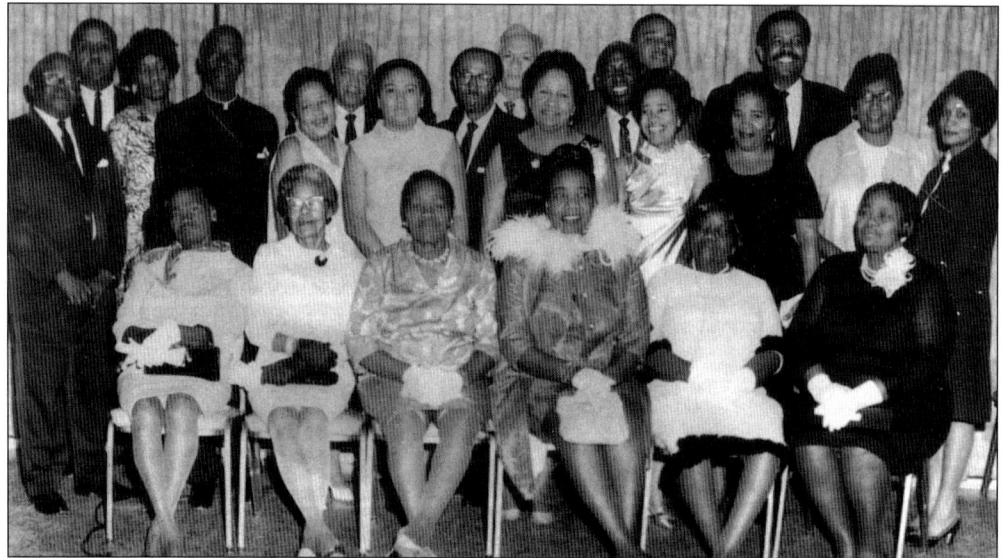

This is a reunion of the Lewis Washington Taylor family in the 1950s. Seated, from left to right, are sisters Claudine Taylor Butler, Crizell Lucille Taylor Robinson, Letisha Taylor Byrd, Wallace Taylor Valentine, Madeline Catherine Casanas (mother), and Victorine Taylor Blake. Other guests and relatives include Willie B. Stewart, Sam F. Howell, Lois Steele, C.K. Steele, Aquilina Howell, Antonio Casanas, Lucille Alexander, Herbert Alexander, Catherine Larkins, Althea Roberts, Annie Lee Roberts, and Fr. David Brooks. Mrs. Casanas was the principal of Ward, a one-room black schoolhouse.

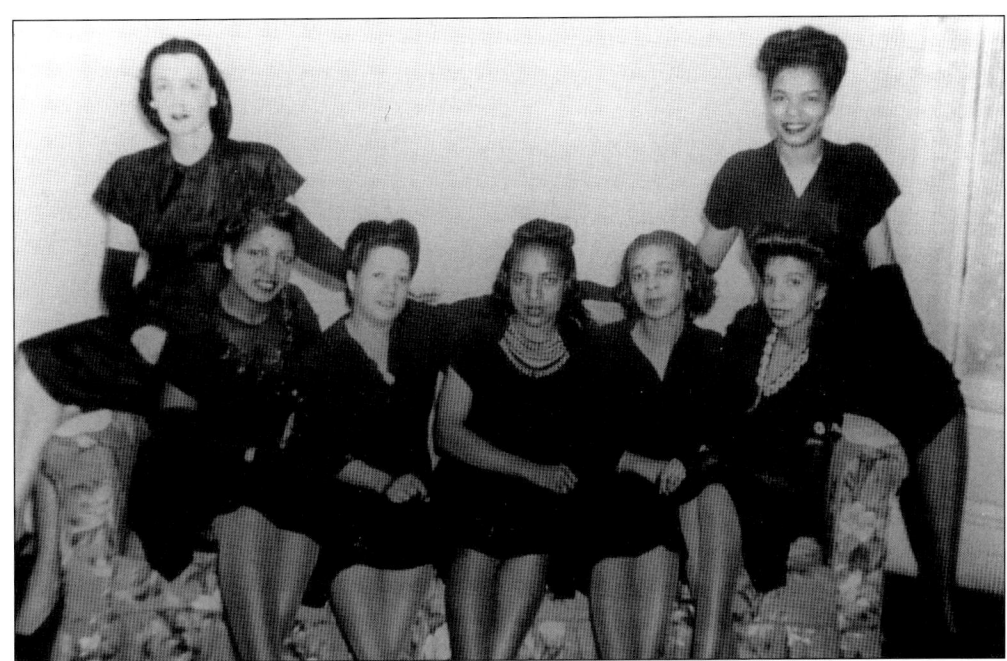

The Delta Kappa Omega chapter of Alpha Kappa Alpha Sorority, Inc. was chartered on January 24, 1947, at the home of Dora H. Anderson. From left to right are members Hilda Foote, Rosa Lee Snell-Bonds, Dora Anderson, Marolyn C. Warner Smith, Charlotte Diggs Griffin, Gloria Hughes, and Eleanor Young-Love. (Courtesy of Charlotte Griffin.)

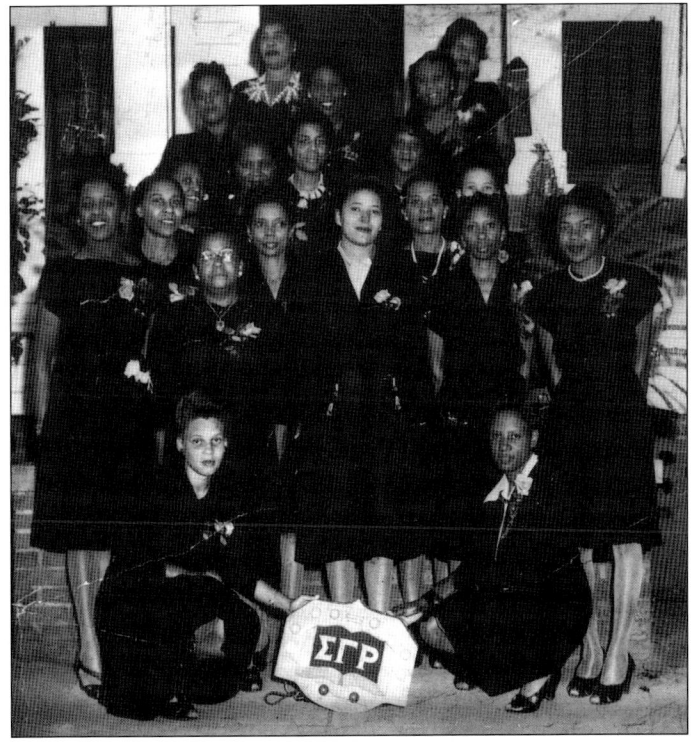

A 1946 Sigma Gamma Rho Sorority graduate chapter chartering ceremony was attended by charter members Elease Twine Spears, Dorothy Walker, Inez Gardner Robinson, Mayola Robinson, Emma Reed, Allie Seabrooks, Minerva Adams, Virginia Abner, Sarah Blackshear, Marie Kilpatrick, Essie R. Jones, Mamie Strong, Jesse Cooper, Ernestine Ford Seabrooks, Laura Fitz, Lucille Brown. Kneeling are, from left to right, Vera Mills and Bessie Weems. (Courtesy of Inez Gardner Robinson.)

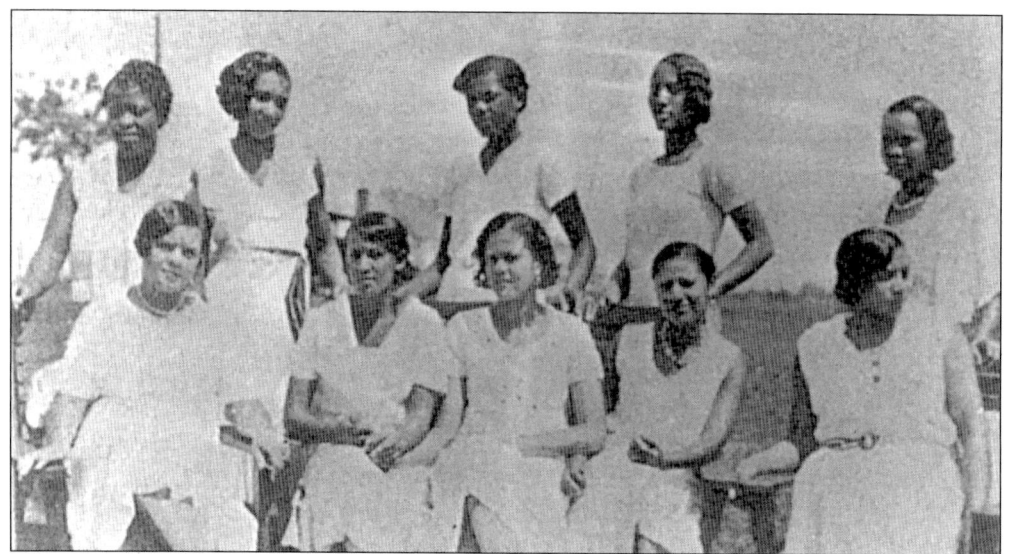

Zeta Phi Beta Sorority's Gamma Alpha chapter was chartered on the campus of Florida A&M College in 1932 with the following members, pictured from left to right: (seated) Ireta Martin Crosby, Ruth Bates Orr, Mary Martin Dansby, Beatrice Hill Stewart, and Anita Prater Steward; (standing) Edna Cross Burton, Sue K. Russell, Susie M. Britt, Ruby W. Anderson, and Ida Lee Bradley. Dr. James Robert Bate, a FAMU hospital intern, chapter founder Ester Johnson, and the Zeta regional director Violette N. Anderson performed the initiation.

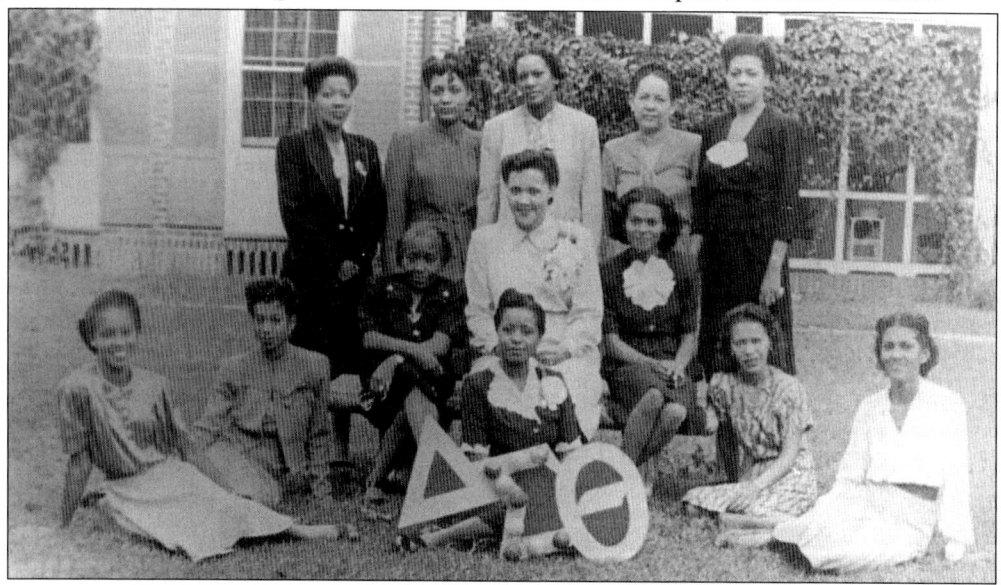

The charter members of the Tallahassee alumnae chapter of Delta Sigma Theta pose for a photograph. From left to right are as follows: (seated on ground) unidentified, Grace Mays Beckett, Gladys P. Anderson, Alverta Nevels Morris, and unidentified; (front row, seated) Lollie M. Fleming, the sorority's regional director at the time, and Madge Hughes Washington; (standing) Mai Alice Norwood, unidentified, Irene A. Decoursey, Hazel Yates Gray (wife of FAMU president William H. Gray), and Mary E. Carnegie. Charter members Yvette Holley Roberts, Glovenia C. Baker, Ruth Lazarus Nabbie, and Yvonne Walker are not shown here. The chapter was established on October 3, 1946.

Collette Warren, a retired educator, was photographed at the annual Harvest Ball, a popular event during the 1950s. The Warrens lived in the historic Frenchtown district. The family home on the corner of Martin Luther King and Carolina Streets was demolished in 1997.

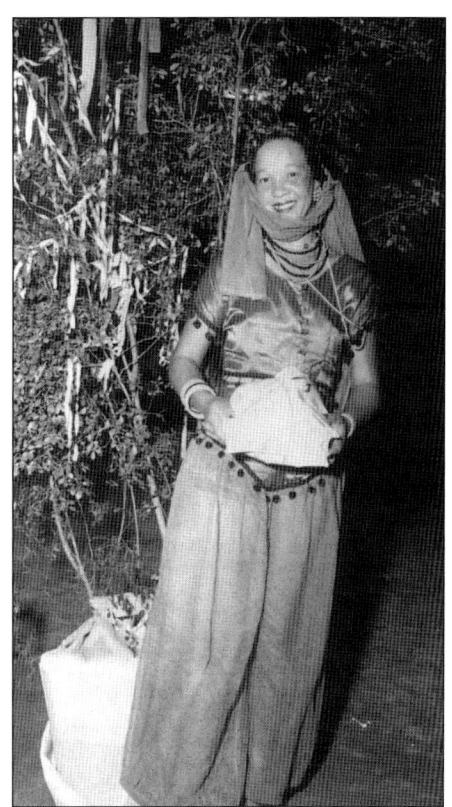

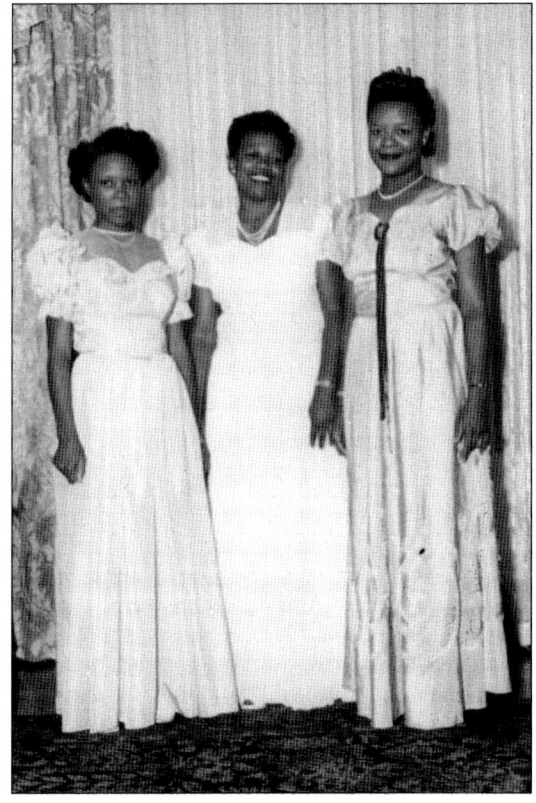

Sisters Vivian, Beatrice, and Johnnie Mae Turner were photographed in 1945 dressed for a piano recital. Their aunt, Lucy Turner, was a well-known piano teacher in Leon County for many years.

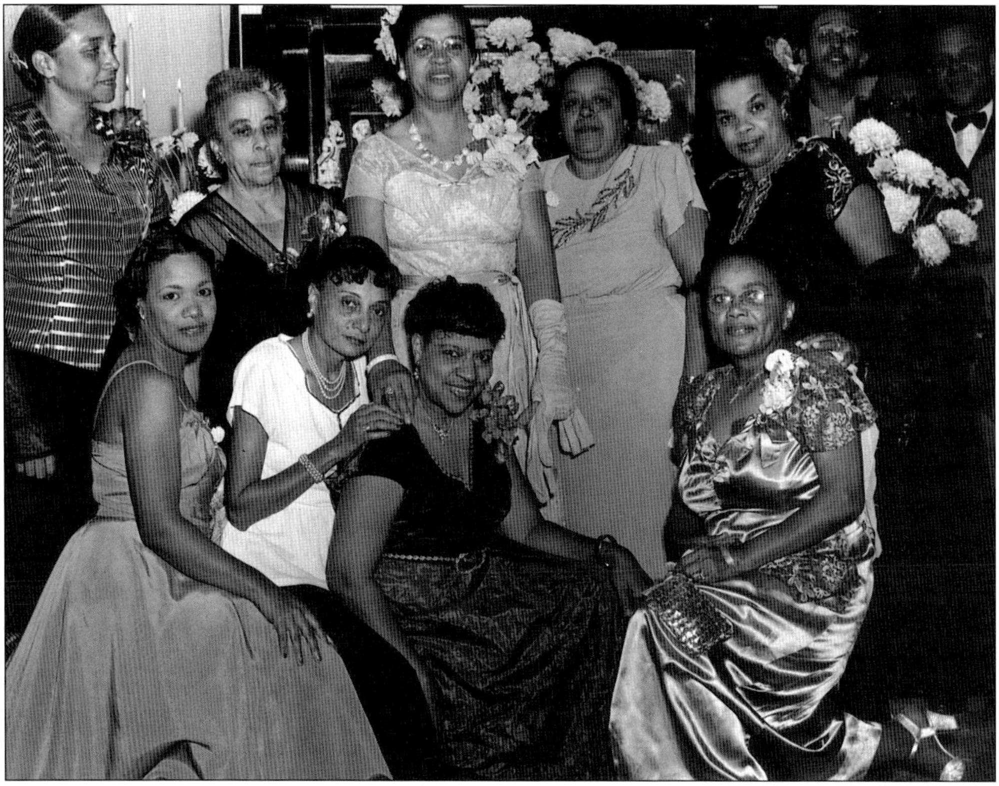

A unique side of Tallahassee and Leon County was the exhilarating social life among the middle class, stimulated by the presence of Florida A&M University. Social scenes often included such personalities as those seen here, from left to right: (kneeling) Inez Jones, Lucy Rose Adams, Clementine Daniels, and Amerique Briggs; (standing) Anita Stewart, Elizabeth Martin, Betty Lee, Birdie Jones, and unidentified.

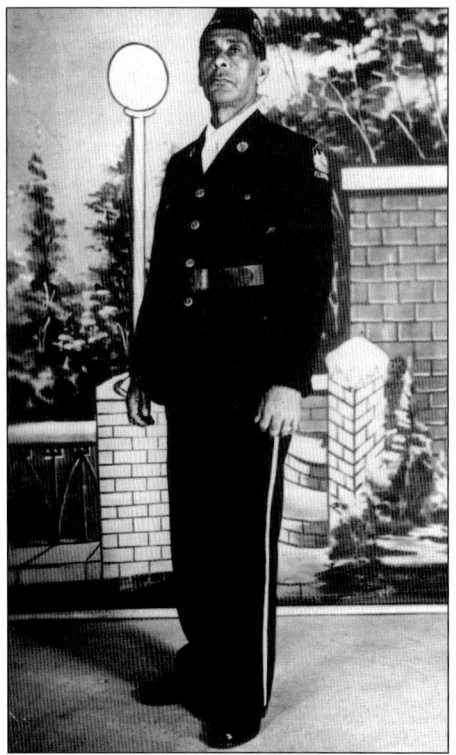

Many African-American servicemen became active in the American Legion after they returned home from war. World War I veteran Divillow Crawford is shown in his veteran's attire, representing Sneed Franklin Post.

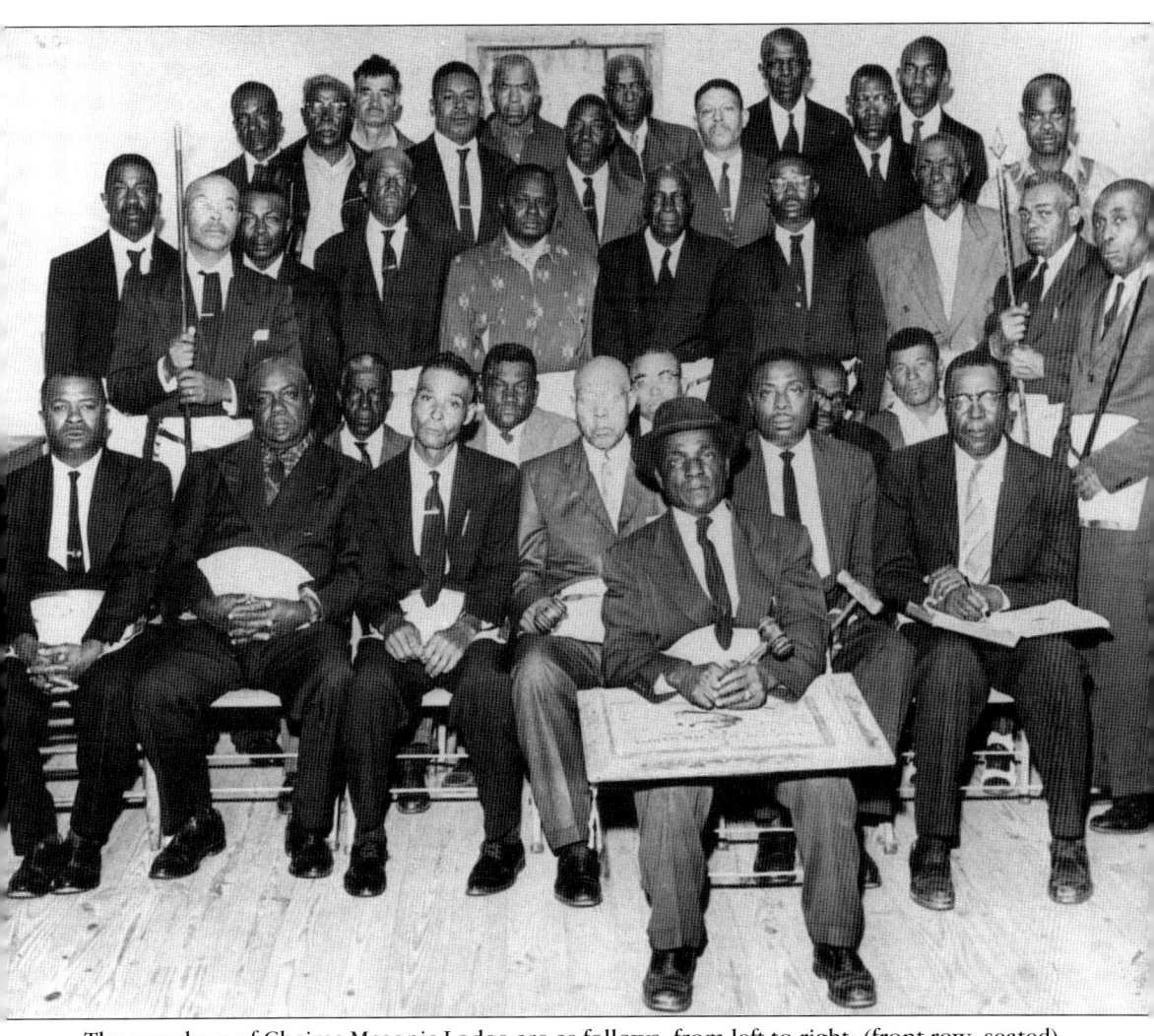

The members of Chaires Masonic Lodge are as follows, from left to right: (front row, seated) S. David Walker; (second row, seated) Horace James, James Williams, James Footman, Wes Robinson, Clarence Lindsey, and Arthur Lindsey; (third row, seated) Jack Jefferson, Otis Dixon, Leonard Duhart, Albert Pompey, and Brook Wright; (fourth row, standing) Roy Leonard, Harry Norton Sr., Richard Leonard, Zack Leon, unidentified, Joe Bright, Willie Hogan, unidentified, Vernon White, and William Robinson; (fifth row, standing) unidentified, Richard Ward, unidentified, Johnny Clay, David Copeland, and unidentified; (sixth row, standing) Arthur Thompson Sr., Eddie Leonard, Isaac Yant, Waymon Thompson, Israel Thompson, and Ralph Wilson.

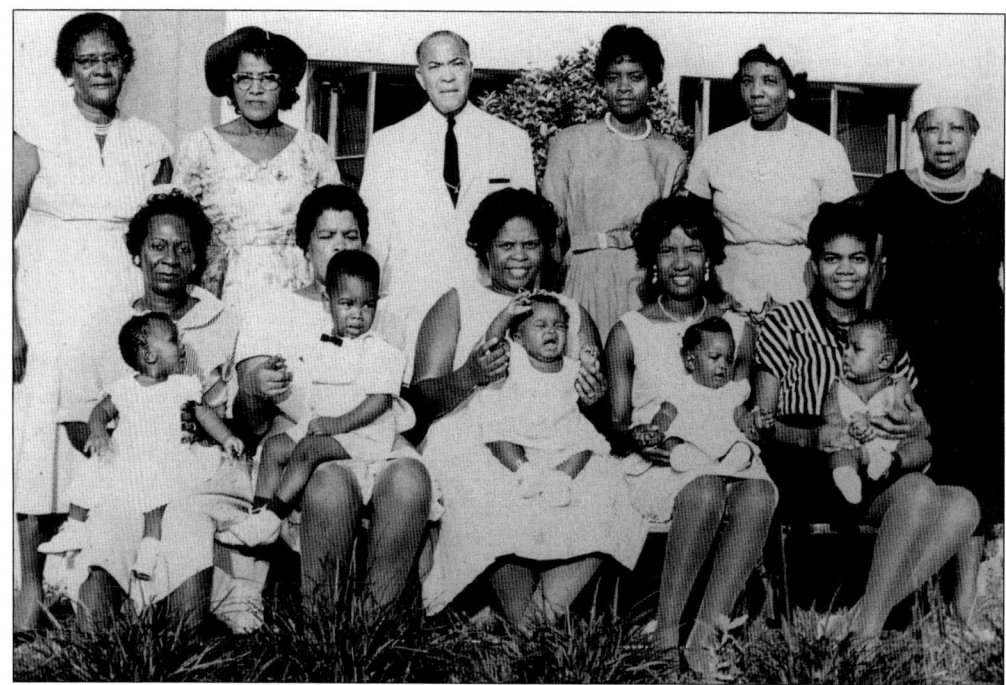

This is a picture of a Bethel AME baby contest. From left to right are as follows: (seated) Delores McCoy and her daughter; Daisy Smith and her grandson Von Kornegay; Patricia Jefferson and her daughter Bridgette; Ann Johnson and her daughter Kim; and Ann Roberts and her son Tony; (standing) Dorothy Tookes, Annie Baldwin, Joseph Franklin, Hattie Robinson, Ella Reed, and Annie Mae Brown.

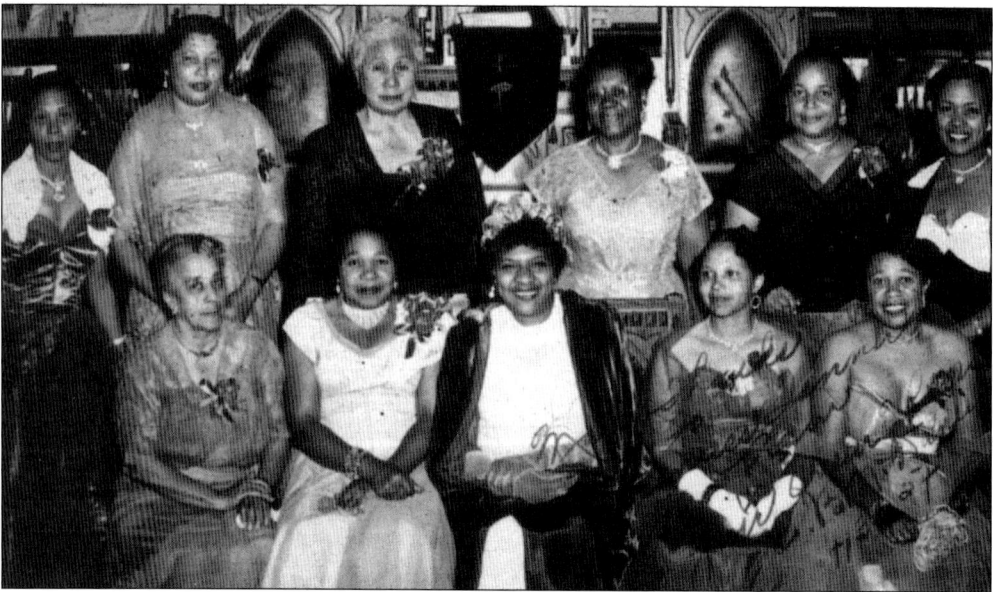

This Miss Bethel AME Church contest was held in 1954. Included in the photograph are the following, from left to right: (seated) Mrs. A.E. Martin, Zelma Harris, Mrs. C.B.N. Daniels, Mrs. Lillie F. Davis, and unidentified; (standing) Augusta Ford Nims, Mrs. Emma Lincoln, Mrs. Lillie Washington, Annie Tanner, Carolyn Harris, and Inez Jones.

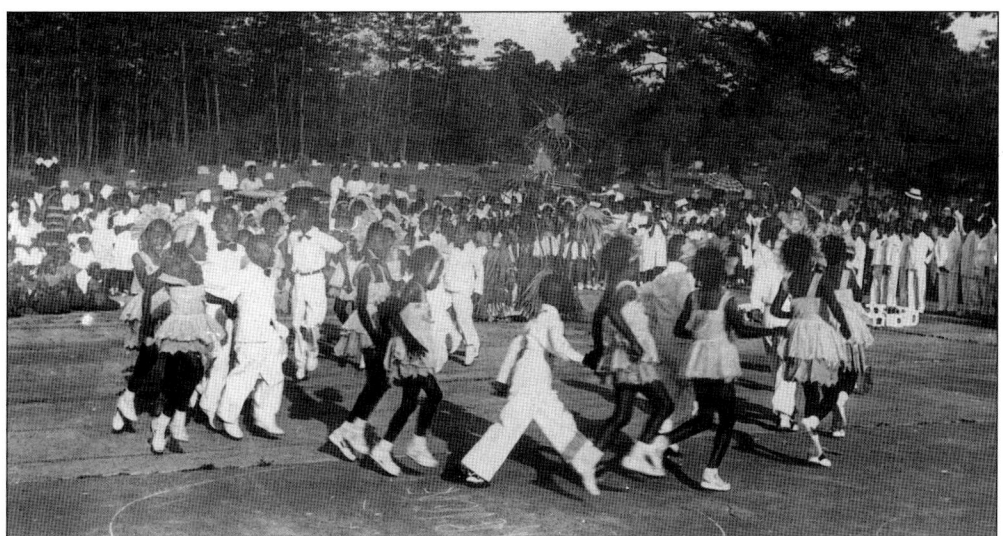

Pictured is a 1946 May Day celebration. During the days of segregation, these occasions were held at each school. Classes were given a theme, a specific costume, and were taught a dance to perform at a community-wide event. Schools were closed for the occasion.

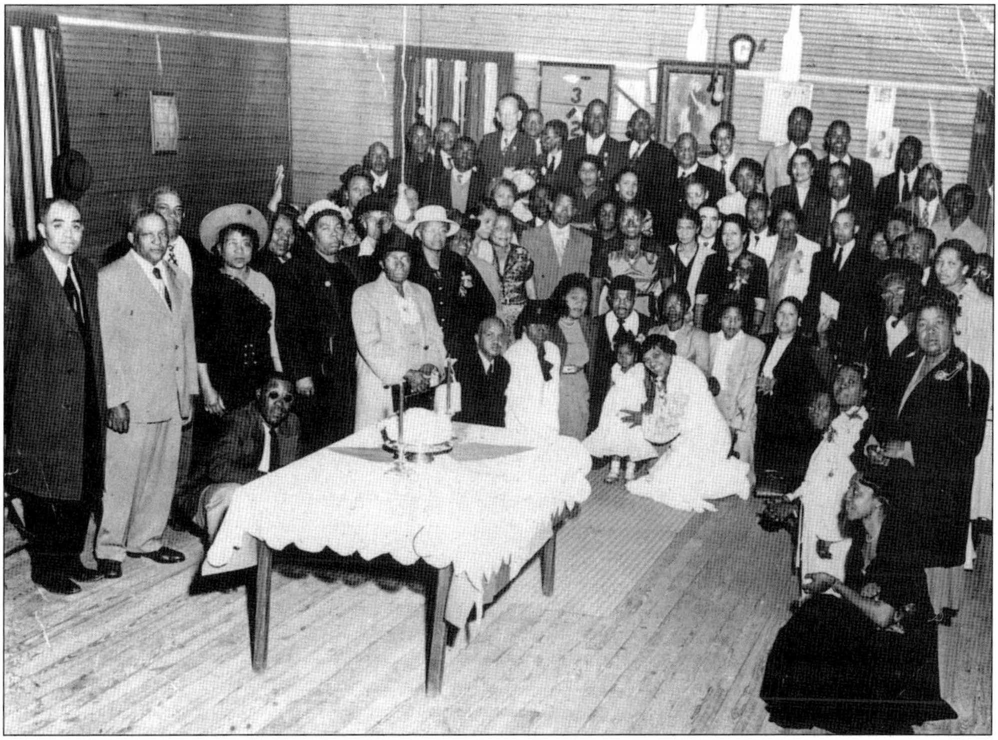

Dignified services among various Masonic Orders and Auxiliaries were commonplace throughout the 1960s. Very elaborate exercises often brought the entire community out to watch as members marched down Macomb Street to the Lodge Hall. Shown are Masons and Eastern Stars at one of these events. The tall gentleman (at the extreme rear, center) is E.A. Pottsdamer, one of Tallahassee's most prominent black citizens. Pottsdamer was an attorney, a property owner, and the owner of a cigar factory.

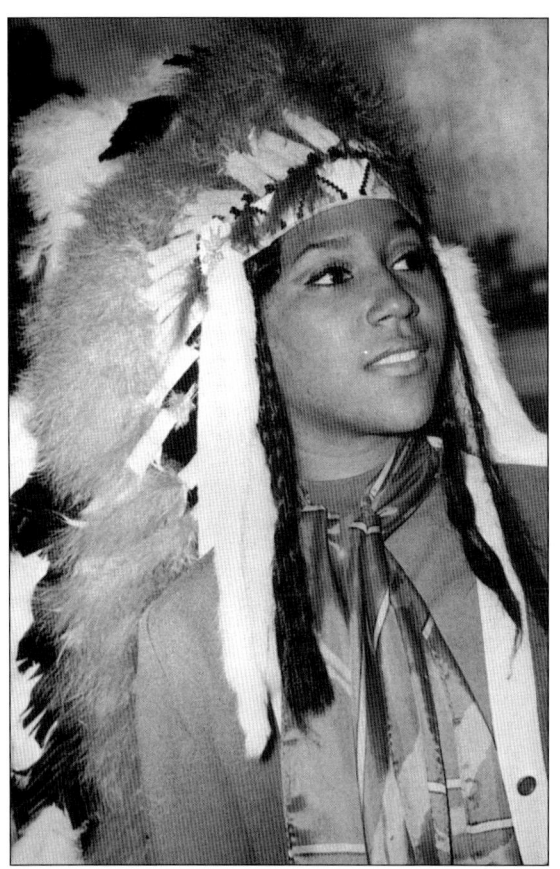

In November 1970, Doby Lee Flowers, a 21-year-old senior in social welfare at Florida State University (FSU), became the first black homecoming queen in the history of the university. She was sponsored by the FSU Black Student Union.

Griffin Junior High School's 1955 Homecoming Parade featured Miss Griffin, Yvonne Cofield (top center), and her attendants Pauline Houzell (top left) and Ida Holloman (top right). Althemese Pemberton (front left) accompanied physical education instructor Edwina Martin, the driver and sponsor. (Courtesy of Ann Roberts.)

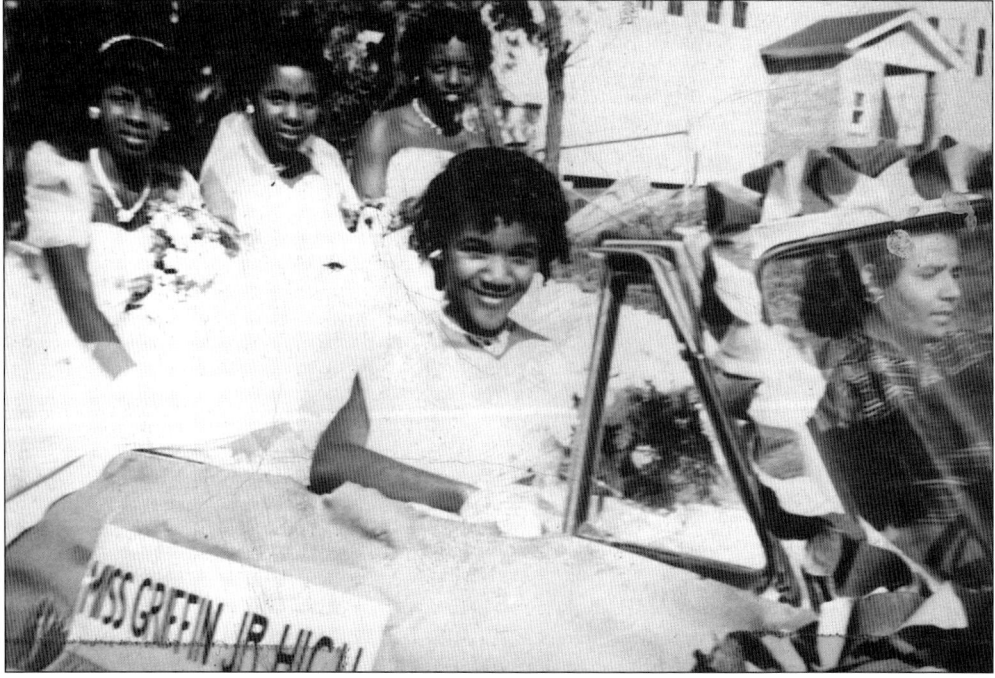

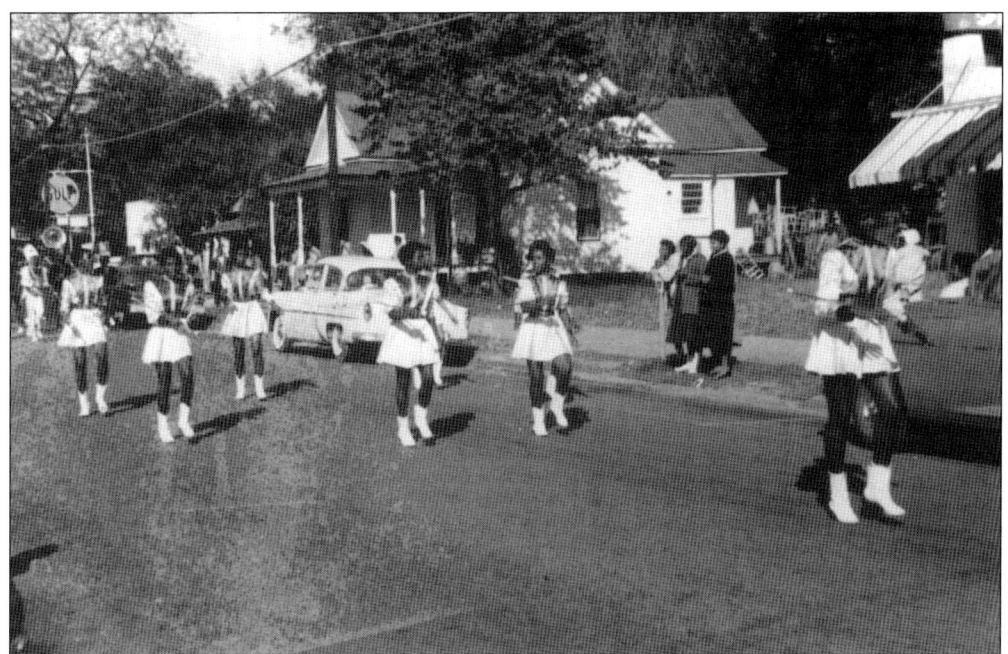

The 1959 Lincoln Homecoming Parade makes its way down Macomb Street in Frenchtown. The Lincoln High Band was led by majorettes, from left to right, Shirley Hunter, Doris Warner, Betty Kelly, Florence Scott, Yvonne Cofield, and Dorothy Speed Eason (head).

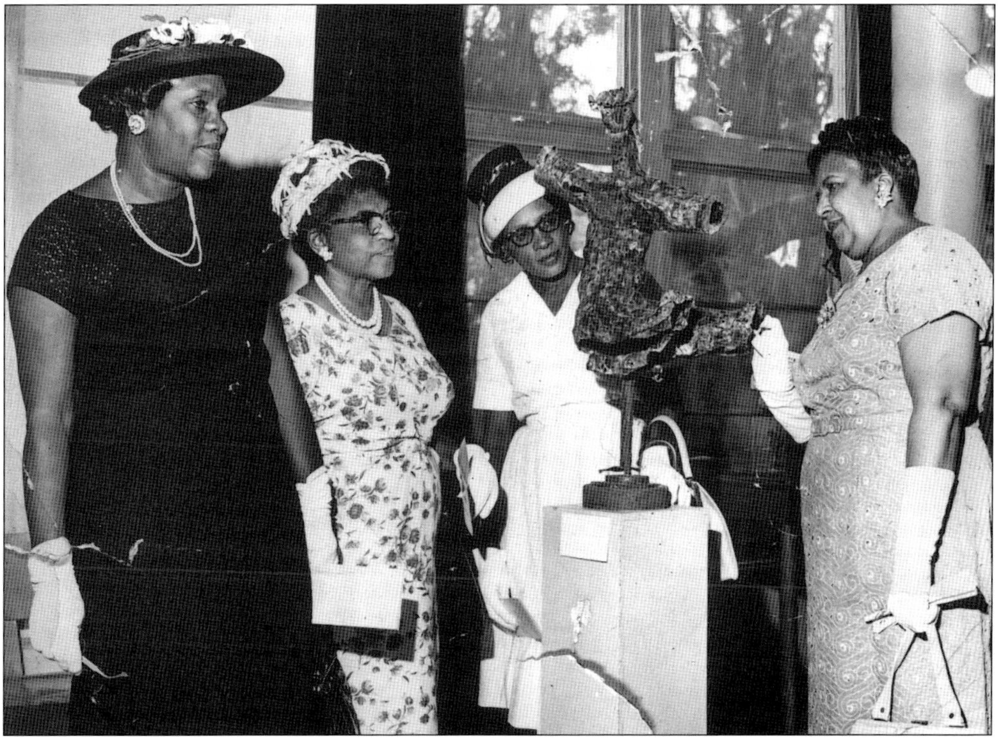

From left to right, Eunice Spencer Carter, Dorothy Gunn Holmes, Bessie Weems, and an unidentified woman appreciate the fine sculpture at Florida A&M University gallery.

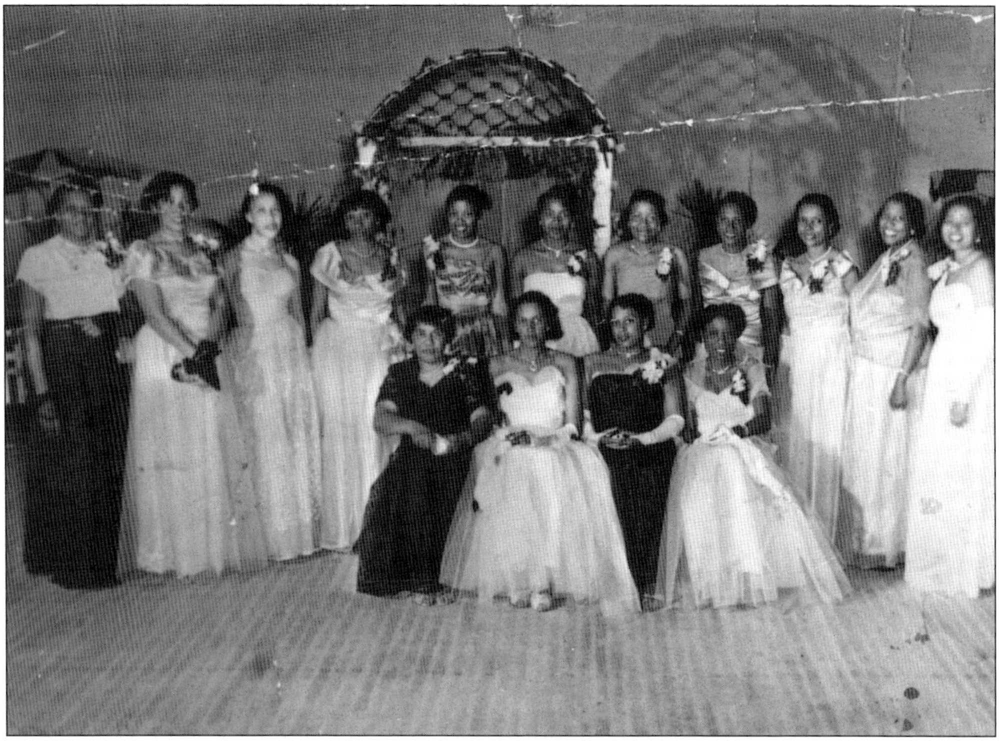

Sigma Gamma Rho charter graduate chapter members attend a social event during Pres. William Gray's tenure at Florida A&M University. Pictured here are the following, from left to right: (seated) Emma Reed, Lillie Davis, Mayola Robinson, and Dorothy Walker; (standing) Marie Kilpatrick, Blanche Holmes, Inez Robinson, Laura Fitz, unidentified, Lucille Brown, Simpkins Jackson, Bessie Weems, Mamie Strong, Alice Seabrooks, and Jesse Cooper.

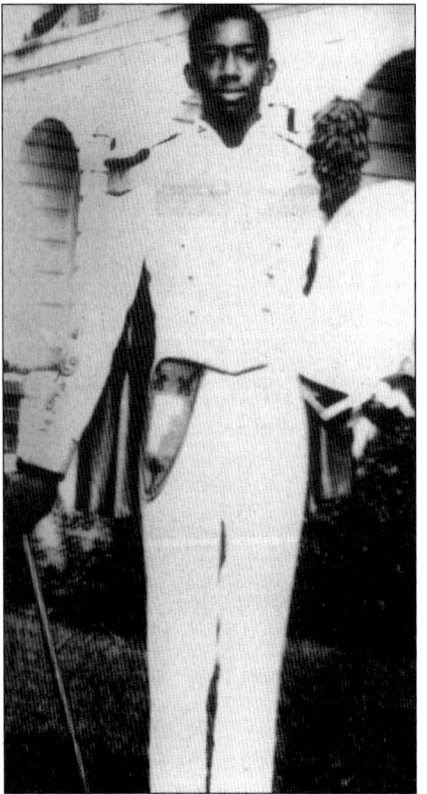

Bishop A.J. Richardson attended Florida A&M University in the 1960s where he was head drum major for the Marching 100. He was elected a bishop in the AME Church in 1996 after serving 18 years as a pastor of Bethel AME Church. He was the first person to be elected a bishop while pastoring a Tallahassee church.

Eight

EDUCATION

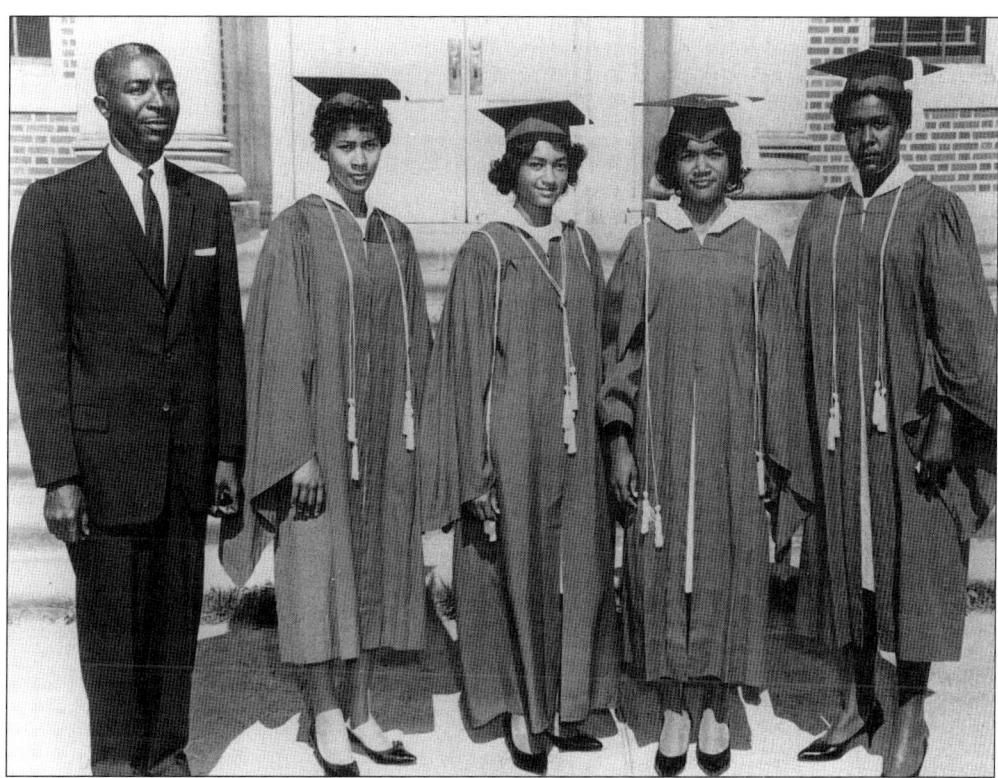

Photographed in 1961 with principal Freeman Lawrence are, from left to right, honor graduates Gwendolyn Oliver, Carol Burney, Althemese Pemberton, and Lillie James. Lawrence attended Greenhowe Elementary School, graduated from Florida A&M University, was principal of Barrow Hill School, and is the only surviving principal of the original Lincoln High School.

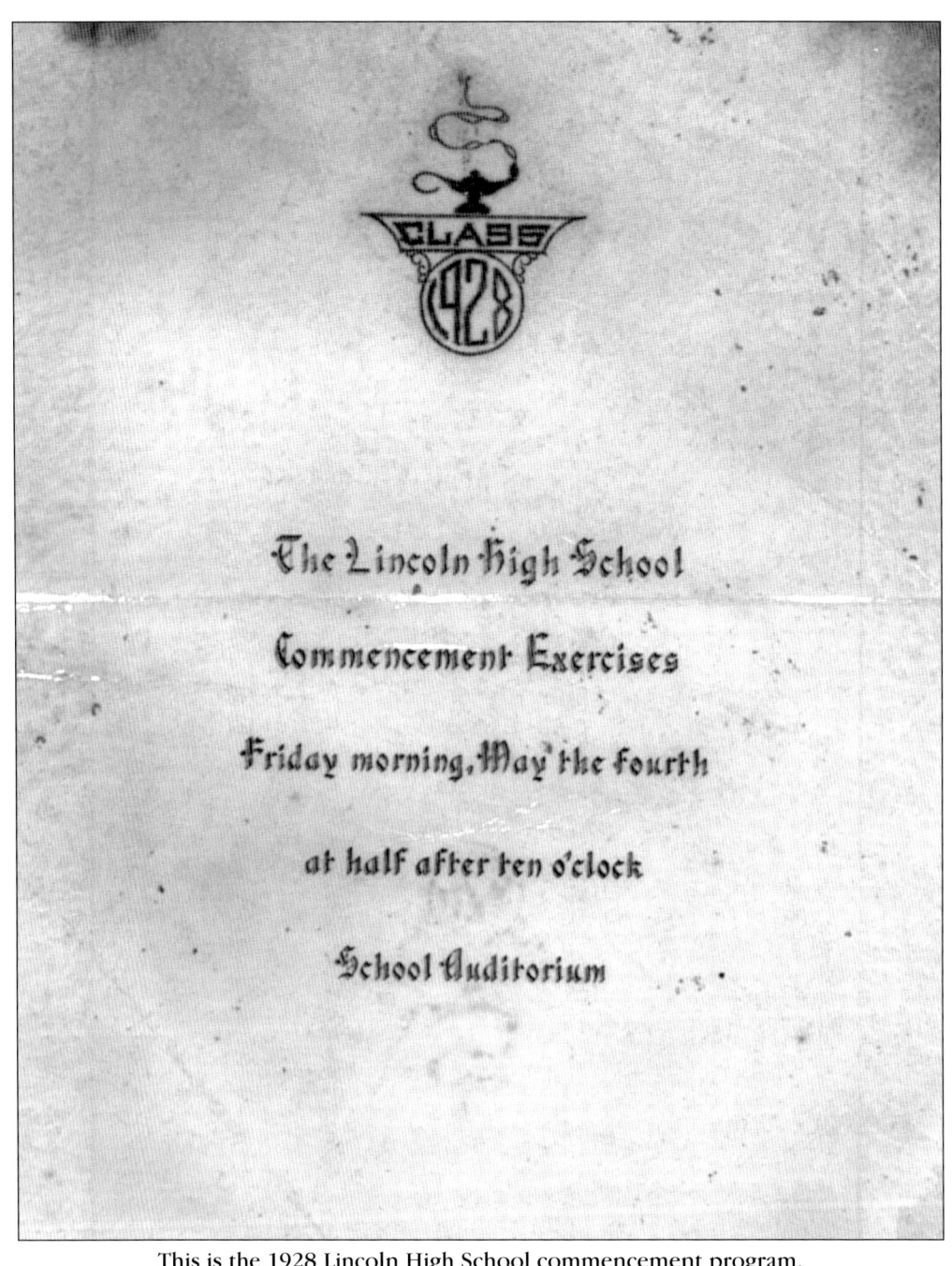

This is the 1928 Lincoln High School commencement program.

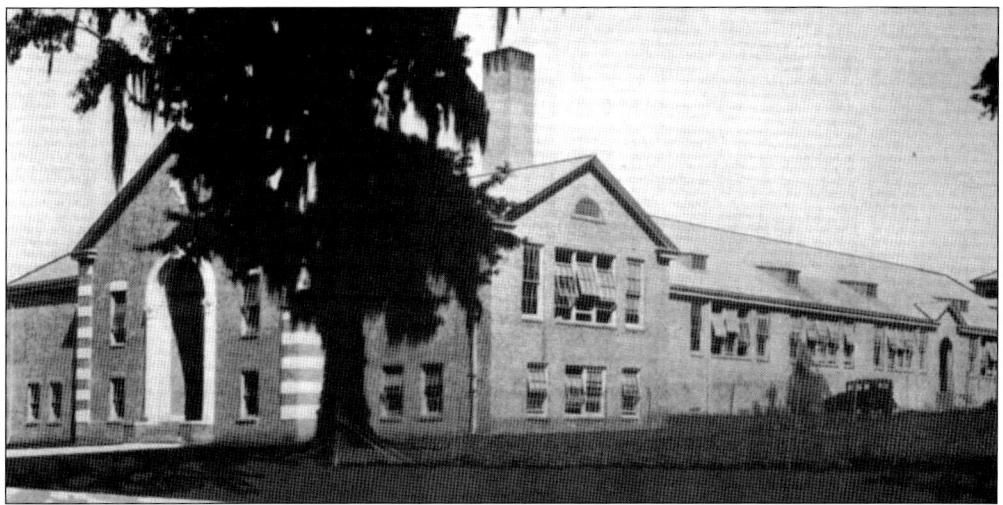

Pictured is the third building occupied by Lincoln School. The original building, which was constructed in 1869 at the corner of Lafayette and Copeland Streets, was destroyed by a fire in 1872. It was rebuilt in 1876 at the corner of Copeland and McCarthy Streets. In 1905, that building was taken over by Florida State Women's College, and the structure seen here was built to house Lincoln. This building still stands on Brevard Street.

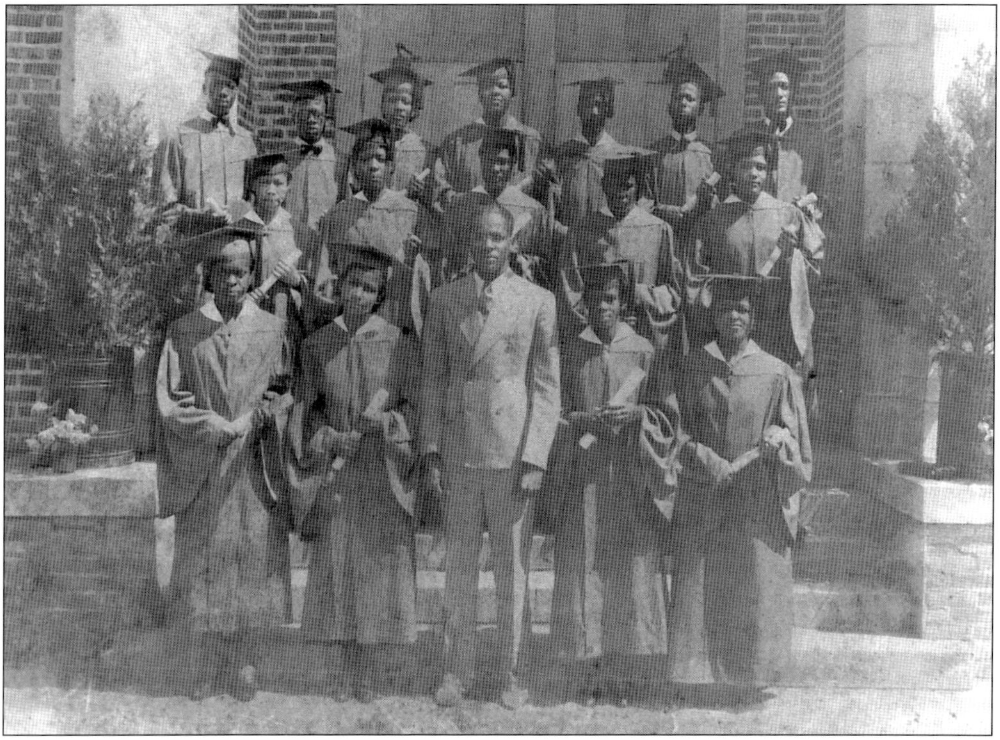

Here is the Lincoln High School graduating class of 1935 with Principal Cecil Walker. During the 1960s, Aquilina Howell (front row, second from left) became the first black assistant superintendent in Leon County. Howell assumed this role during the desegregation movement, having previously served as the district supervisor of curriculum and a teacher in Leon County schools.

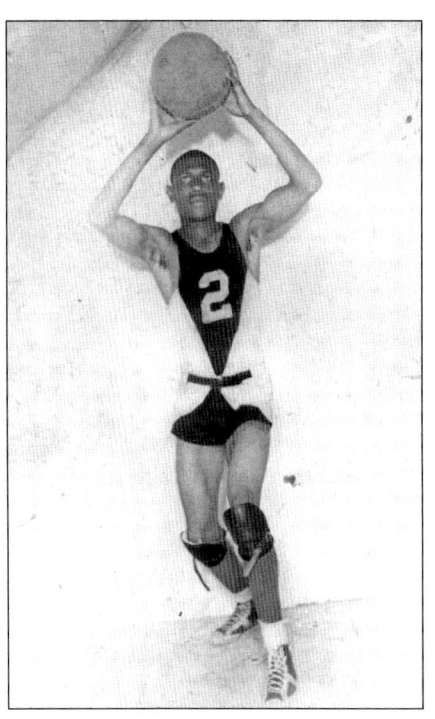

George Holiday was a star on the original Lincoln High School basketball team. Holiday later became a chef at the historic Floridian Hotel, a position he held for many years. The hotel no longer exists.

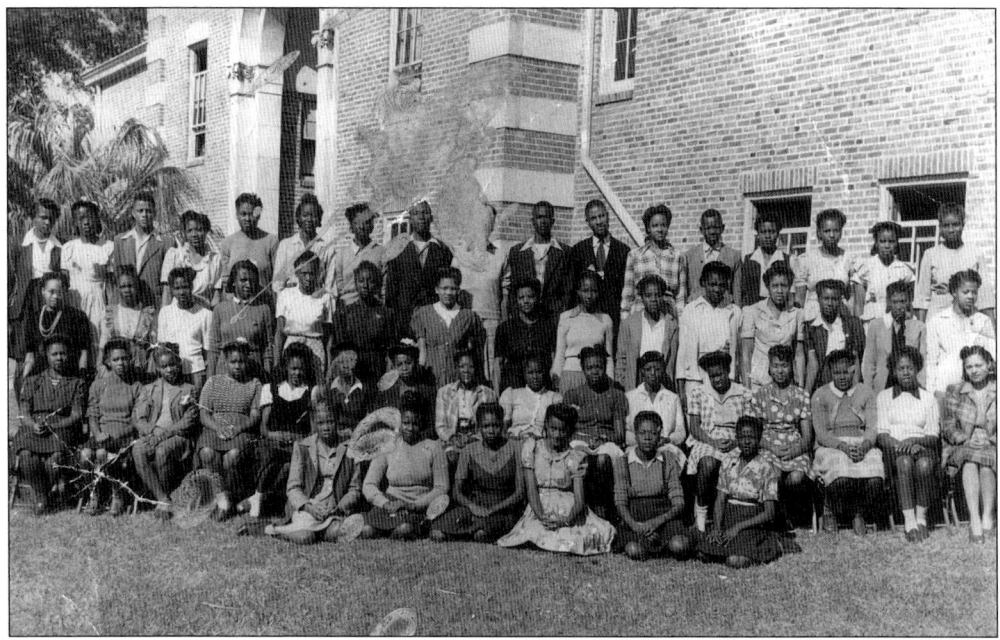

This 1934 Lincoln High School photograph includes Johnnie Twine, Lula Randolph, Armentha Abrams, Carell Hargrove, Alice Prior, Mary Donnie, Mrytle Edward, Rosa Lee Davis, Lena Young, Allene Monroe, Lillia Stevens, Clara Speed, Mary Graham, Anita Davis, Mable Blake, Mary Speed, Zera Henderson, Elizabeth Acon, Jimmy Lee Davis, Cora Allen, Katie Banks, Hazel Starks, Charlotte Jenkins, Wilford Anderson, Aquita Oliver, Florida Hudson, Vernon Floyd, Harold Clack, Antonio Casanas, Vera Ward, Phillip McMahon, Celia Hawkins, and Buelah Pratt.

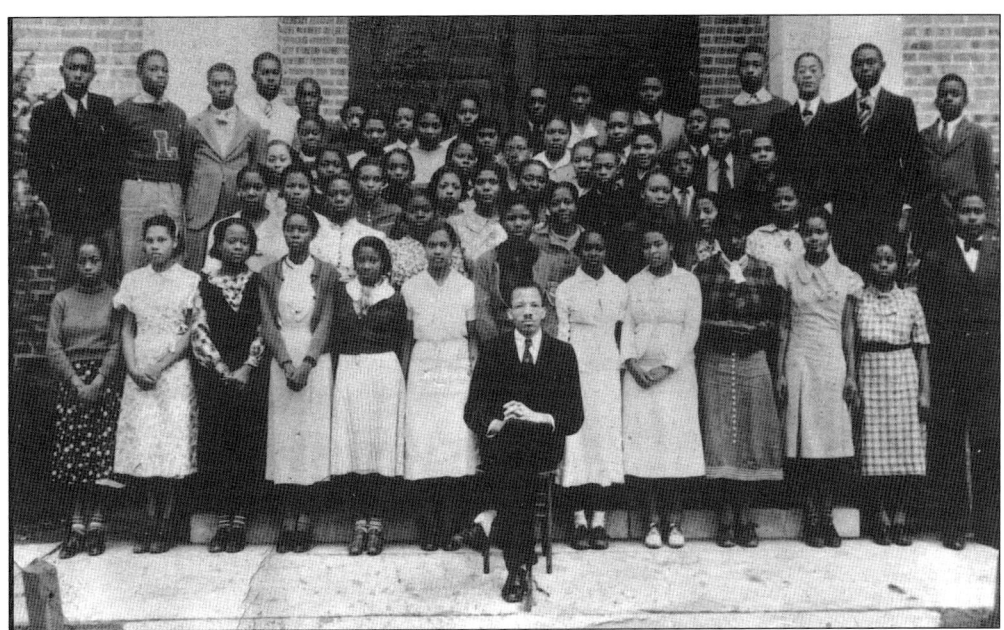

These are Lincoln High School seniors with class advisor Mr. McPherson in 1939. William Sanford is in the back row, second from the left.

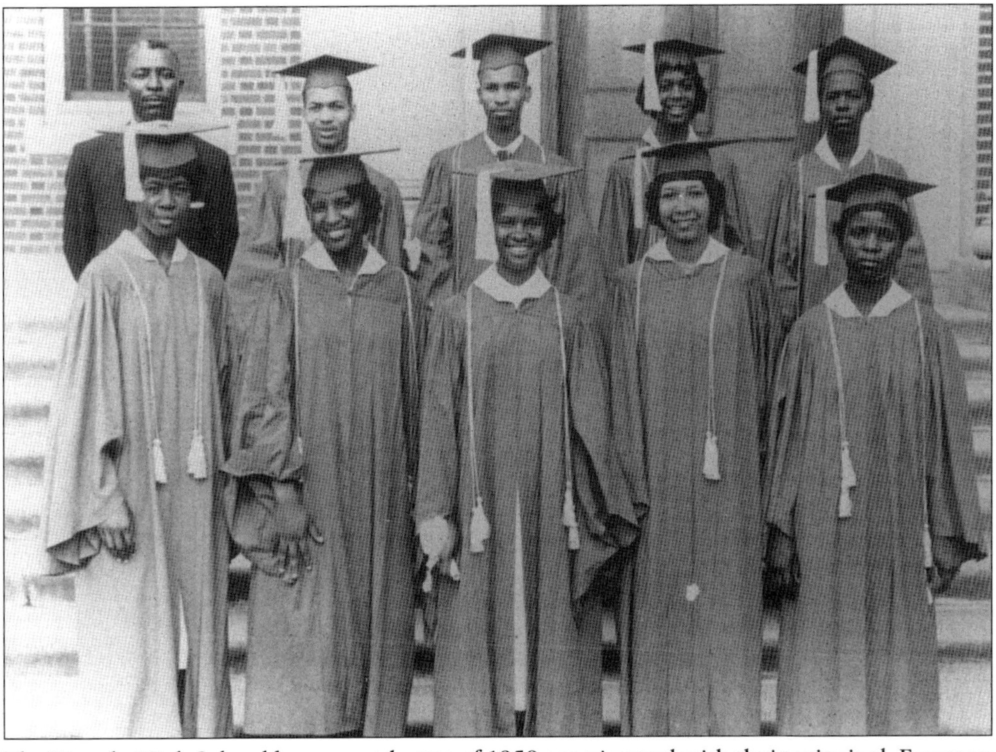

The Lincoln High School honor graduates of 1959 are pictured with their principal, Freeman Lawrence. From left to right are the following: (front row) Evelyn Pemberton, Delores Bright, Gloria Manning, Daisy Williams, and Hannah Walker; (back row) Lawrence, Robert Burney, Eugene Harden, Wyneva Johnson, and Hattie Ayers.

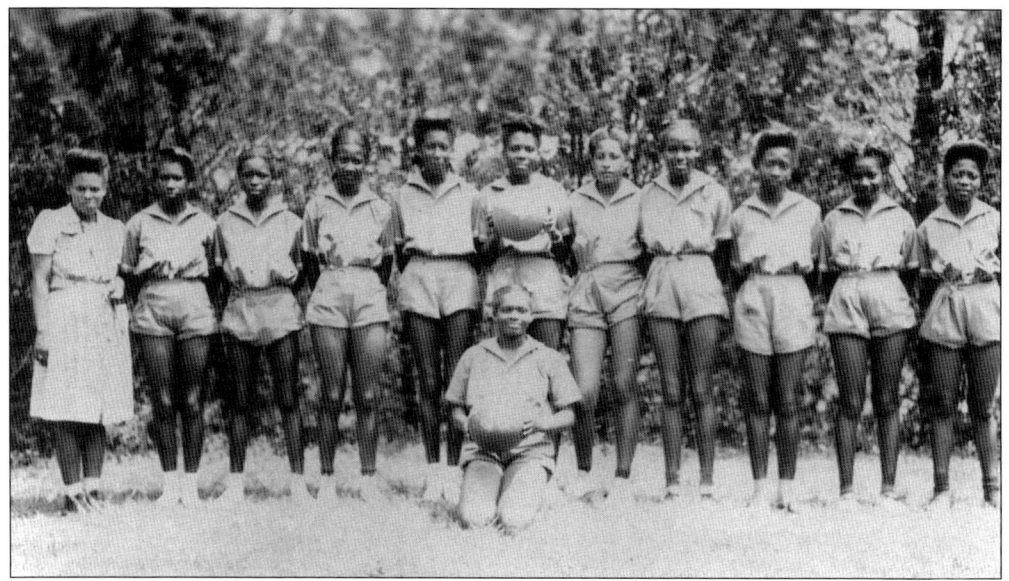

Members of a Lincoln High School girls basketball team in the 1950s are seen here with their coach, Vera Mills. From left to right are the following: (kneeling) Bernice Bryant Hunter; (standing) Mills, Dorothy Wynn, Dorothy Allen, Deloris Adams, Hannah Duhart, Mary Alice Caldwell, Emma Wilson, Ernestine Doyle, unidentified, Evelyn Thompson, and Bernice Littleton Simmons.

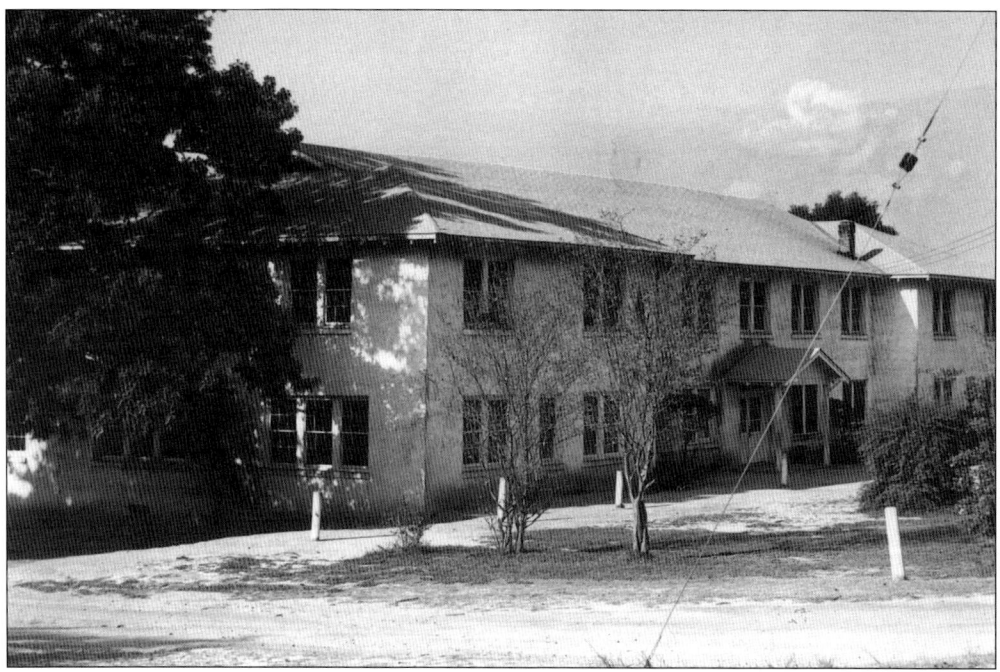

Griffin Normal and Industrial Institute was established in 1905 to provide an education for African Americans. The school was named in honor of Rev. Henry Griffin, the first pastor of St. Mary Church #1, the first Primitive Baptist Church in Florida. The school was founded by the Florida State Primitive Baptist Association and graduated many students before closing in 1954.

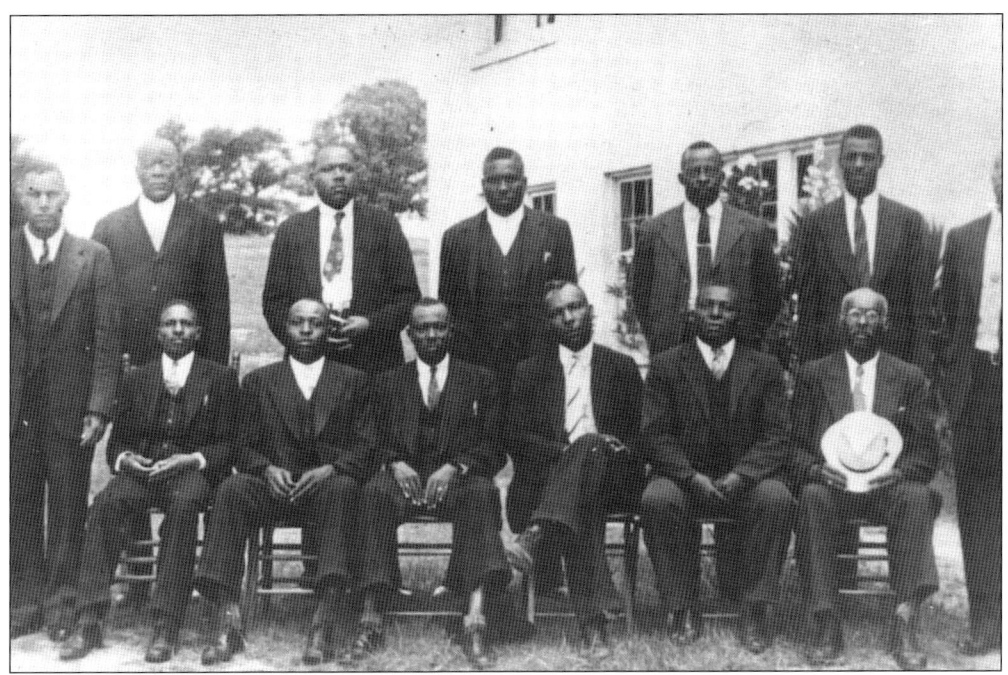

The ministers of the Florida Primitive Baptist Association and the founders of Griffin Normal and Industrial Institute pose for a photograph. They are, from left to right, as follows: (seated) unidentified, Rev. Gus Hill, Rev. Lee Vaughn, Rev. J.H. Hobb, unidentified, and Rev. Tom Bisbee; (standing) Rev. C.P. Allen, Rev. A.L. Ganious, unidentified, Rev. ? Daymon, Rev. Alex Harrison, Rev. Philip Davis, and Rev. William R. Perkins.

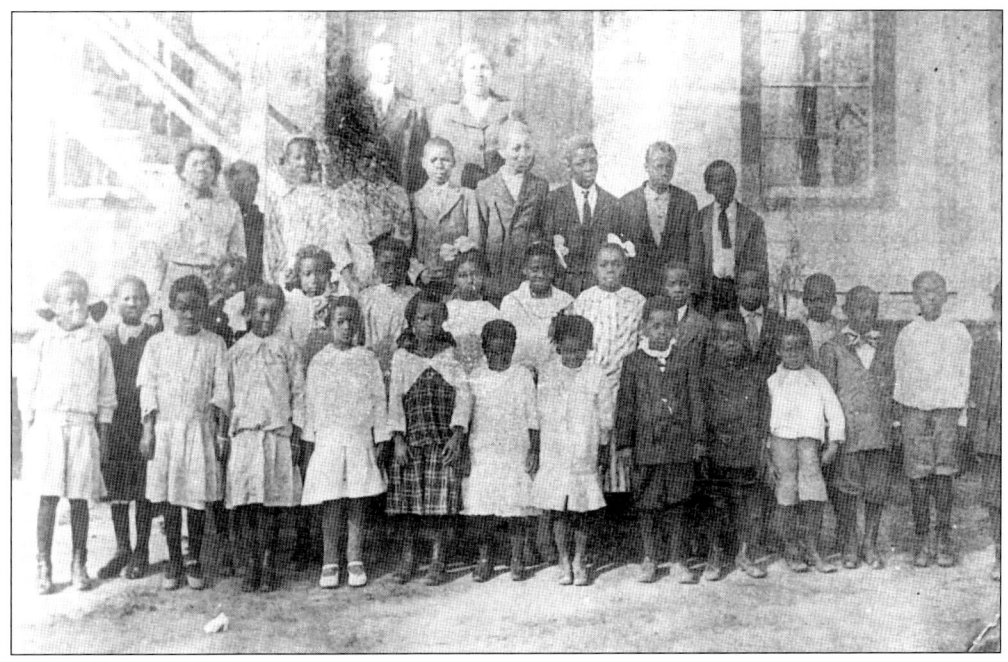

This is a class during the 1920s at Griffin Normal and Industrial Institute.

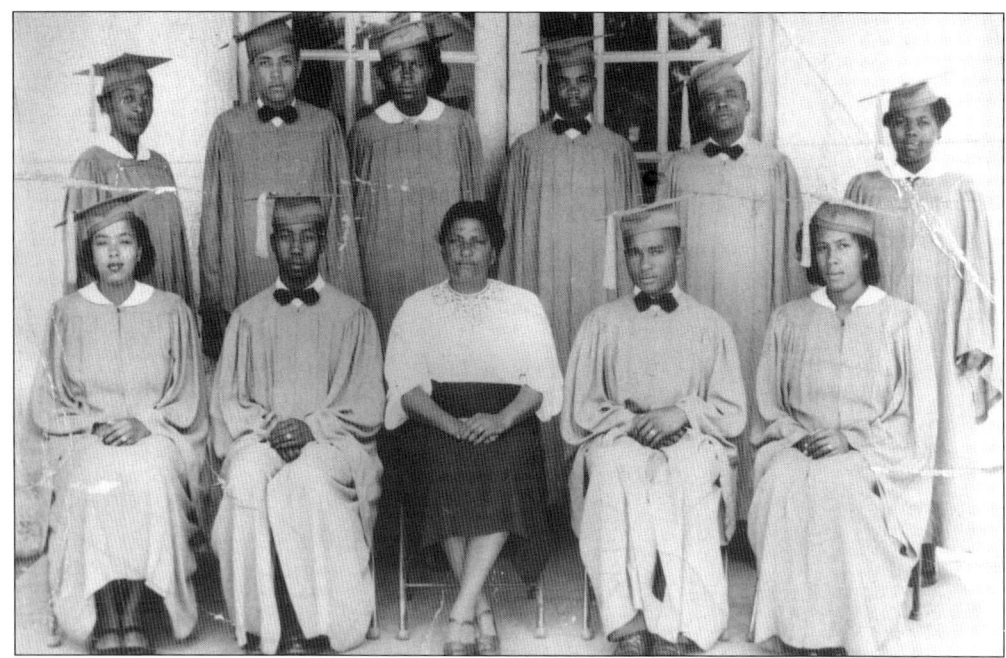

This adult graduating class of Griffin High School in the 1940s included the following, from left to right: (front row) Lucile Bryant Paul, Billy Wells, directing teacher Laura Ziegler White, Clinton Smith, and Viola Drew Thompson; (back row) L.R. Rhunett Paul, Alpha Nims, Sophia Simmons, Ernest McKinley, Raleigh Heyward, and Ruby Williams.

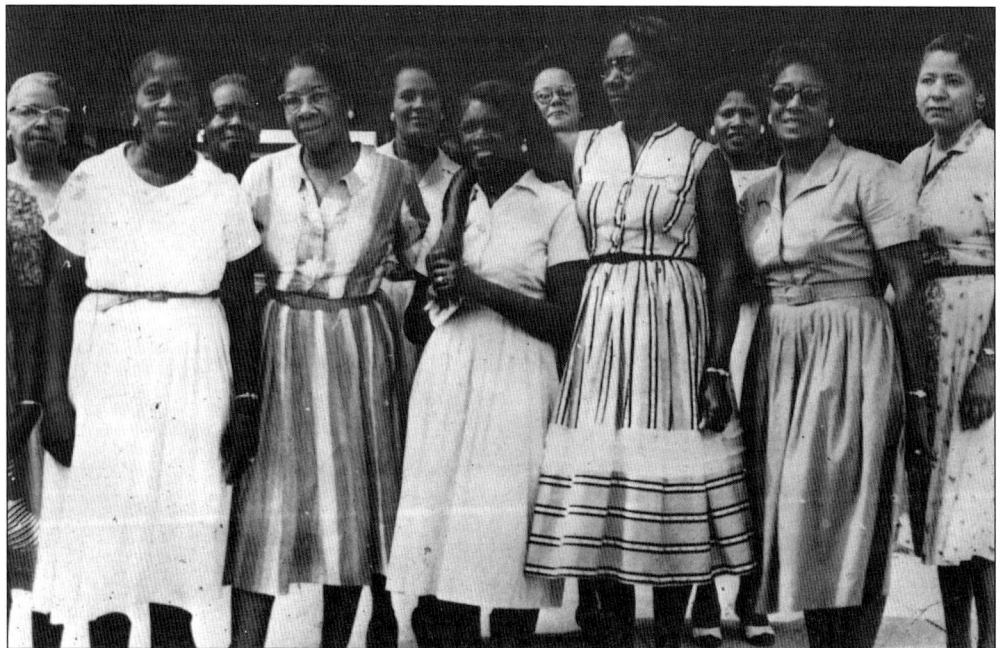

Griffin teachers who served in the 1930s–1950s pose for a photograph. From left to right are as follows: (front row) Olivia Brown, Ruth Jones, Bernyce Clausell, Iola Douglas, Emma Booker, and Jesse Cooper; (back row) Paralee Webb, Daisy Hall, Hilda Gardner, Edith Martin Strong, and Lessie Sanford.

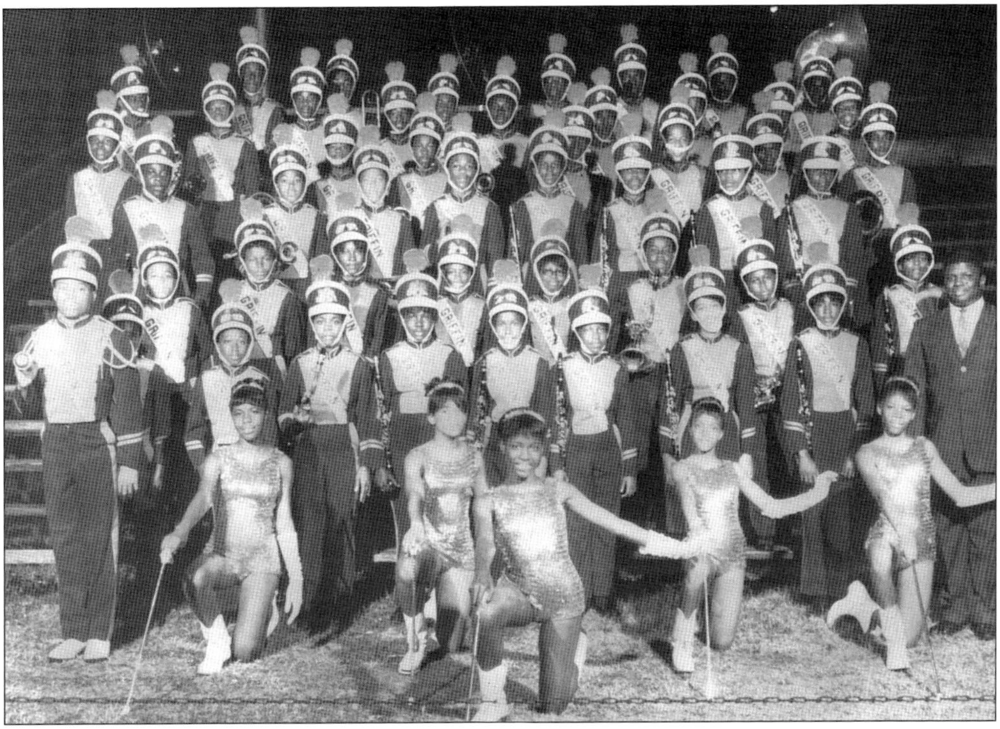

Members of the Griffin Junior High School band, in the 1950s, are poised for a homecoming parade. The band's director is Hamilton Hollins, and the majorettes are, from left to right, Beverly Pemberton, Cheryl Seals, Shirley White, Joyce Williams, and Ronica Brown.

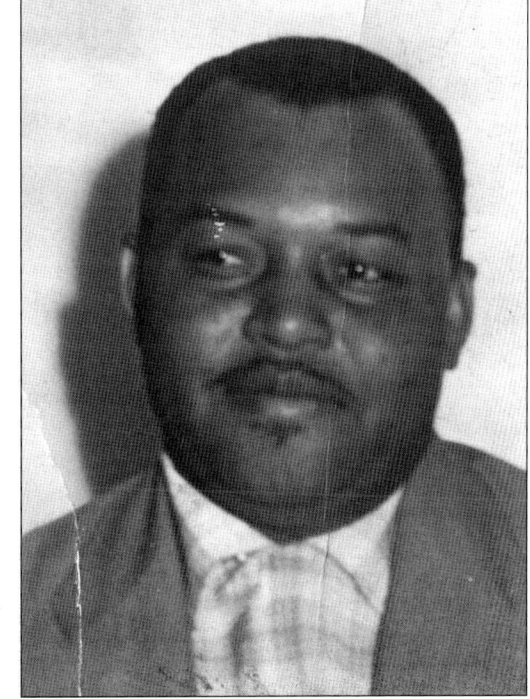

In the 1940s, Roy Rolle organized the first band at Griffin Normal and Industrial Institute, which was later renamed Griffin High School. After the school was phased out as a high school, Rolle served as the director of bands at Lincoln High School until his death. He also played the saxophone with the Lawyer Smith Band for many years.

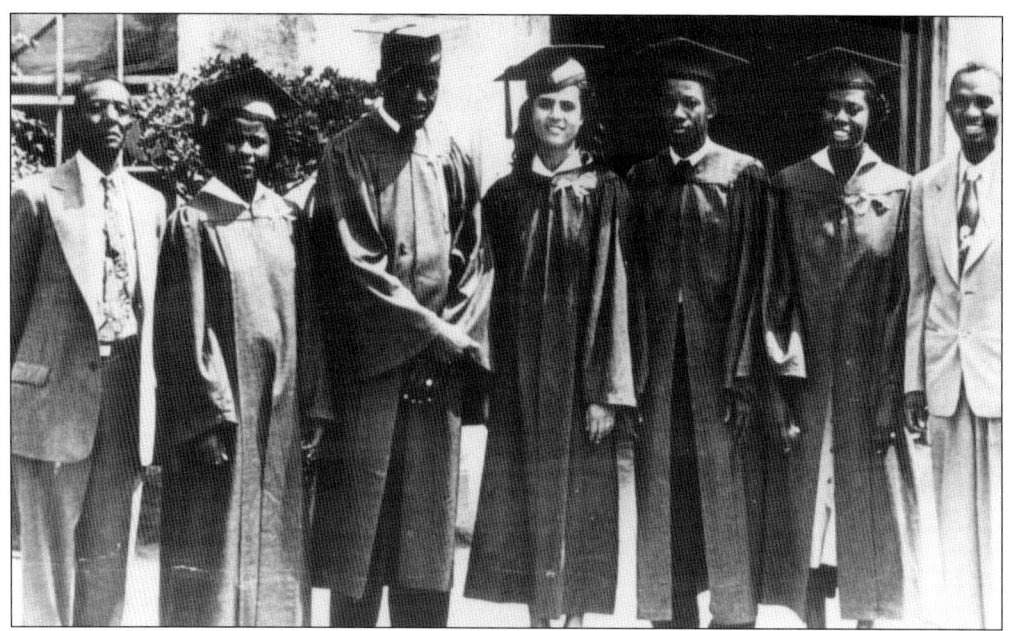

Griffin's 1949 graduating class included, from left to right, Principal William R. Perkins, who served from 1914 to 1961; Fannie Barnes; Moses Pemberton Jr.; Edwina Martin; Barry Moten; Fannie Wilkerson; and Assistant Principal Edwin Norwood Sr.

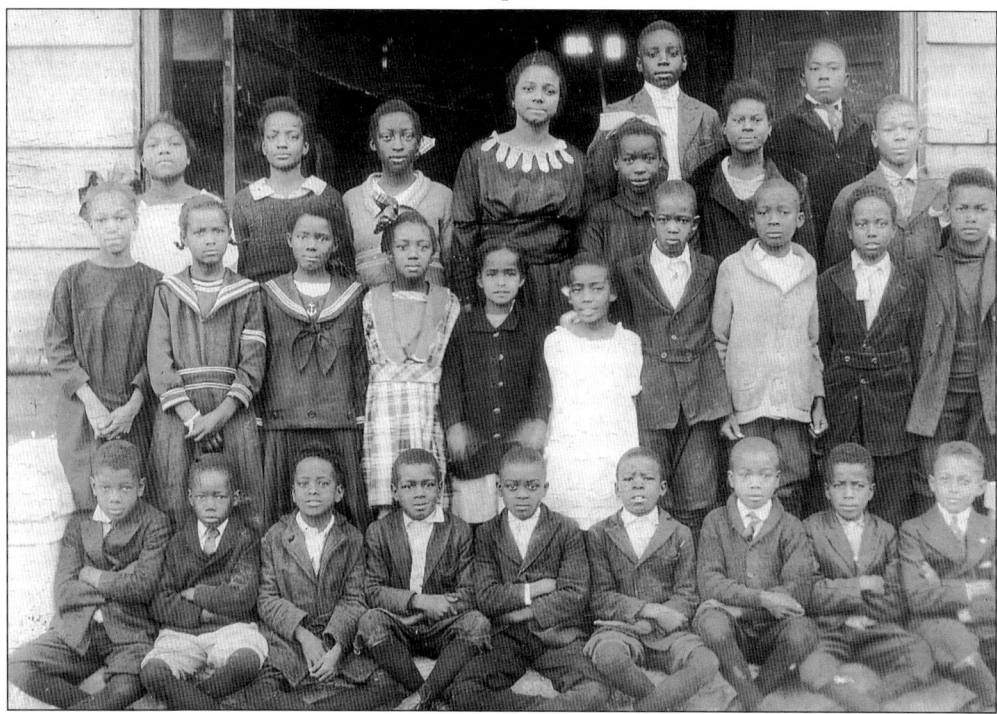

Anita Stewart (center), photographed in the 1940s with students, began her professional career in Tallahassee at Lucy Moten, now Florida A&M University Developmental Research School. The school served grades kindergarten through 12th. Stewart later served as a professor of physical education at the university until her retirement.

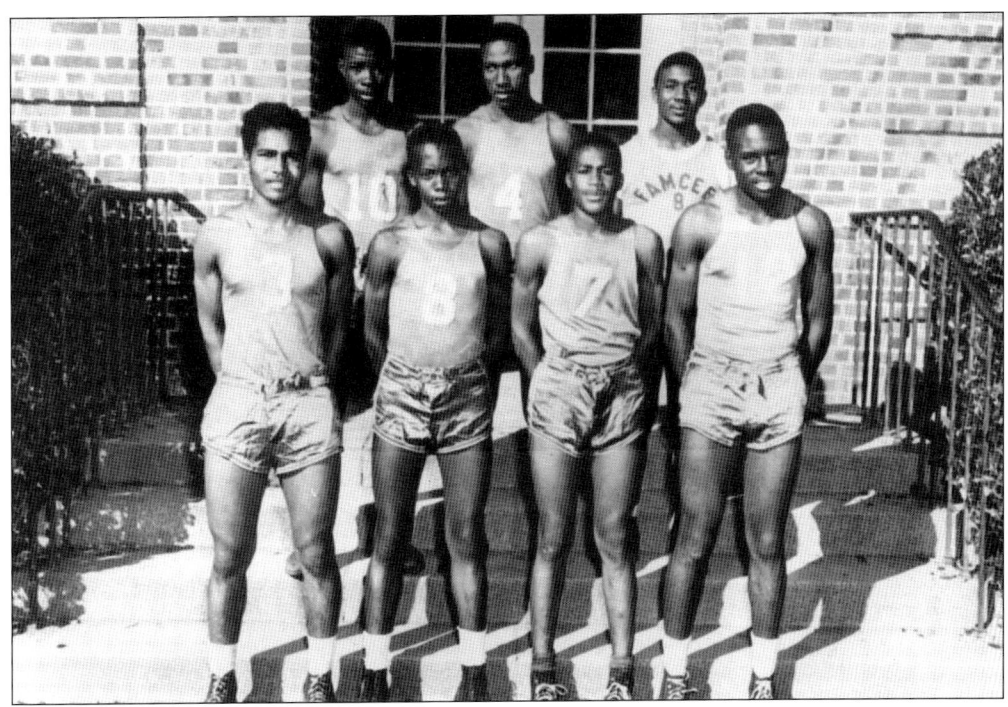

The boys basketball team at Lucy Moten consisted of the following, from left to right: (front row) Timothy James, Joseph McKinney, Henry Parker, and James Corbin; (back row) Clifford Danzler, Glenn Whitaker, and John D. Chandler. Corbin was named to the Florida Board of Regents by Gov. Jeb Bush in 1999.

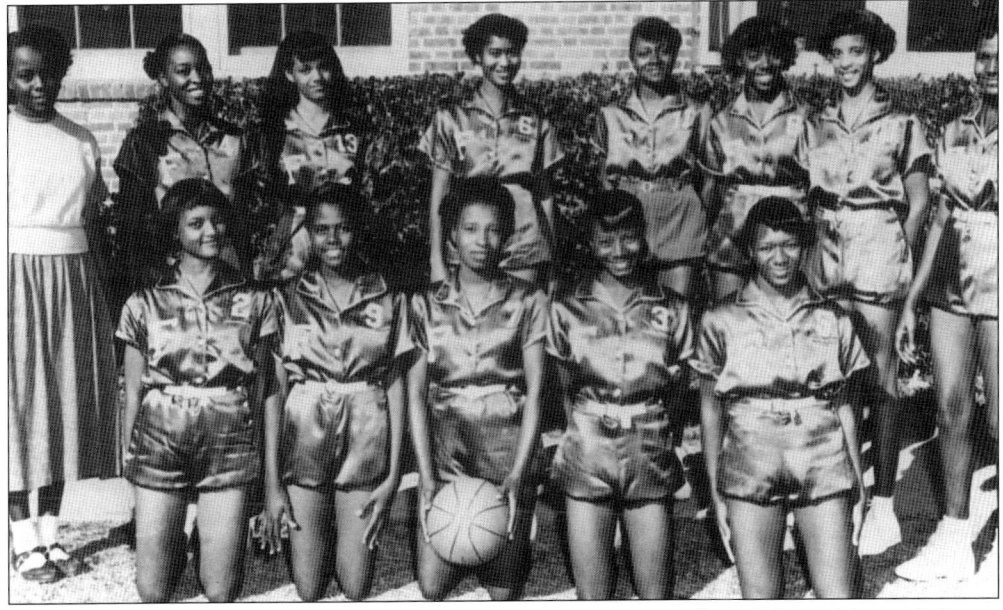

These members of the girls basketball team at Lucy Moten are, from left to right, as follows: (kneeling) Connie Robinson, Thelma Corbin, Dorothy Hogan, Hazel Nelson, and Gracie Gaines; (standing) Laura Mae Vaughn, Mildred Nicholson, Barbara Nims, Erie Lee Ryan, Gertrude Marshall, Catherine Paremore, Patricia Ford, and Mary Hill.

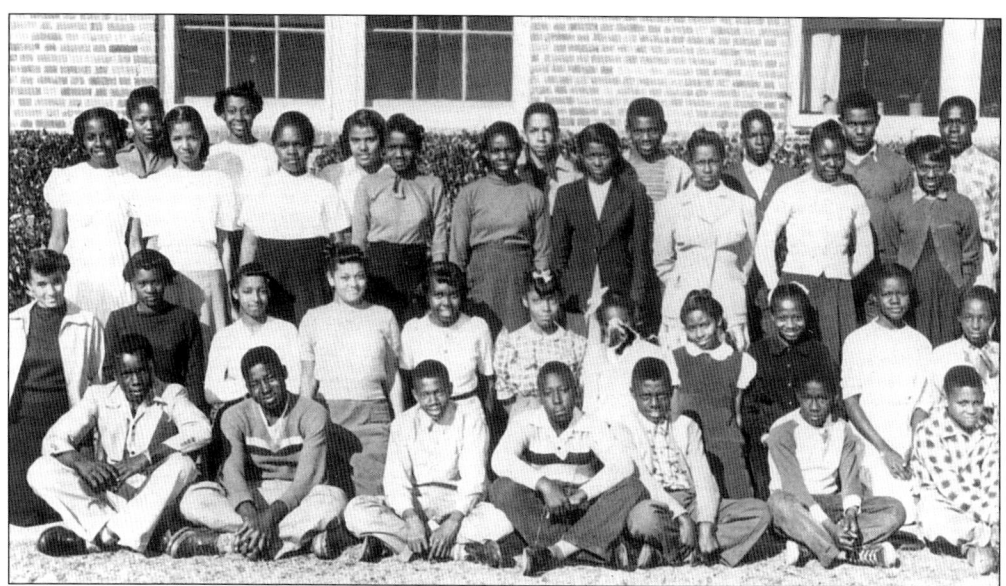

Pictured, from left to right, are the following members of a Lucy Moten class: (front row) Ray Baker, Freeman Bryant, Alzon Colquitt, Lawrence Beasley, Jonas Hope, William Brown, and Eddie Jefferson; (second row) Barbara Jones, Rosa Jackson, Lakay Beasley, Pauline Davis, Judy Lewis, Francis Triplett, unidentified, Inesta Beasley, Annie McKinney, Rebecca Governor, and Alice Morris; (third row) Elaine Hunter, Bertha Howard, Sammie Spencer, Ritchie Maddox, Dorothy Pittman, Mildred Chester, Virdell Chester, Shirley Haynes, and Emily McPherson; (back row) Laura Wilson, Gwendolyn Edwards, Frankie Jackson, William Oats, John Wyche, Troy Springer, Henry Trueblood, and Robert Davis.

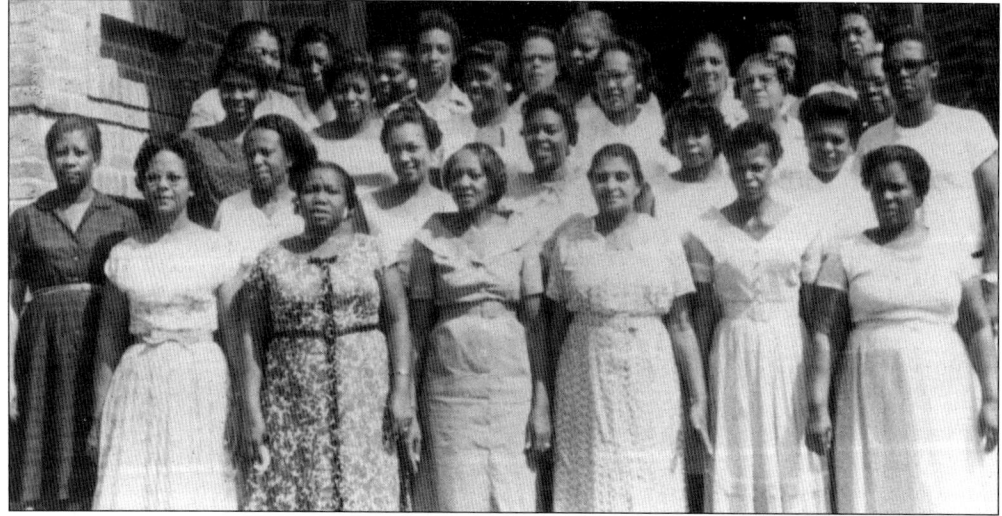

In 1950, the teachers at Bond Elementary School posed for this picture. From left to right they are as follows: (front row) Larenuia B. Gaines, Marazine M. Brown, Marie Kilpatrick, Lucille Bright, Ruth Allen, and Louise Acosta; (second row) Lucille Williams, Rosa Johnson, Inez Jones, Lucille Brown, Frances Ferrell, Queenie Marshall, and Charles Hayeling; (third row) Juanita Hollis, Majorie Williams, Annie Nelson, Cherrie Williams, Sarah Blackshear, ? Spearman, and Annie Pinder; (back row) Karell Hargrove, Dorothy Bell, Estelle Pelham, Dorothy Gaiter, Delores Williams, Emma Field, Mayola Robinson, and Fannie Pridgeon.

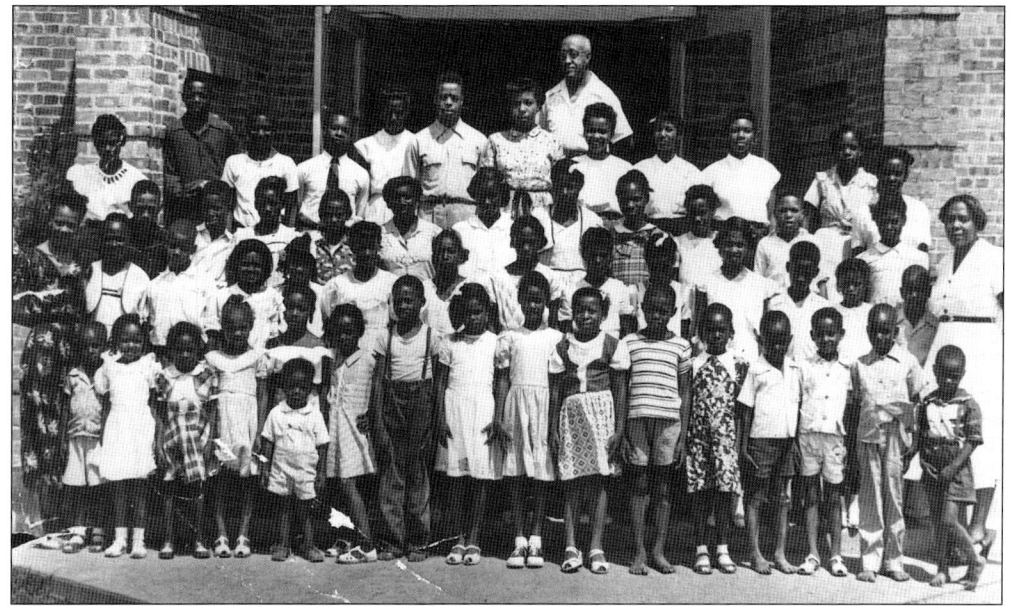

Classes at Bond Elementary School were photographed during the 1940s with Clarence Nasby (top row, center), an itinerant art instructor for "colored" schools from the 1930s through the 1950s. Nasby's tenure was before art was placed in school curriculums and before the district began hiring full-time art teachers.

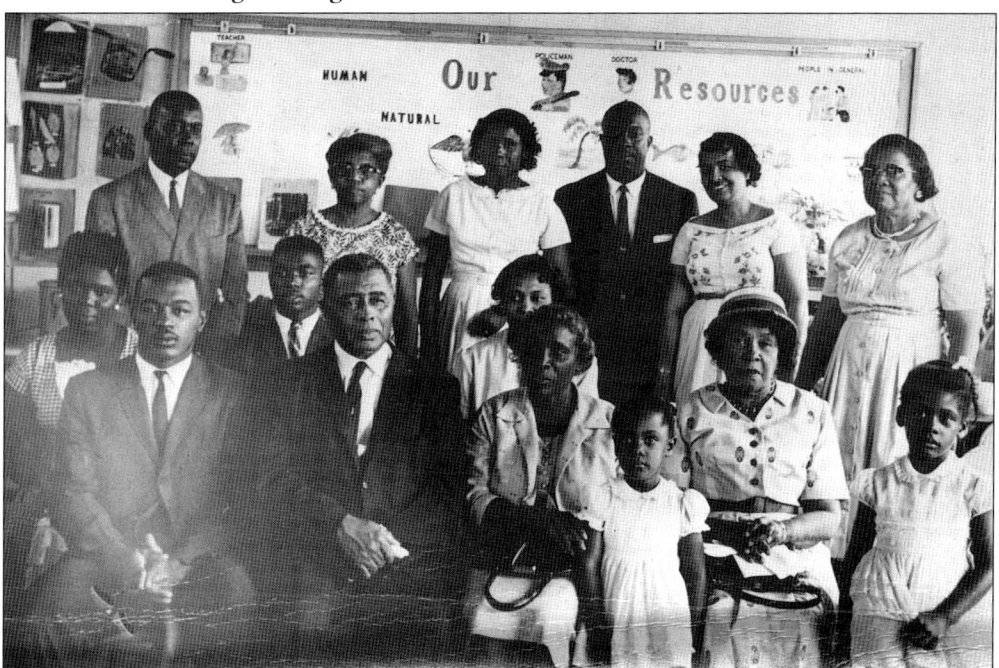

Here is a Parent Teachers Association (PTA) function during the 1950s at Riley Elementary School. In attendance are Emory Collier, intern; Rev. S.R. Bright; Modeste Duncan; Fadra Glenn, baby contest winner; Mary Hicks, supervisor of FAMU interns; Allie Mae Glenn; Principal Luther Williams; Dorothy Holmes, Jeanes supervisor; Mattie Green, PTA Queen; Dr. Devurn Glenn; A.C. Ware, directing teacher; and Mrs. R.E. Richards, sixth grade teacher.

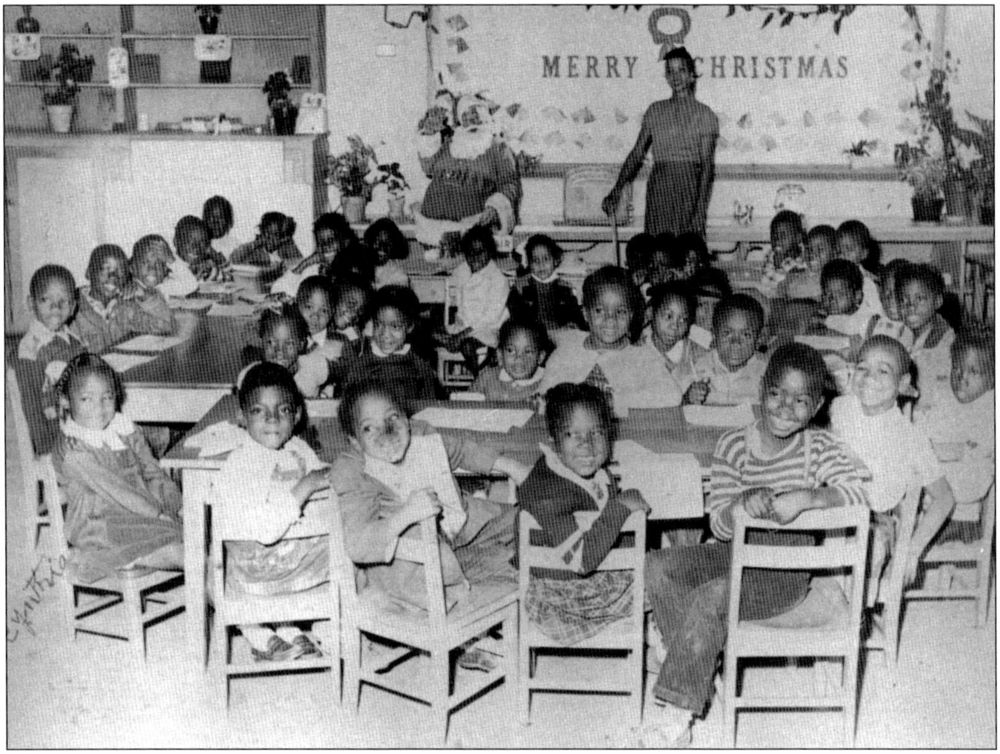

Kate Warren Condra is pictured here with her class at Riley Elementary School in the 1950s.

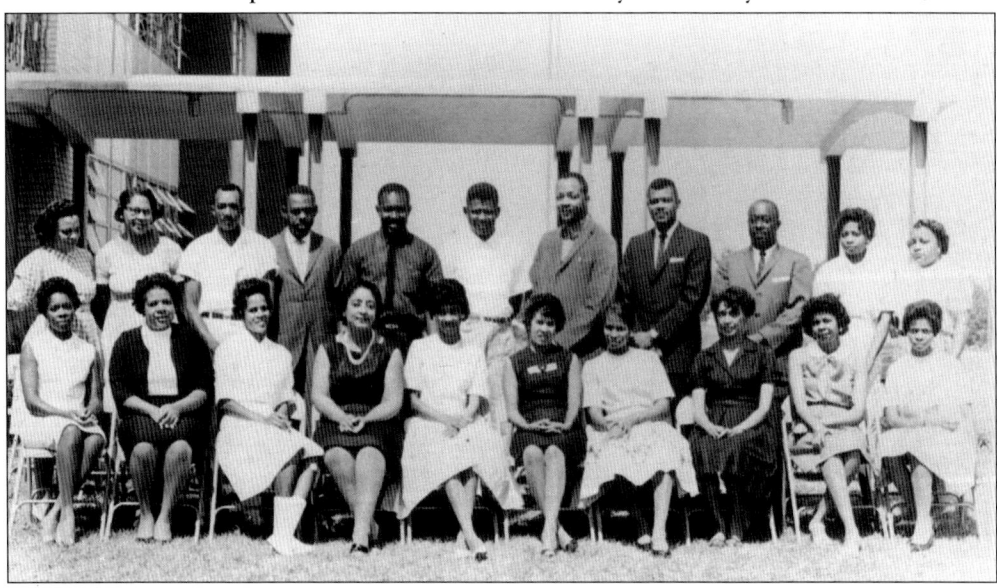

The Nims teachers are pictured here with their principal, Dr. Devurn Glenn. They are, from left to right, as follows: (seated) JoAnn Barnes, Virdell Stevens, S. Glenn, Lavada Beasley, Hortense Tookes, Gussie Mallory, Lillie D. Davis, unidentified, Jacquelyn Thomas, and unidentified; (standing) Vera Mills, Minerva Adams, unidentified, Henry Murphy, Sylvester Peeples, Charles Herout, Alphonso McPherson, Alonzo Williams, Devurn Glenn, Emma Wade, and Edith Landers.

From left to right are the following Raney School teachers in the 1940s: (front row) Collette Warren, A.C. Ware, and Jean Brewington; (middle row) Emma Goldwire, Clarisse McPherson, and Mayola Robinson; (back row) Bertha Chester Ranson and Principal Raymond Fields.

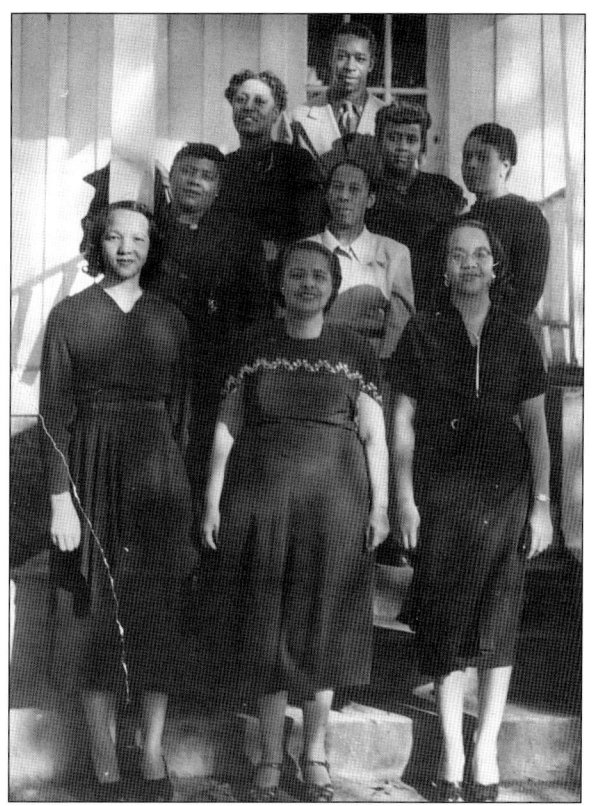

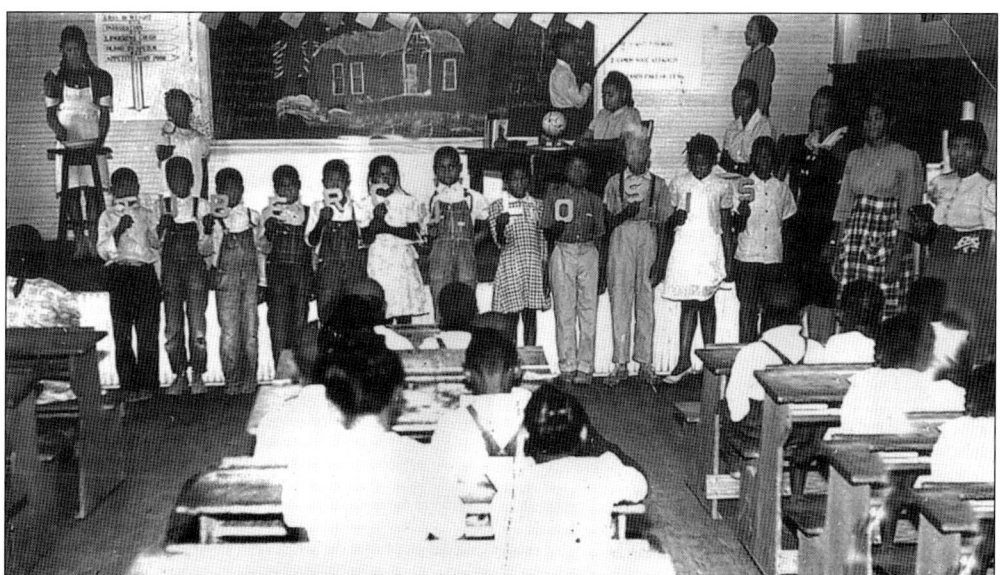

A Raney School elementary class in the 1940s is seen here with Dorothy Gunn Holmes, the last Jeanes supervisor in Leon County. White philanthropist Anna Jeanes donated funds to build schools for African Americans in the South and provide supervision for these schools. The Raney School building still stands at Centerville and Lonnbladh Road.

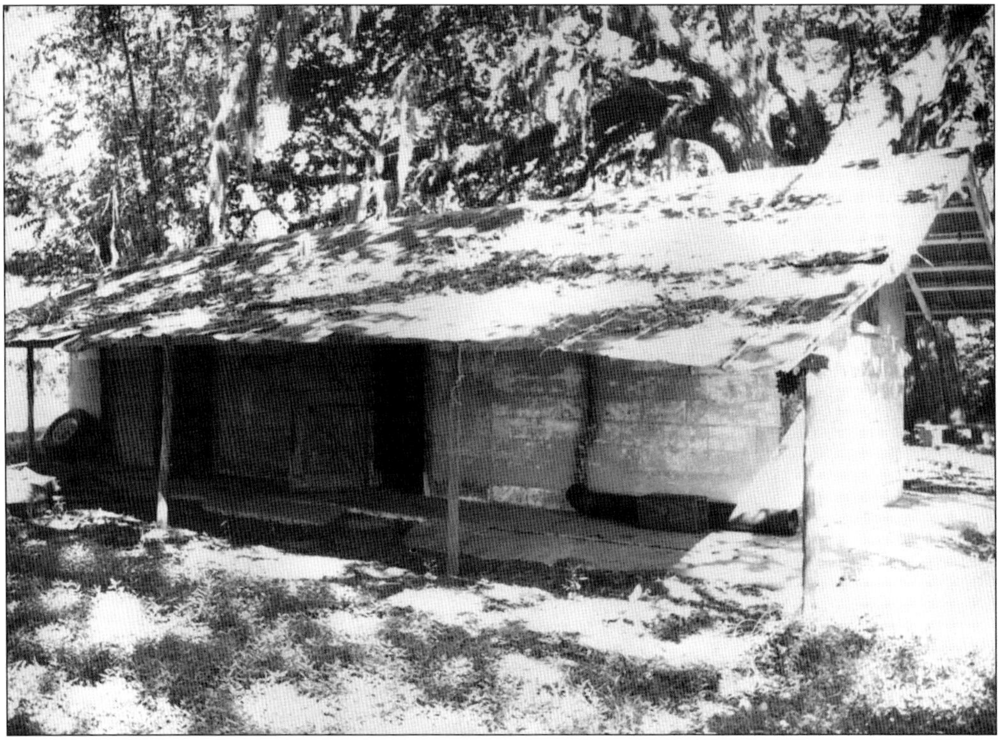

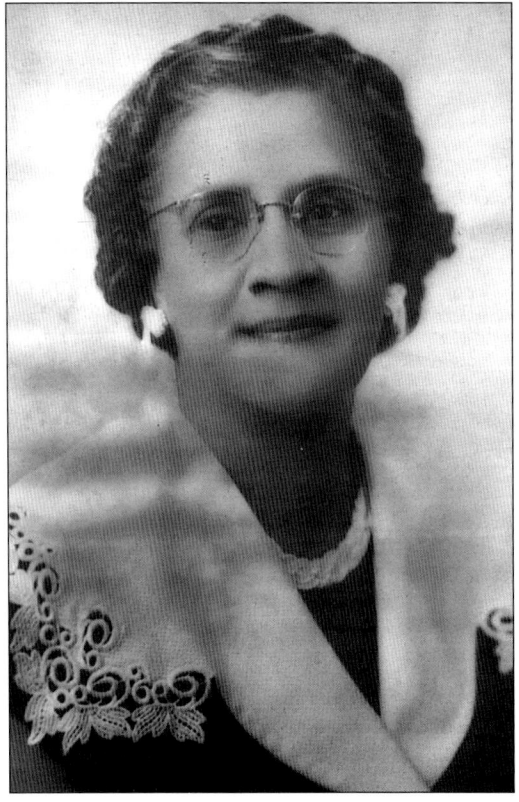

This field house (physical education), photographed by Debra Start-Herman, is a vestige of the "separate but equal" doctrine that existed in public education through the 1960s. This structure is on the site of the former Concord Negro Schoolhouse on State Road 59. One of the main school buildings also remains and has been renovated as a private residence.

Annie L. Gordan Perry (1891–1966), the mother of FAMU's sixth president, Benjamin L. Perry, was one of 16 children. She was born in Maury County, Tennessee, and graduated from the Tuskegee Institute. Mrs. Perry later enrolled at FAMU and earned a diploma in elementary education in 1928, a bachelor of science in 1945, and a masters degree in 1956. She was the first Jeanes teacher-supervisor for Leon County.

Nine
WORSHIP

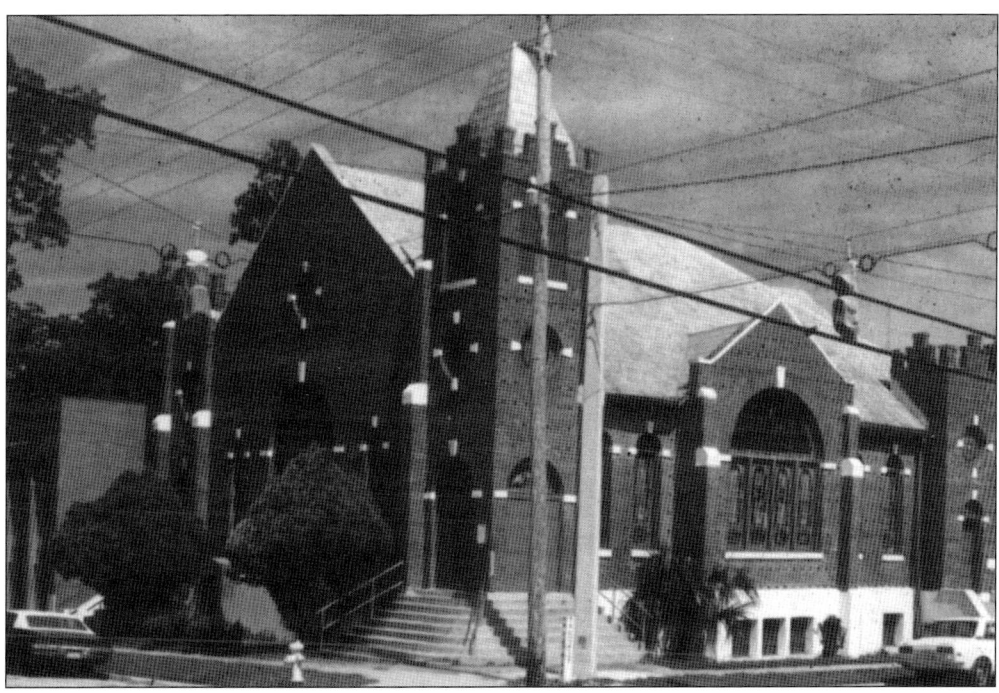

On February 20, 1866, the Rev. Robert Meacham, assisted by Bethel Missionary Baptist Church preacher James Page, laid the cornerstone for the Bethel African American Episcopal Church on Duval Street. Rev. Charles Pearce organized the church on March 1, 1866. The AME Church embraced and demonstrated through its leaders a philosophy of the "inseparability of political creed from religious duties." Many of their ministers and bishops served in politics during the Reconstruction and Post Reconstruction eras.

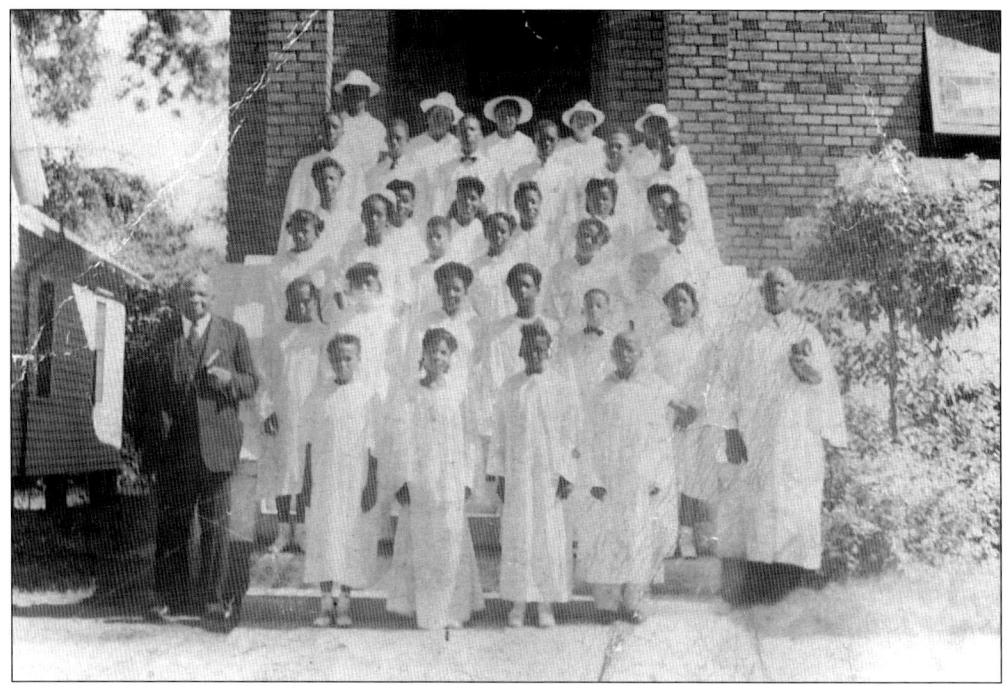

The Bethel AME Church choir is pictured here with their pastor, Rev. Noah Z. Graham. A glimpse of the parsonage is on the left. The parsonage was demolished in the 1950s.

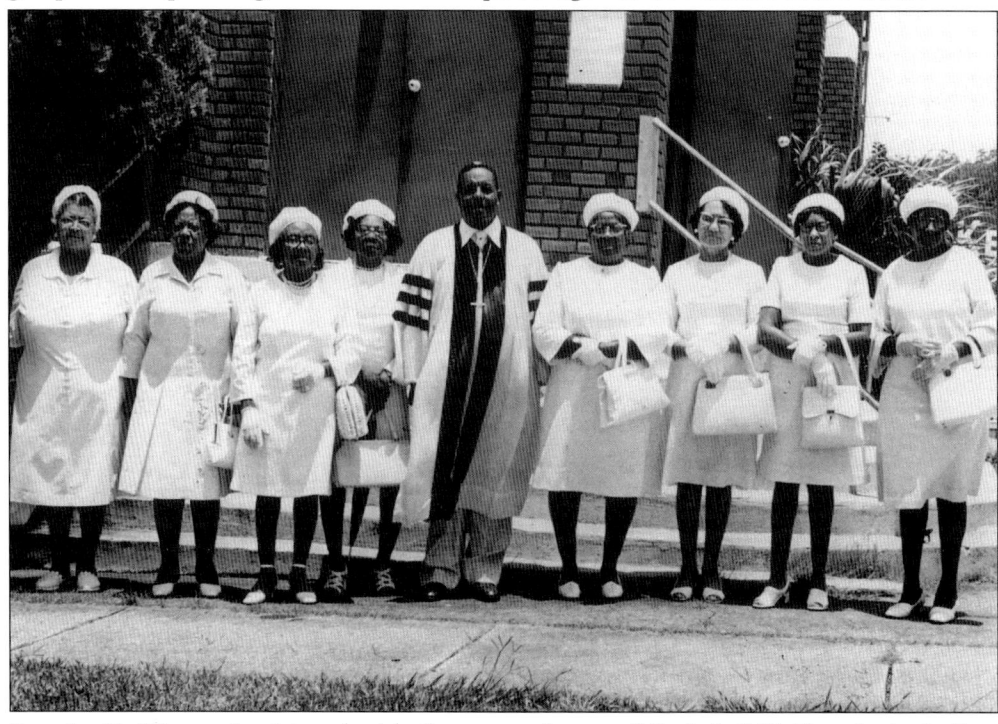

Rev. Ira D. Hinson is pictured with the stewardesses of Bethel AME Church, including, from left to right, Mrs. P.B. Roberts, Annie Tanner, Fannie Richardson, Nancy Shaw, Alberta Oliver, Clara Weaver, unidentified, and Mary Thurman.

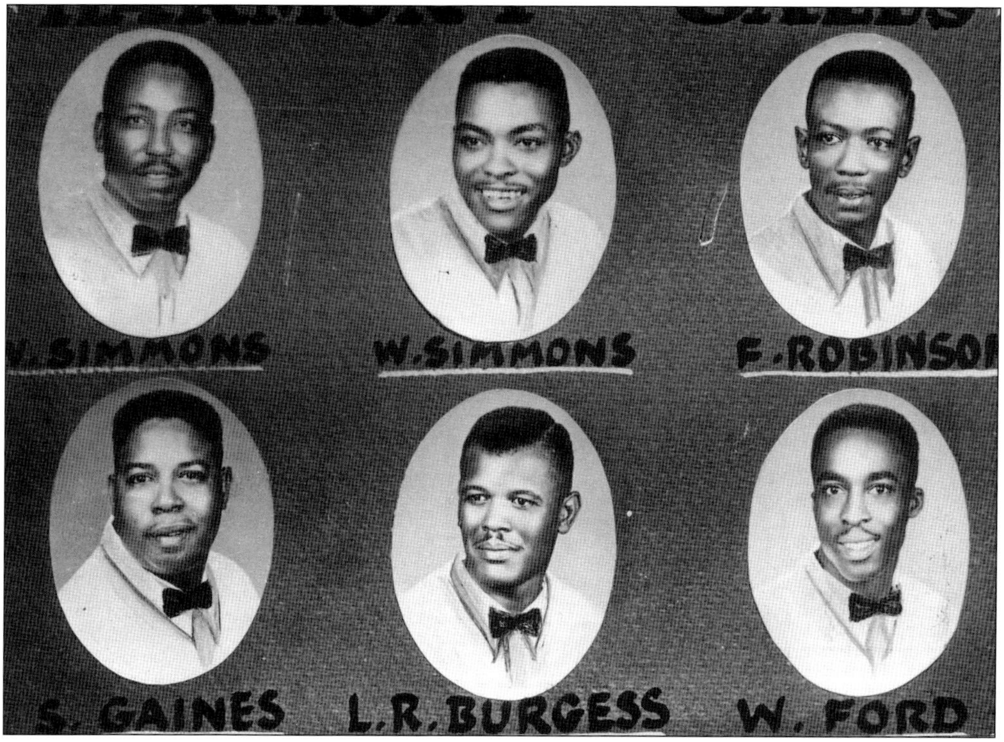

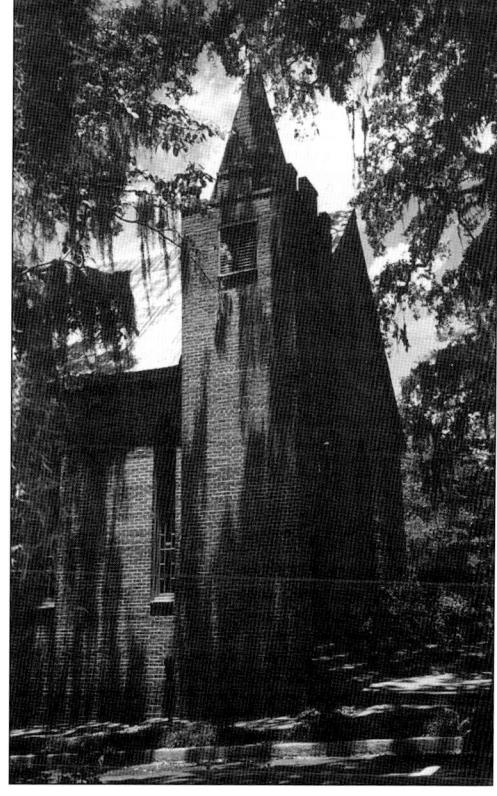

The Original Harmony Gales Quartet was organized in 1957 with the following members, seen here from left to right: (top row) Wesley Simmons, Willie Simmons, and Fred Robison; (bottom row) Seth Gaines, Leroy Burgess, and Washington Ford. Leroy was the lead singer. Wesley Simmons was a pioneering black police officer and Seth the first black bus driver in Tallahassee. In 1959, the quartet was the first black singing group to have a regular spot on a local television station, WCTV; they appeared each Sunday from 10 to 11 a.m.

After 1865, St. James Christian Methodist Episcopal (CME) went directly under the control of "colored" pastors. The church has the unique distinction of serving as a hospital for wounded Union soldiers, mothering the Tallahassee AME Church, being the birthplace of the public school system of Leon County, and establishing the first Bible vocational school for black youth with the Rev. E. W. Spearman, John Gimore Riley, and Mrs. R. Dames as instructors. (Photographed by Byron Spice, Riley Museum volunteer, 1998.)

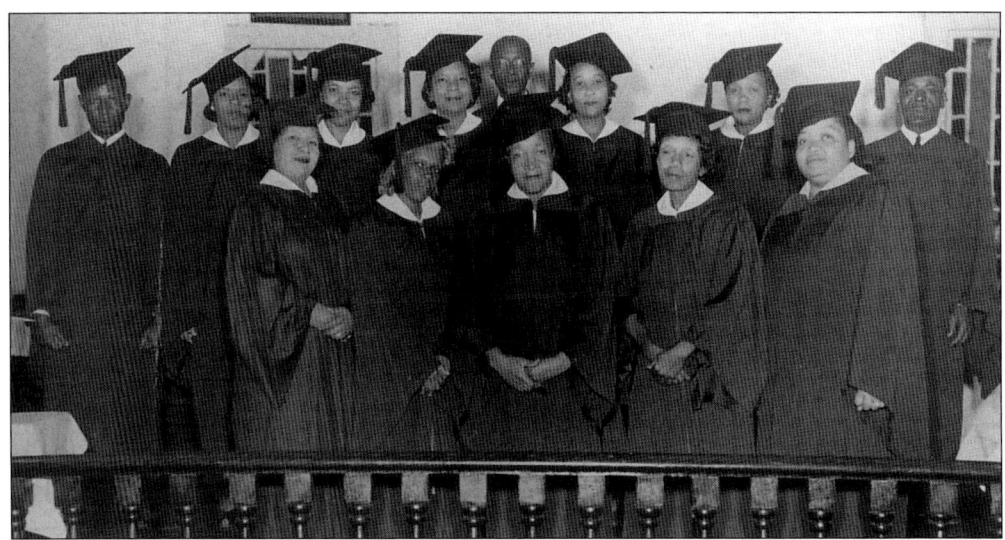

The St. James CME Church choir is seen here in the 1940s. Some of the choir members are Alease Twine Spears, Mattie Pope, Hazel Twine Jones, Estelle Young Gray, Horace Reese, and Nancy Johnson.

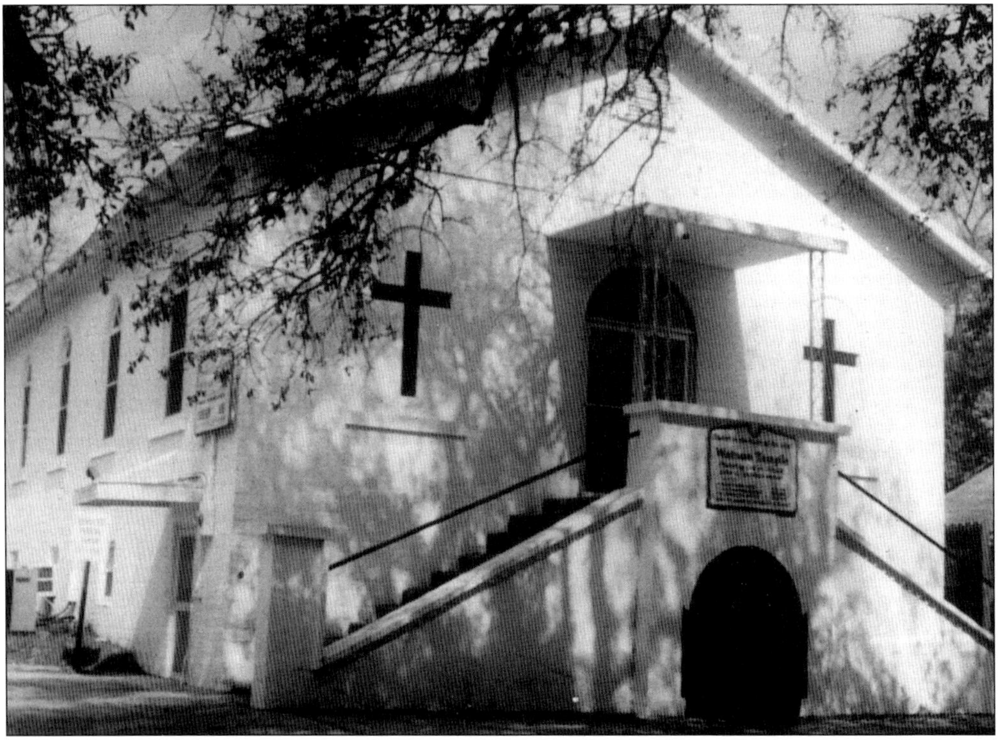

Watson Temple Church of God in Christ was established in the 1930s on Boulevard Street. Elder Zed Brown was appointed pastor by W.R. Nesbitt. Elder Stennis Watson joined the fellowship and eventually became pastor, leading the congregation to obtain land at Georgia and Dewey Streets. After Watson's death, Elder Turner Grier became pastor and completed the building. Others pastors over the years included Elders Owen Smith, W.R. Nesbitt Jr., R.L. McCloud, and Elbert Lee Sheppard.

Elder Stennis Watson was the driving force behind the establishment of Watson Temple Church. He was the grandfather of Sam, Obadiah, and Mary Sims, who still reside in Tallahassee.

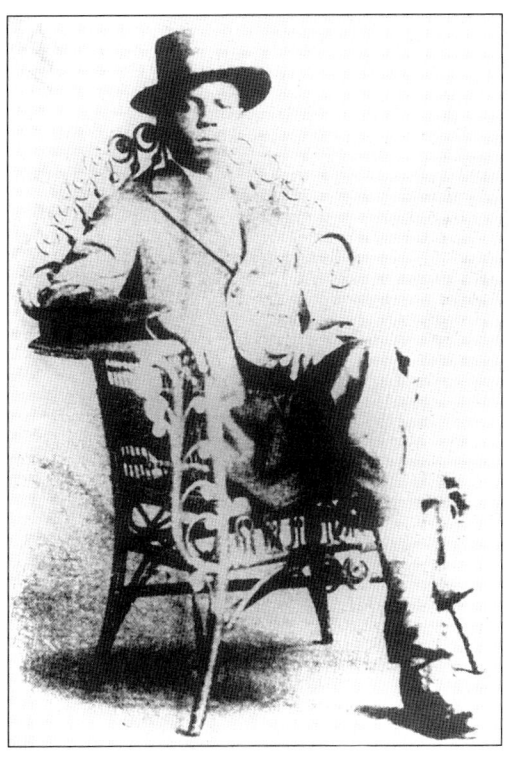

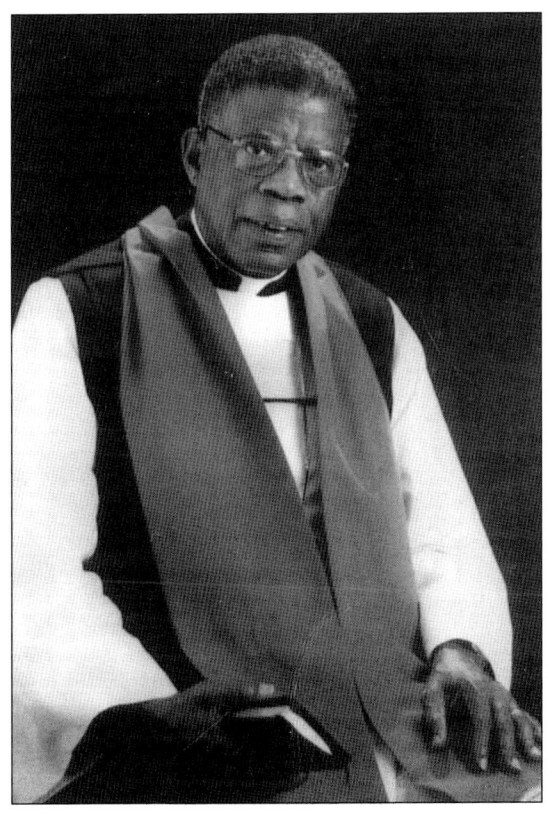

Bishop Elbert Lee Sheppard (1928–1998) served as presiding prelate of the Western Florida Ecclesiastical Jurisdiction, Church of God in Christ.

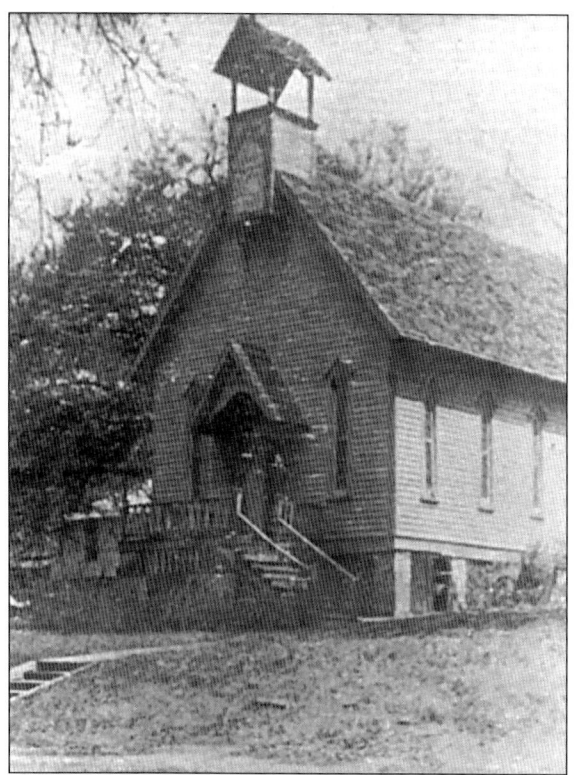

St. Michaels All Angels Episcopal Church was established in 1882. Bishop J.F. Young took charge of the mission congregation, and six years later, a building was erected on Park Avenue at Duval. The church was given its name by Bishop E.W. Weed and has been located on other sites, including Martin Luther King at Lafayette, 501 S. Boulevard, and, currently, Melvin Street. Past bishops include Frank A. Juhan, Edward H. West, and Frank S. Cerveny.

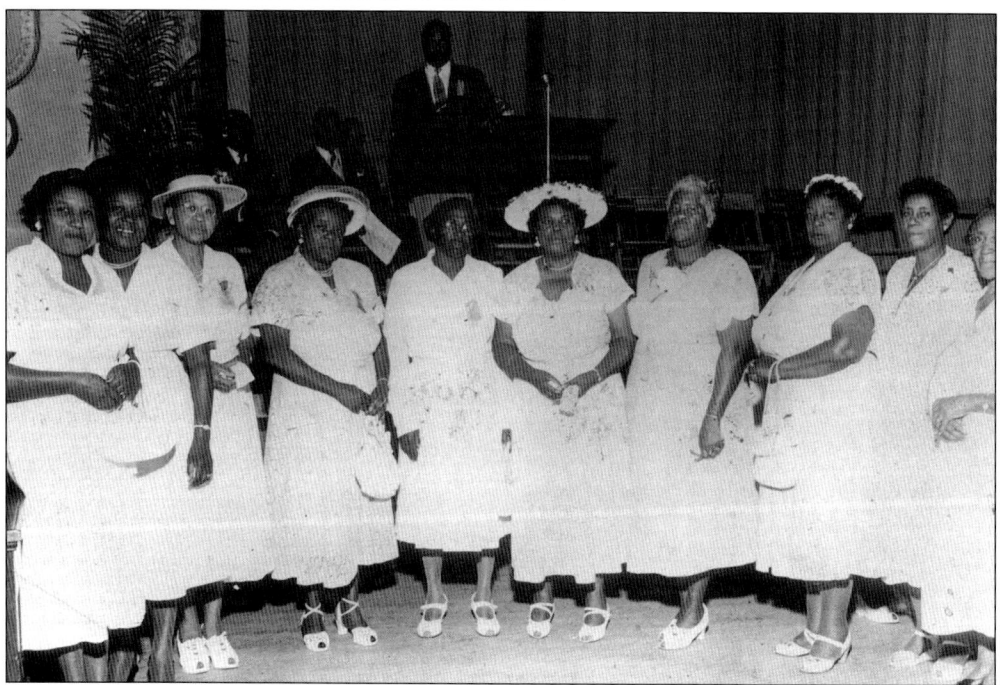

This is a 1940s picture of the Florida Primitive Baptist Women's Congress at their State Convention Queen's Contest. Those identified include Lilla Holiday (fourth from left), Mary Pauline Allen (sixth from left), and Alice Gainous (seventh from left).

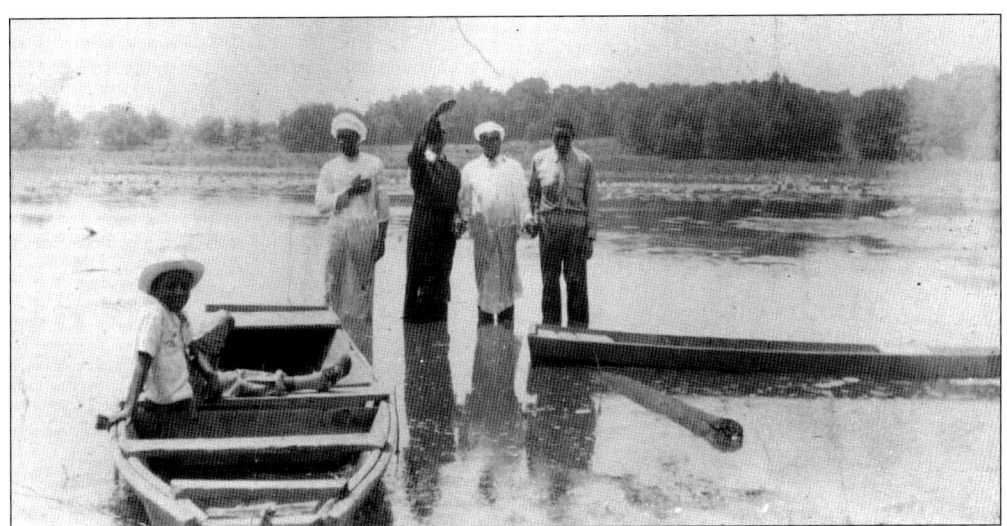

Rev. T.S. Lofton baptizes converts in the chilly waters at Buck Lake.

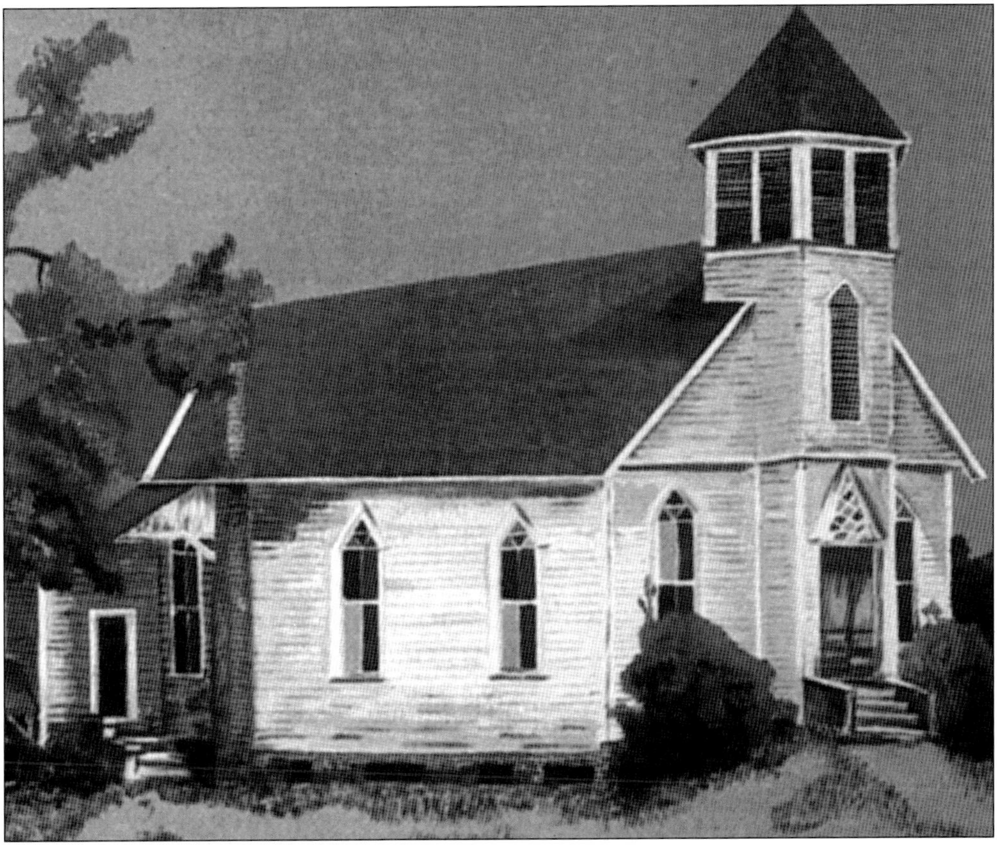

St. Mary Primitive Baptist Church #1 on West Call Street is the oldest Primitive Baptist Church in Tallahassee. The church was pastored for many years by Rev. Capus P. Allen, who was also the moderator of the Florida Primitive Baptist Association and the secretary of the Primitive Baptist National Convention of the USA. A historical document shows the church's address as 454 West Call Street and telephone number, during Allen's tenure, as 516-R.

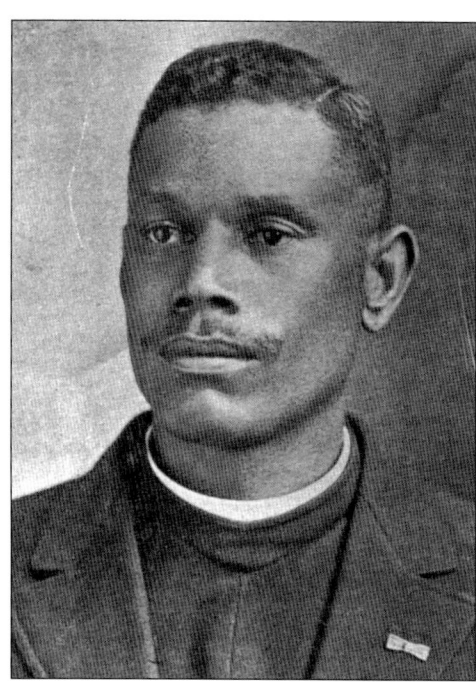

Rev. Capus P. Allen was the pastor at St. Mary Primitive Baptist Church #1.

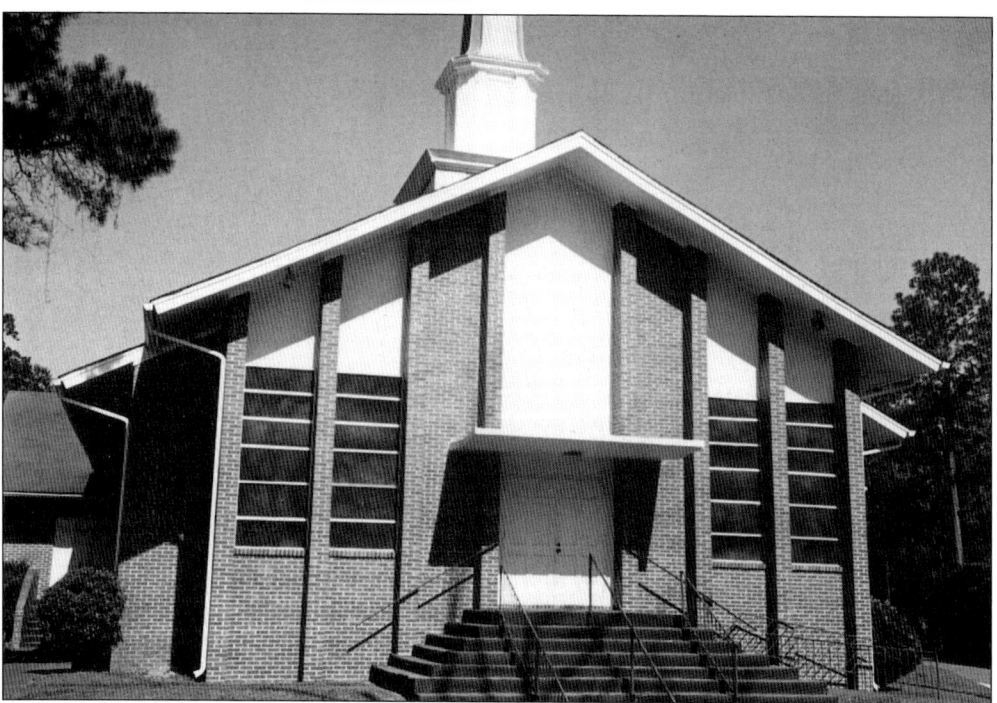

Philadelphia Primitive Baptist Church began in 1903 with a group who met on Dent Street. The church's formal organization occurred in 1905 with Elder A.R. Pender, Deacon ? Johnson, and Mother ? Wells as officers. The pastors have included Elder Pender (1905–1912), Elder Mack Davis (1912–1919), Elder T.B. Bisbee (1919–1925), Elder Alex Harrison (1926–1933), Elder Thomas Abrams (1933–1936), Elder A.L. Gainous (1936–1940), Elder William Atkins (1940–1947), and Elder Moses G. Miles (1948–1996).

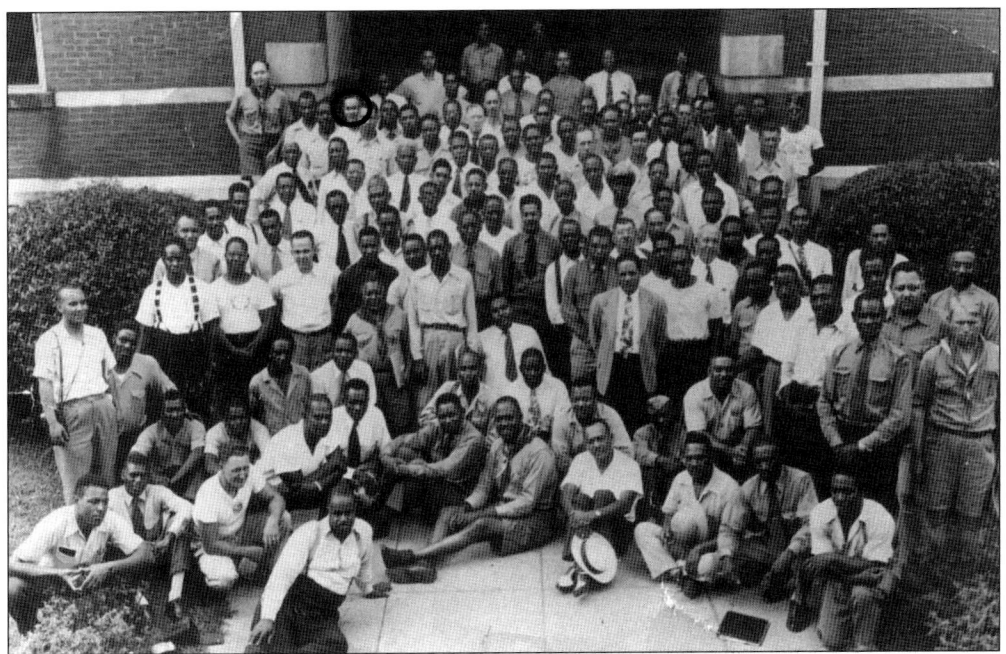

Many churches included the establishment of Boys Scout troops as an extension of their ministry. Male church leaders, including Florida A&M University's sixth president, Benjamin Perry Jr., Bartow Duhart, and John Swilley, organized and worked with youth in the Boy Scouts for many years. Shown are scout leaders at a conference in Atlanta, Georgia, in 1947 with Swilley (circled) in the back.

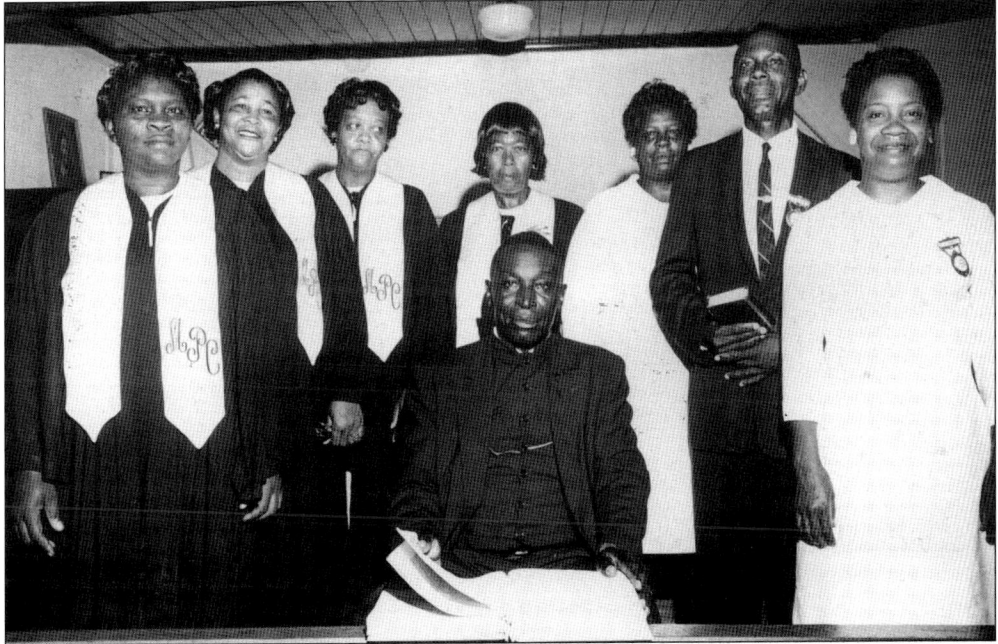

Rev. Sam Mann is pictured at Lake Hall Church on Thomasville Road with, from left to right, choir members Bessie Harden, Annie Henry, Bessie Mae Houston, Violet Payne Anderson, Mary Davis, Ike Gilliam, and Selona Diggs.

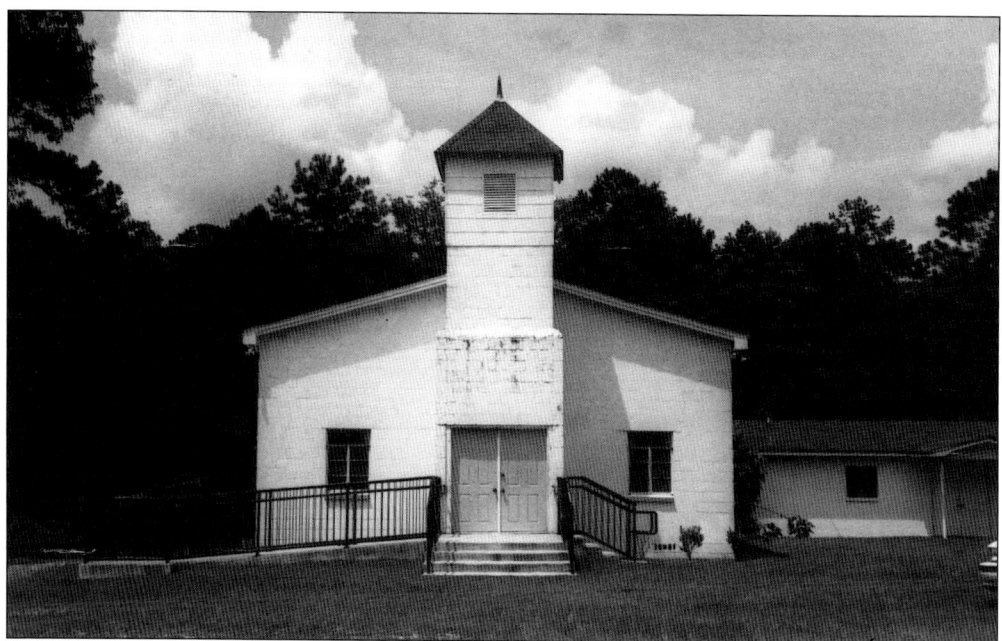

Concord AME Church, in the historic Miccosukee Community, was rebuilt in 1956. Its original trustees were Jesse Harley, W.L. Hall, J. Livingston, Aaron Nathan, F.H. Hall, S.M. Murry, and Edith Robinson. Rev. D. Ward Nichols, LLD, was bishop, Rev. A.W. Thompson was presiding elder, and Rev. S. Stewart was pastor.

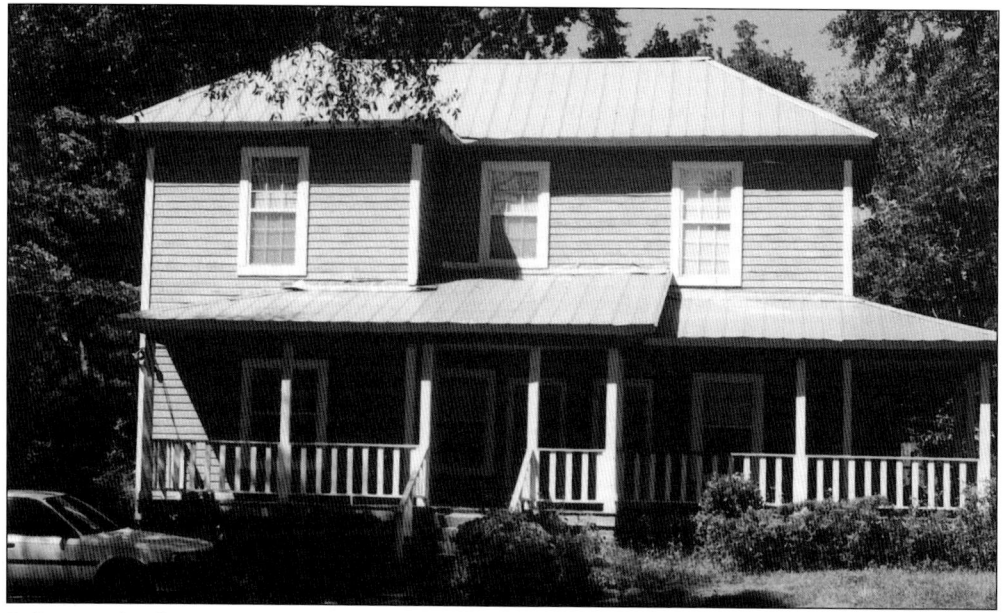

Religious leaders inspired people not only through their sermons but through their accomplishments, which often included ownership of businesses, property, and homes. This historic residence is a prime example of the lavish lifestyle of Rev. Jessie Starks and his wife, Frances, who built this house, which still stands majestically in the Frenchtown community. Reverend Stark was one of the first pastors of Bethel AME Church and built the first parsonage at Bethel next to the church on Virginia and Duval Streets.

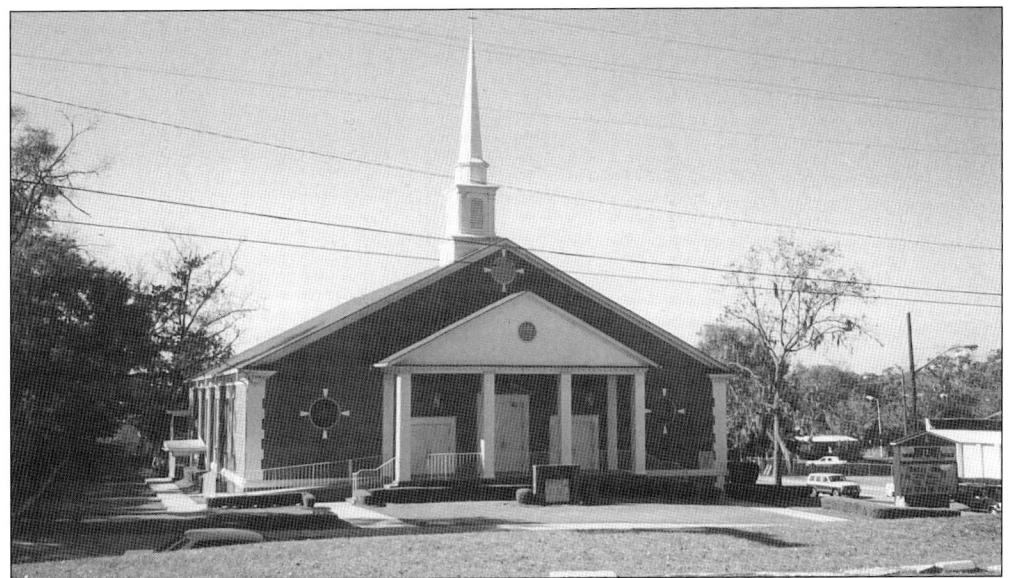

Shown is the Bethel Missionary Baptist Church. By June 1868, the Tallahassee Missionary Baptist Church, founded by the Rev. James Page in 1866 and originally situated on Bel Aire Road, had a Sunday school large enough to occupy 12 teachers. Church activities included Sunday school picnics at Lake Bradford and fund-raising festivals at the courthouse. In March 1869, trustees purchased a lot in the northwest addition of the city from Philip J. Pearce for $250 and constructed the present church building on Martin Luther King Boulevard, between Call and Tennessee Streets.

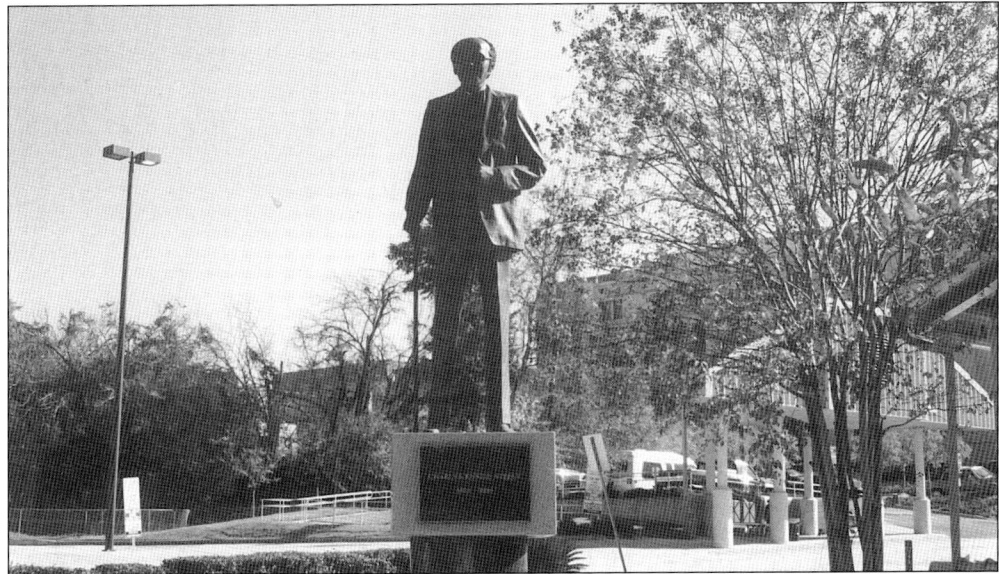

This statue of Rev. Charles Kenzie Steele was erected at the Tallahassee Bus Terminal, at the corner of Tennessee and Adams Streets, in acknowledgment of the substantial involvement of Reverend Steele in the Civil Rights Movement. As president of the Inter-Civic Council, Reverend Steele led the bus boycott that resulted in open seating on city buses in the 1960s. In addition to his leadership on the civil rights front, Reverend Steele also pastored the Bethel Missionary Baptist Church.

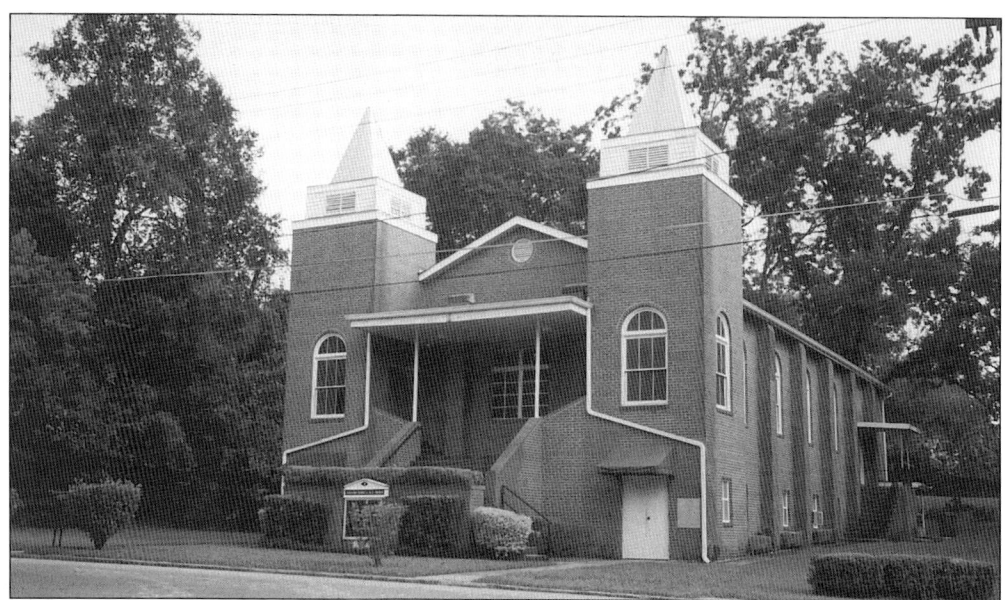

Around 1800, two struggling AME churches—Houston Chapel and Fountain Head—merged to form Fountain Chapel AME Church, shown in this photograph. The former was located in the eastern section of Tallahassee and the latter on Old Carabelle Railroad between the present Orange Avenue and Springhill Road. The consolidated church building was erected in 1902 on Eugenia Street in the Villa Mitchell community. The property for the church was donated by Rev. A.L. Spencer. Some of the church founders were Hillis Lincoln, Monroe Hinson, George Patterson, Robert Hall Oston, H.H. Jugger, and Nathan Brooks.

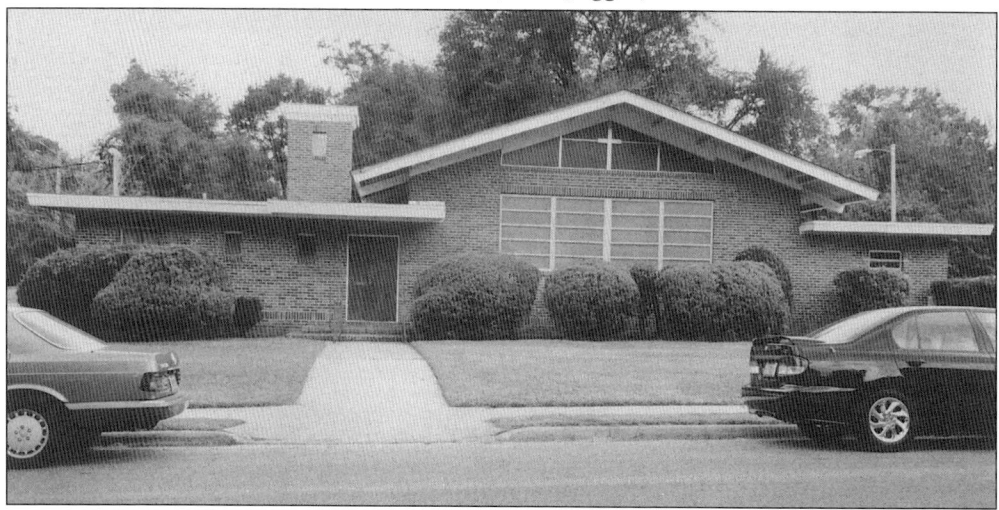

Shown here is Trinity Presbyterian Church. On July 29, 1953, the Rev. J. Metz Rollins, who holds bachelor and doctor of divinity degrees from Johnson C. Smith University, became the first pastor of a small band of Christians seeking to identify with the Presbyterian Church. The first congregational workshop was conducted in August 1953 in the sanctuary of Saint Michaels All Angels Episcopal Church. Their first regular service was held on April 30, 1953, in the manse at 223 South Boulevard. On January 31, 1954, the Trinity University Presbyterian Church U.S. was formerly organized in Lee Hall Auditorium on the FAMU campus. On April 29, 1962, a new edifice was completed at Gore and Pasco Streets.

Ten

LEGACY OF AVERY

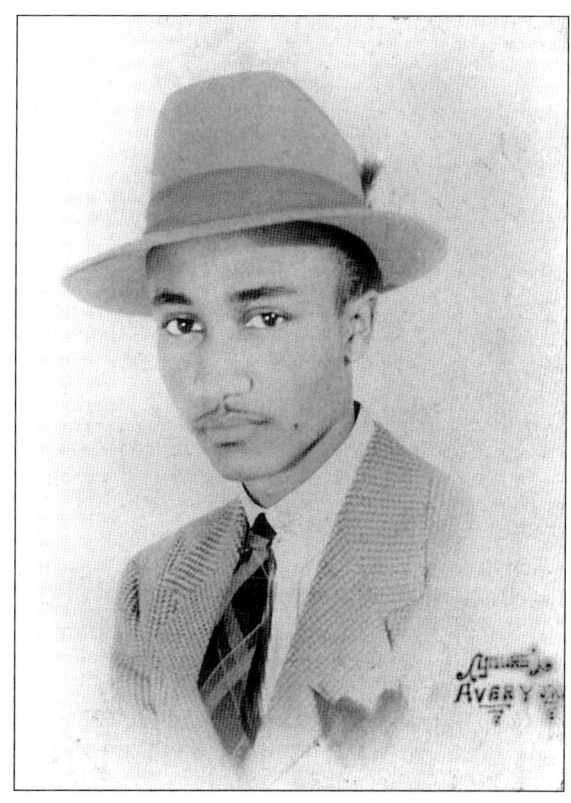

Joseph H. Avery Jr. captured classy women, zoot-suited men, brown sugars, and persons of distinction at his studio on Virginia Street. The studio closed in 1950 when Avery moved to Royal Art Studio in Jacksonville. In 1960, he relocated to Washington, D.C. and became chief of the photo lab with the U.S. House of Representatives, a position he held until his retirement in 1995. Many African-American homes in Tallahassee have in their collection at least one Avery photograph.

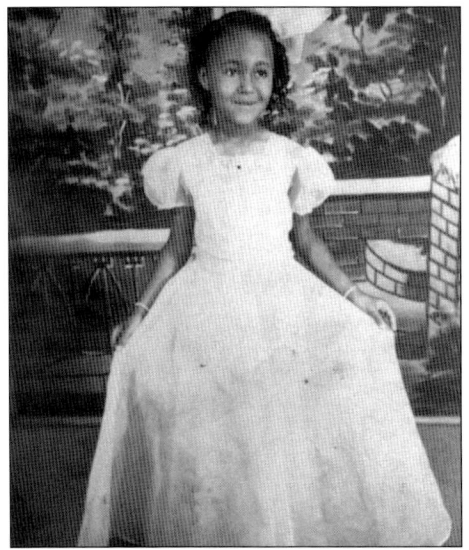 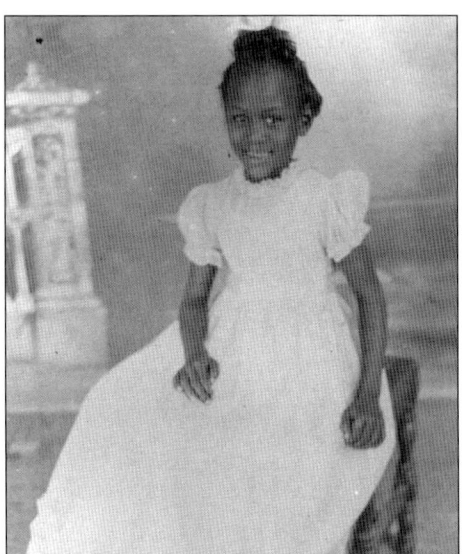

Left: Johnella Reid Bell is the daughter of John Reid and Bennie Mae Washington. A product of the "baby boomers" generation, Johnella is seen here at age nine as one of the annual May Day celebration queens. Her grandparents were early settlers in the historic Frenchtown area.
Right: Eddie Mae Davis Mordica, seen here at age ten, was born in the historic African-American community of Springfield. Mordica's family once owned and operated a laundry in this community at the corner of Brevard and Dean Streets. The community, during the early to mid-20th century, was a thriving commercial and residential corridor.

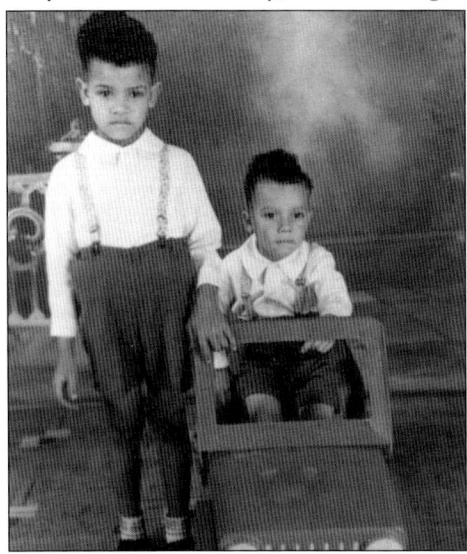 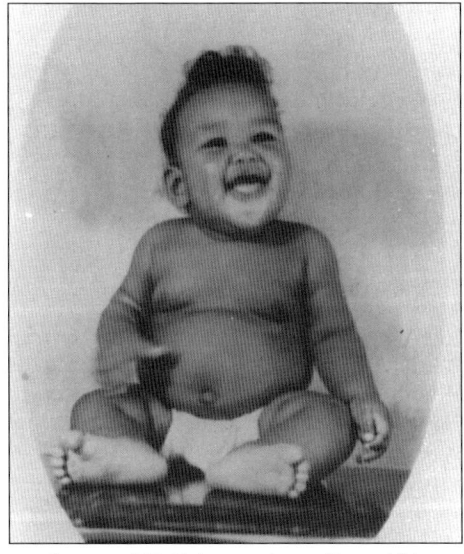

Left: Theodore and Alfred Nims are the grandsons of one of Tallahassee's earliest African-American families. They descended from a line of prominent black businessmen, including Pete, Joe, and Robert Nims. This photograph was taken at Avery Studio in the 1940s.
Right: Ivory Richardson, also photographed in the 1940s, was the son of Kate Warren Richardson Condra and Jimmy Richardson. Ivory was raised in the historic Frenchtown neighborhood, attended the Old Lincoln High School, and matriculated at FAMU. His grandparents, Robert and Annie Richardson, owned a business on Frenchtown's Macomb Street.

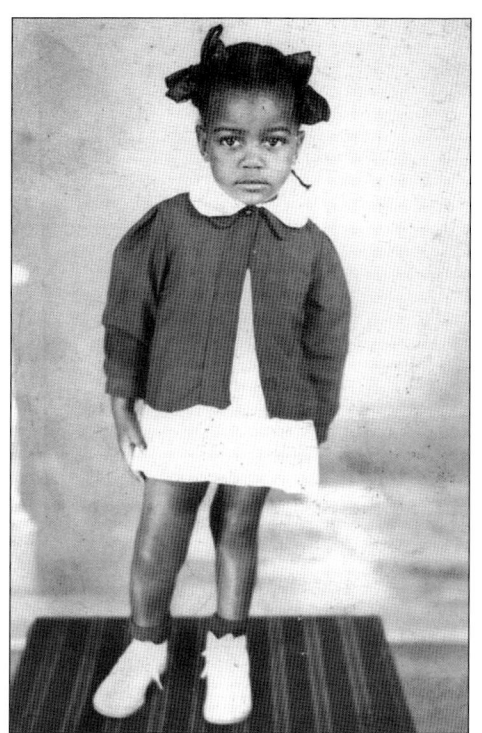
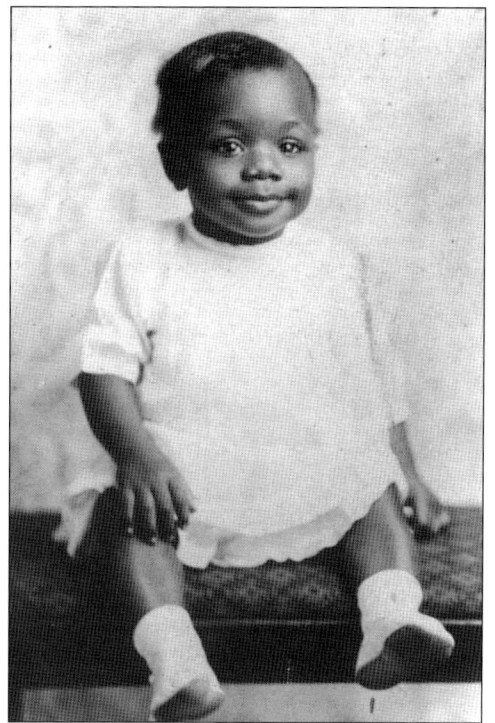
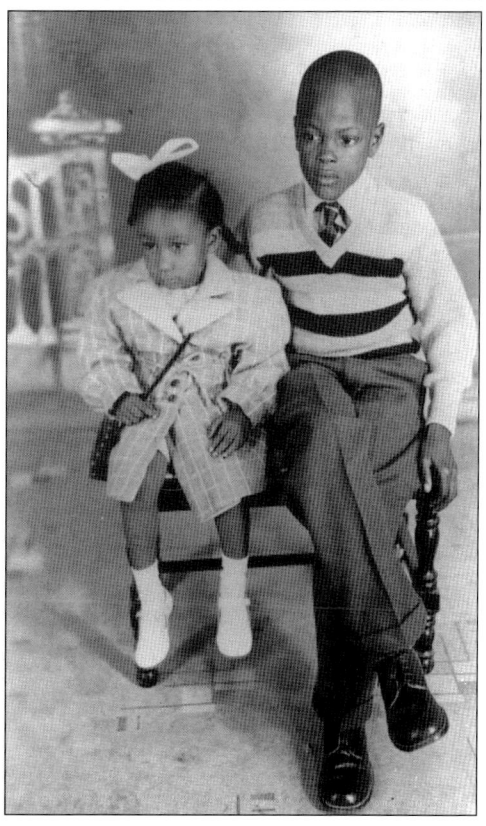

Above Left: Anthon "Ann" Roberts is the daughter of Pete Birdie and Simon Roberts and the granddaughter of AME bishop Robert Anthony Grant, for whom she is named. Raised in the Frenchtown district, she attended the Old Lincoln High and graduated from FAMU. Roberts resides in the home on West Carolina Street that was purchased by her family in 1936.

Above Right: Moses Pemberton Jr. is seen here at the age of six months. Born in 1932 on Waverly Plantation, Moses graduated in 1949 from Griffin High School, matriculated at FAMU, and served in the USAF. He lived in Orlando for many years before retiring to Tallahassee in the 1980s.

Right: Janice McCloud Bryant and Howard Jackson were childhood neighbors during the 1950s and 1960s. Janice, the daughter of Bennie Osborne McCloud Moseley, and Howard, the nephew of Lucille Brown, lived next door to one another on Macomb Street in the Frenchtown neighborhood.

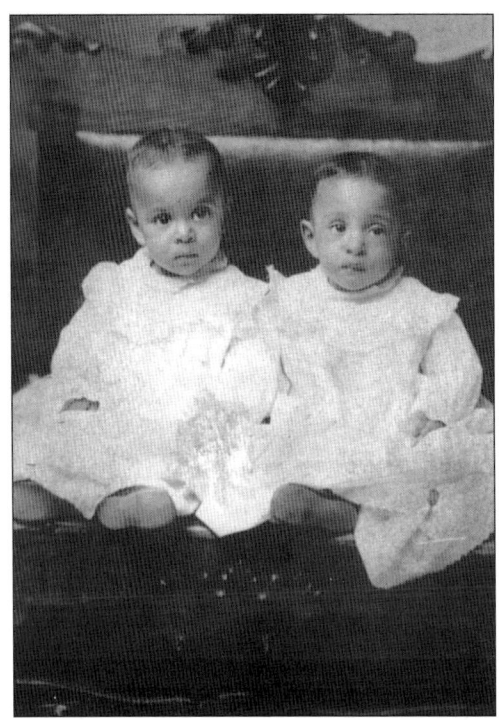

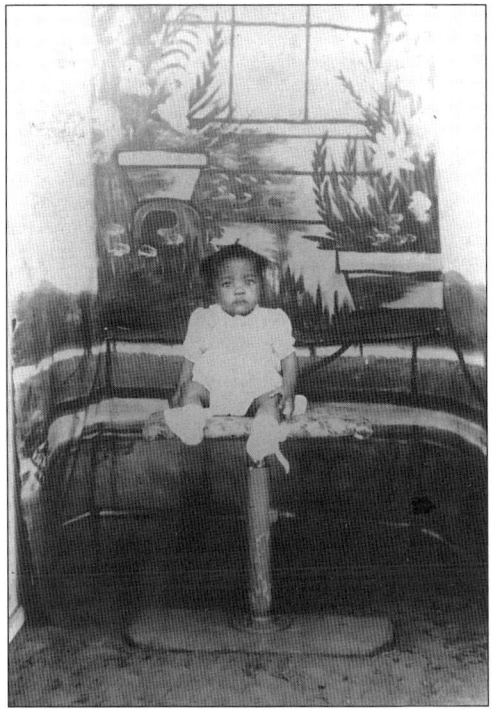

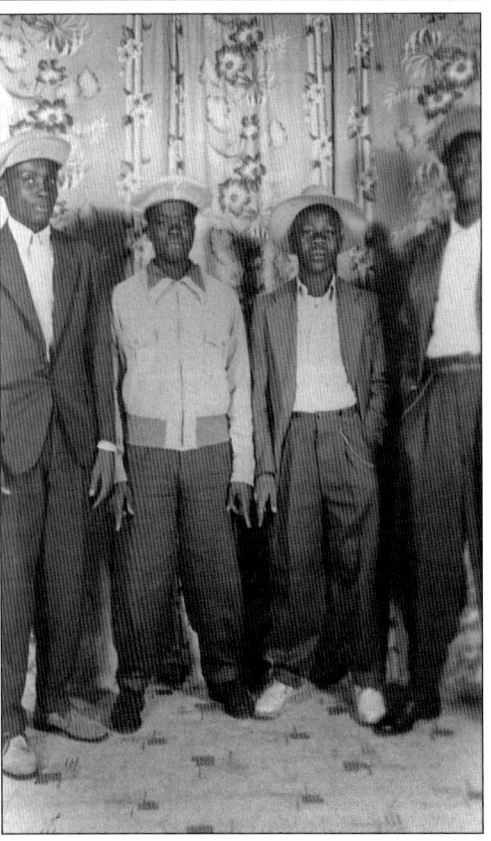

Above Left: Earl Henry West and his sister Ruth West Avant are captured in this Avery photograph. Earl moved to Tallahassee during World War I and remained until his death in the mid-1990s. He worked as a waiter at one of downtown Tallahassee's hotels and was a butler/servant at the governors mansion during the tenure of Leroy Collins. He retired as a waiter from Morrisons Cafeteria.

Above Right: This photograph of Barrie Roberts Ashcroft was taken at Avery Studio in 1947. Barrie is the daughter of Pete Birdie and Simon Peter Roberts; Pete Birdie's family moved to Tallahassee immediately following the Civil War. In the 1980s, Barrie and her sister Robbie restored the home of a cousin, Margaret Yellowhair, on Martin Luther King Boulevard, and now Barrie lives there. Yellowhair was a 1904 FAMU graduate.

Left: A popular fashion of the 1930s and 1940s is depicted in this Avery photograph. Jimmy Reid and friends, in their youthful splendor, sport zoot suits and jive chains for the camera.

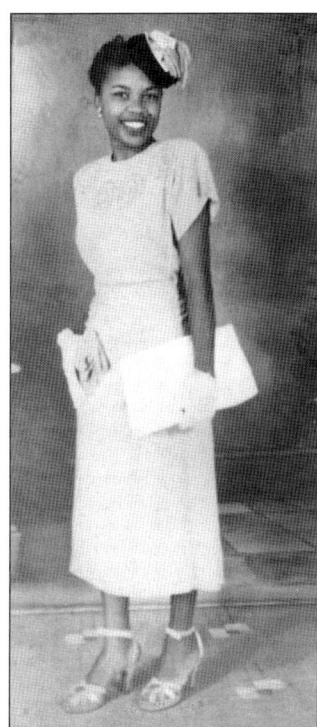 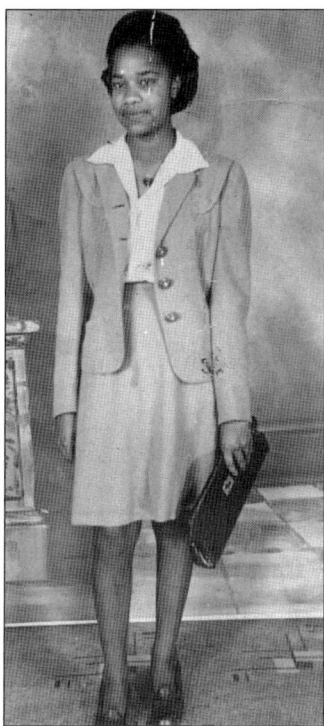 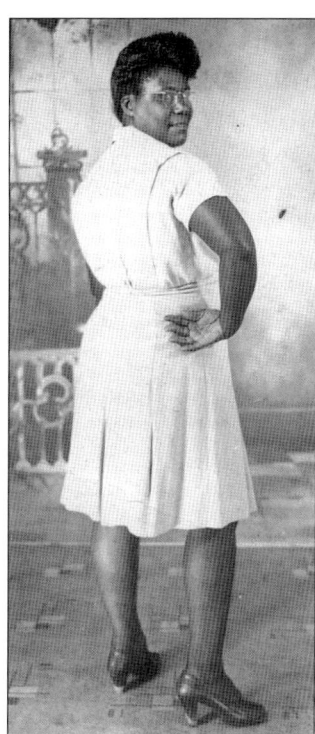

Left: Lucille Baldwin Holiday Brown was born on Suwanee Street in the Smokey Hollow community to Mr. and Mrs. Dallis Baldwin. The Baldwins co-founded St. John, now New St. John Church. Lucille was the first black public county librarian.

Center: Lucille Casanas Alexander is the daughter of an elementary school principal, Madeline Casanas, and band leader and cabinetmaker Aurelio Casanas. A nurse by profession, Lucille is the widow of Rev. Herbert Alexander, a former FAMU professor and one of Tallahassee's civil rights leaders during the 1970s and 1980s. The home in which she grew up, the Taylor House on Georgia Street, is being restored as a Frenchtown historic home.

Right: Mrs. Frances Brown Carter is shown here in the 1940s. A homemaker, she was born in 1904 and lived most of her adult life on Macomb Street in Frenchtown with her husband, Willie Carter. Her early roots have been traced to the Carroll Quarters and Bretton Hills communities of Tallahassee. Mrs. Carter was the mother of Genevieve C. Lathrop and Willie "Son Baby" Carter Jr. Her husband was an automobile mechanic at Rhaney Cawthon on Brevard Street for many years.

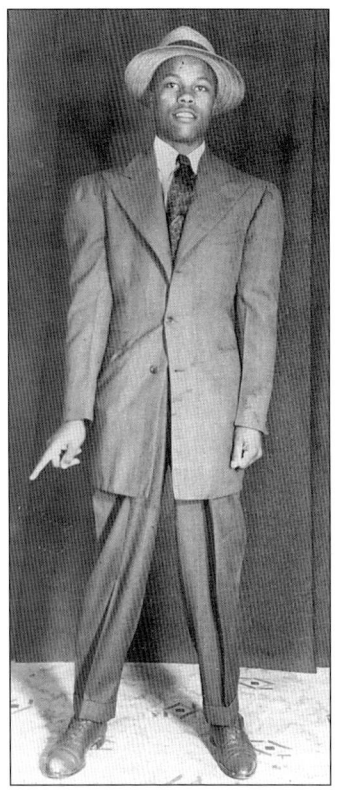 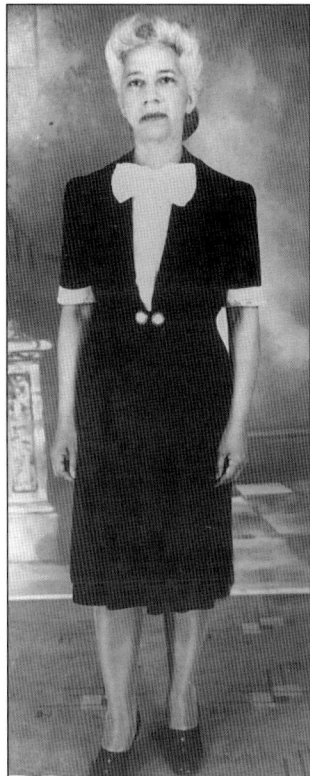 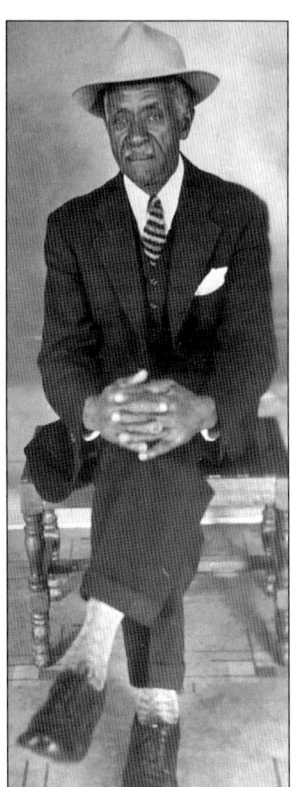

Left: Rayfield McGhee was one of the eleven children of Samantha and Ellis McGhee. He graduated from FAMU and taught in the Alachua County public schools. His brother Alphonso was the first graduate of the FAMU Law School.

Center: Mrs. Clyde Isler Eaton, a sophisticated lady, poses at Avery Studio in the 1940s. Eaton purchased a home in the 1930s on Virginia Street in the historic Frenchtown community. She was a part-time nurse at Campbell's Hospital and also taught at Ward, a one-room schoolhouse for black children located on Springhill Road. One of her grandsons, Rev. Theodore Houston, a pharmacist, is the supervisor of pharmaceutical services for Capital Health Plan in Tallahassee.

Right: Senior gentlemen, such as Austin Porter III (shown here), often dropped into Avery's after church to pose for pictures. A few of these photos are still in the collection of families who were residing in Tallahassee during that era.

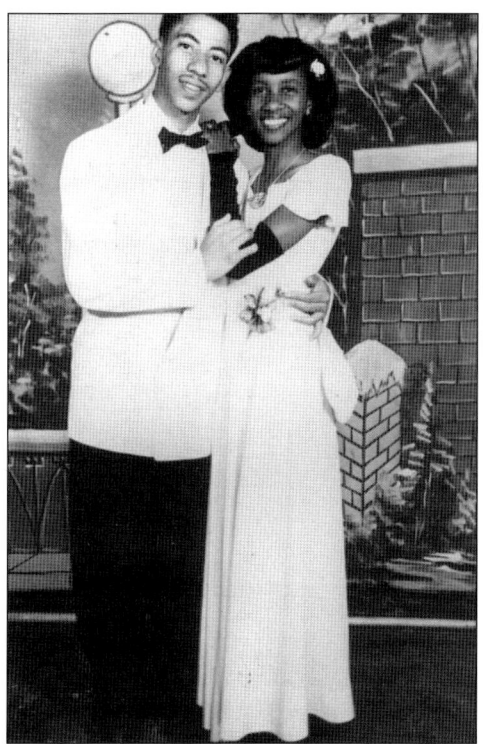
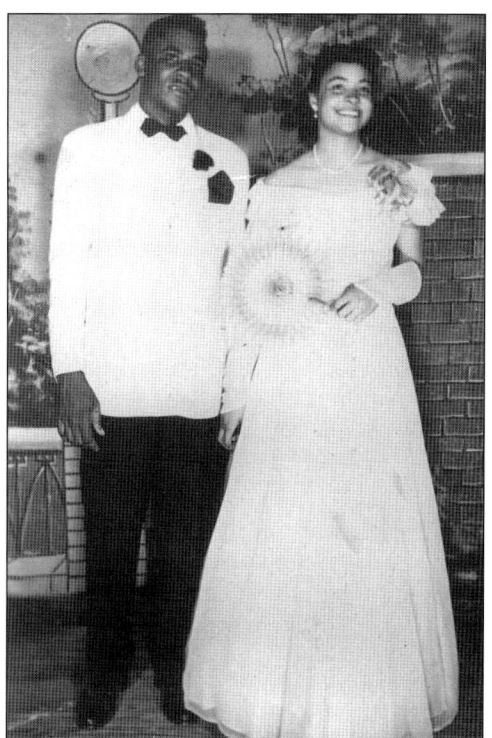
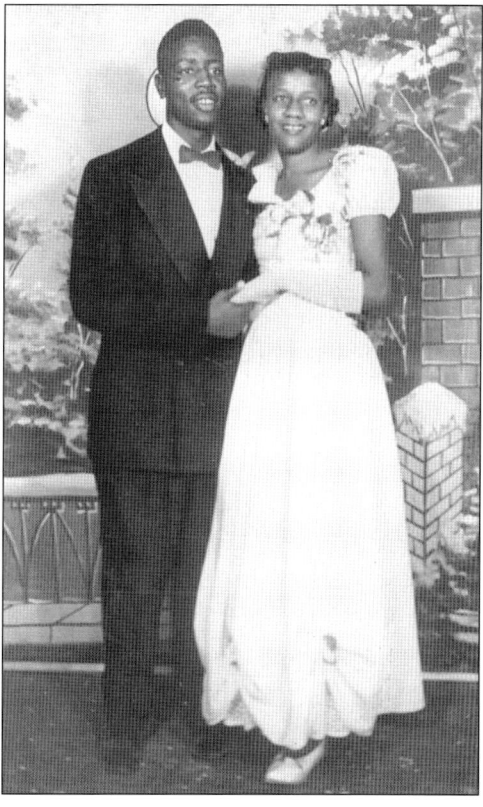

Above Left: Shown in this Avery photograph are Edward Wynn and Lucille Richards at their 1950 Lincoln High School prom. The prom was a community highlight for Tallahassee's teens. Many couples stopped by Avery Studio to savor and preserve the special night.

Above Right: This unidentified couple also attended the 1950 prom. When the Avery Studio closed in the 1950s, many photos were left behind, like this one. The Riley Museum of African American History and Culture has a project underway to identify such images.

Right: Corine Davis (Bridgewater) and her unidentified escort were photographed by Avery in 1949 as they prepared for the big event of the school year—the junior-senior prom. Corine was the daughter of Rev. Philip H. Davis, who was a pastor and served as chief evangelist of the Florida State Middle Florida Baptist Association. Corine moved to Salt Lake City and was supervisor of social workers. She had a daughter, Norma Hart.

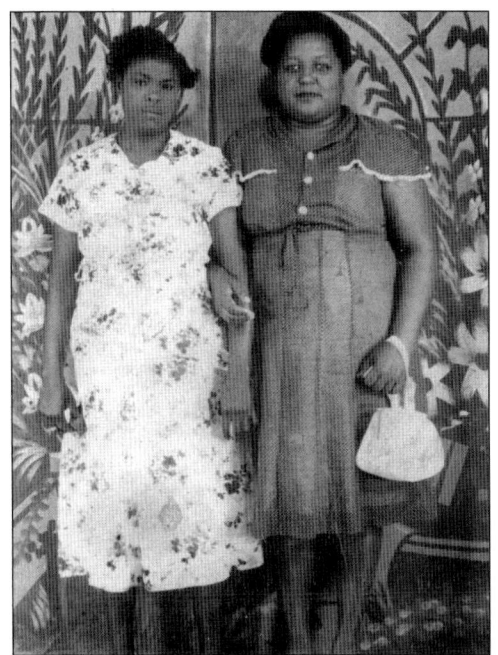 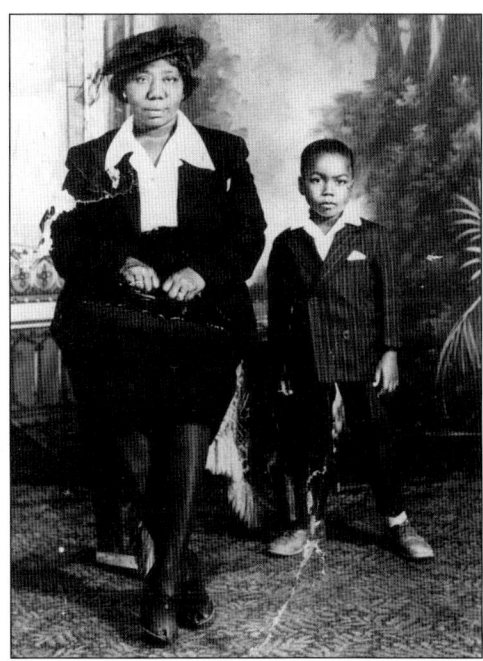

Left: Mrs. Marietta Hall (right) is pictured with her friend in front of one of Avery's famous backdrops. Hall and her family owned land in the Miccosukee community where family members Flora Hall, Jean Harrison, and others still reside. Her family was instrumental in the 1888 establishment of Concord AME Church.

Right: Mrs. Josephine Baker and her great nephew Glover Martin Jr. are shown in the 1940s. Glover is one of nine children of Glover Sr. and Christine Martin. Glover Sr. worked in the labs at Florida State University and sold peanuts so that all his children could attend college. His children—Gwendolyn, Glover Jr., Freddie, Jacquelyn, Harold, Lavern, Reginald, Carolyn, and Sheryl—graduated from FAMU with honors, and four earned medical degrees.

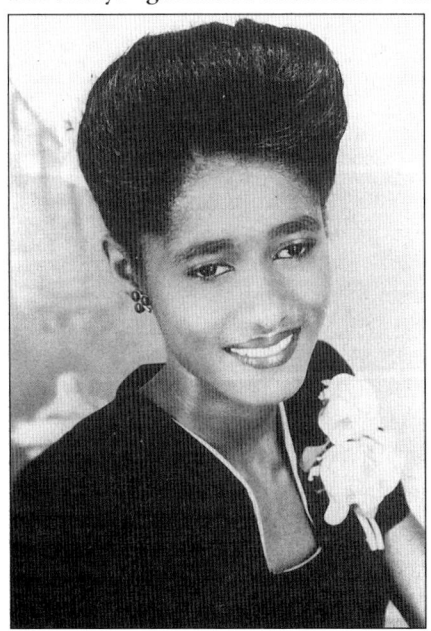

Cleo Pearl Abrams (Rawls) was the daughter of Rev. T.J. Abrams, a former pastor of Philadelphia Primitive Baptist Church, and Mrs. Susie Armentha Abrams. Her mother taught at Station I and Pineview Schools. Cleo graduated from Lincoln High School in the 1940s and attended FAMU. She taught in the public schools at Inverness and Ocala, Florida, until her retirement. Her other siblings were Armentha, Anita, Thomas Jr., Josephus, and Audrey. Audrey is the widow of All-American halfback Willie Gallimore, who played for the Chicago Bears.